The Debasement

of

HUMAN
RIGHTS

The

Debasement

of

HUMAN
RIGHTS

How Politics Sabotage
the Ideal of Freedom

AARON RHODES

ENCOUNTER BOOKS
New York • London

First American edition published in 2018 by Encounter Books,
an activity of Encounter for Culture and Education, Inc.,
a nonprofit, tax exempt corporation.
Encounter Books website address: www.encounterbooks.com

Manufactured in the United States and printed on
acid-free paper. The paper used in this publication meets
the minimum requirements of ANSI/NISO Z39.48–1992
(R 1997) (*Permanence of Paper*).

FIRST AMERICAN EDITION

LIBRARY OF CONGRESS CATALOGING-IN-PUBLICATION DATA

Names: Rhodes, Aaron Anthony, 1949– author.
Title: The debasement of human rights : how politics sabotage the ideal of freedom /
by Aaron Rhodes.
Description: New York : Encounter Books, 2018. |
Includes bibliographical references and index.
Identifiers: LCCN 2017045279 (print) | LCCN 2017052447 (ebook) |
ISBN 9781594039805 (Ebook) | ISBN 9781594039799 (hardcover : alk. paper)
Subjects: LCSH: Human rights—Philosophy. | Natural law.
Classification: LCC JC571 (ebook) | LCC JC571 .R489 2018 (print) |
DDC 323.01—dc23
LC record available at https://lccn.loc.gov/2017045279

Interior page design and composition: BooksByBruce.com

Contents

Acknowledgments
and Dedication

I am grateful to all those who have been encouraging and helpful in the process of publishing this book, especially to Adam Bellow, Tom Palmer, Anne Pierce, Lorna Rhodes (my sister), and of course Roger Kimball and his colleagues at Encounter Books. I wish to express particular thanks to Carol Staswick for her fine work in editing the book.

Part of the work on this book was supported by a grant from the John Templeton Foundation to the Freedom Rights Project, which allowed me to work with three colleagues, Jacob Mchangama, Paulina Neuding and Guglielmo Verdirame, on the conceptual problems of human rights. I owe much to each of them. The book also benefited from research done by Marine Testut during her time as an intern. The Woodrow Wilson Center for International Scholars provided a research fellowship in 2013 for study of the Soviet dissident human rights movement in the Kennan Collection.

My colleagues in religious freedom advocacy, Willy Fautré, Kamal Fahmi, Dominic Zoehrer and Peter Zoehrer, have given important moral support for my efforts.

My wife, Anna Sunder-Plassmann, herself a human rights activist, supported our family during most of my work on the book, and I am deeply grateful for that and for her wise counsel. I dedicate this book to Anna, to our daughters Leah and Rivkah, and to my sons Daniel and Nathan.

A Threat to Freedom

The international community's concept of human rights lacks intellectual and moral integrity. It is corrupted by political ideas. A debased and contradictory understanding of human rights has allowed the concept to be exploited by authoritarian states to justify their denial of liberties and to denigrate free societies, and has encouraged ideologues to pursue political agendas under the cover of human rights. While the struggle to protect individual freedom is increasingly marginalized, the idea of human rights has been so loosely applied and so distorted that it is now used to justify restrictions on basic individual freedoms and to advocate the global regulation of an immense range of social and economic activity. The concept of human rights is now rarely informed by the ideas and principles that originally gave it meaning. It has become so much associated with ideological agendas and frivolous demands that few take it seriously anymore. The idea of human rights has been emptied of the moral force that once inspired people around the world seeking freedom and democracy.

The result is profoundly deleterious to the way we think about human rights and apply the concept through international law and institutions. To have any hope of addressing the problem, we must identify the source: the falsehood at the heart of the international community's definition of human rights. It is a definition that mingles protections of basic individual freedoms with guaranteed state entitlements. It mixes natural rights with those established by positive law. It blurs the line between what is and is not a *human* right; it degrades the idea of natural rights, thus eroding the moral foundation upon which the entire edifice of human rights rests.

In this book, I show why economic and social human rights, so named under international law, are not universal human rights. Economic and social rights such as the "right to social security" and the "right to an adequate standard of living" are not simply different *kinds* of human rights; they are demonstrably not human rights at all, for they are based on different principles. They are rights granted by states, reflecting political values that are not intrinsic to human beings; they are collective, not individual rights; they embody political values and goals, and do not accord with the essential nonpolitical and nonpartisan character of authentic, universal human rights. They derive from particular political interests and passions, while authentic human rights are based on our common human nature and on reason, the basis of their universality.

In past decades, some have criticized the assertion that economic and social rights are universal human rights to be respected and applied in the same way as fundamental natural rights. Scholars and jurists have shown their weaknesses as human rights—that they are vague and cannot be enforced, and do not deliver what they promise. Conservatives have disparaged economic and social rights as left-wing political utopianism. But serious critiques of economic and social rights are not widely appreciated in the current atmosphere of human rights inflation, while the international community and human rights organizations have succumbed to political and intellectual bullying on the subject. In recent years, acceptance of economic and social rights as human rights has become the norm and an unquestioned dogma, thanks largely to leftist ideological pressure and the heavy-handed influence of United Nations officials. The international human rights system is rapidly developing with a focus on extending these rights.

What is not generally recognized is how this focus has compromised the capacity of the international human rights system, and of civil society, to protect individual liberty. The issue thus needs to be reopened forcefully, to expose the problems of economic and social rights in theory and in practice. The issue needs to be addressed in both practical and philosophical terms, showing what has happened to human rights, and why it has happened.

In what follows, I examine the mingling of human rights with politics at the heart of the international system. The concept of human rights was opened up to ideological interpretations, and the field has been invaded by actors with political agendas. The international human rights system is losing its credibility under the influence of economic and social rights, leading to destructive doubts about the very idea of universal, internationally codified human rights as a standard for governments and a North Star for people everywhere in search of security, peace and freedom. The human rights package has become too big, too contradictory, too political. Any meaningful clarification of international human rights discourse hinges on removing or marginalizing the extraneous notions that have confused and debased our concept of human rights, and refocusing on protecting individual political freedom. This in turn requires a renewed understanding of the moral and intellectual foundations of human rights.

The need for this renewal is acute, because the cultivation and preservation of the human soul demand free societies. Particularly in the modern world, states and ideologies have shown their power to dehumanize through propaganda; to invade and manipulate the spheres of individual privacy and civil society; to censor and control the flow of information; to abuse the dignity of the individual with high-tech police-state tactics and biomedical technology; and to drain individuals of moral responsibility and accountability with intrusive and paternalistic bureaucracies that limit freedom and choice, and sap our initiative and creativity. Today, the very idea of freedom is challenged by fascistic, nationalistic regimes and by political Islam, but perhaps even more insidiously by the complacency and moral lassitude, and indeed the illiberalism of many members of liberal democracies themselves. Yet the people of free societies cannot defend the concept of human rights in its corrupted and weakened form without also bowing to those who seek to limit individual freedom; indeed, the concept is being used as a weapon against freedom. The modern world needs authentic human rights more than ever, but has largely forgotten their meaning.

As a human rights advocate, I am convinced that clarifying the way we understand and apply human rights is essential to the future of freedom. I ask you, the readers, to open yourself to my arguments even if you start by opposing them. I have come to my conclusions about the nature of human rights through many years of working in the trenches, in both advocacy and investigation. You will already have detected a political prejudice on the side of classical liberalism—a belief that the purpose of governments should be to protect individual rights and freedoms, and to foster civil society. My experiences in dealing with the ravages of communism and authoritarianism have convinced me of the superiority of governments that restrain themselves and defer to individual freedom and civil society. I own up to my own prejudices, but my purpose here is not to make a political argument against socialism or welfare states. I am in favor of government services to assist citizens in need; I am in favor of communities pooling their resources to guarantee minimum standards of living and health, if they so decide. But these are political questions that should be settled in democratic processes. Human rights serve to protect a fair political process, but they should not serve political goals. The consequences are woeful when they are misused in that way.

Eastern Europeans

I began my direct engagement in international human rights after a period of work in Eastern Europe in the years following the end of the Communist regimes. In the late 1980s, as an administrator at Boston University, I had tried to assist the late Polish philosopher and intellectual entrepreneur Krzysztof Michalski in his efforts on behalf of intellectuals in the captive nations of Eastern Europe. In 1991, Michalski invited me to his Vienna-based Institut für die Wissenschaften vom Menschen (Institute for Human Sciences) to run a European Union–funded project to help reform universities and research institutions in Hungary, Poland and Czechoslovakia. Both before and after the events of 1989, the Institute brought together many of the leading intellectuals of Eastern Europe to help them get up to speed in their disciplines by meeting and working with Western colleagues in a propaganda-free environment, and to promote an inclusive Europe. The project on university reform was overseen by a committee headed by Lord Dahrendorf.

Attached to an inchoate liberalism and with an intuitive hatred of communism, I encountered, in my work around the region, the detritus of "real state socialism." My Eastern European colleagues were among the most intelligent and hard-headed people I had ever known—tenacious, principled, disciplined and shrewd. They had survived the forty-five-year nightmare of Soviet-dominated communism—after the murder of millions of their fellow citizens and the plunder of their societies by Nazi Germany—and had come out with their souls intact. They also recognized in themselves what one of them called the "childish irresponsibility" of marginalized intellectuals in totalitarian societies, with the melancholy luxury of narrowed possibilities. The Communist state had framed their lives with rigid rules and coercive enforcement, restricting their choices while providing prefabricated solutions to the existential dilemmas of freedom. Now they faced rising prices and the collapse of the social welfare apparatus, as well as the ruthless opportunism of former Communist *apparatchiks*. They strove to suppress their nostalgia for the slow pace and economic security of the past, as they coped with the burdens of supporting themselves and their families in the turmoil of the transition years.

In his New Year's address after the Velvet Revolution in 1989, Václav Havel told his countrymen in Czechoslovakia that they lived in "a contaminated moral environment." My Eastern European friends had experienced and analyzed what happens when unconstrained state power marches under the banner of economic and social rights. The Second World War had killed millions and ruined the infrastructure of their societies, but communism had devastated their moral infrastructure. Institutions, including universities, were virtually all controlled by cynical opportunists who had made their way through the ranks of the Communist Party; all of the deans at the Law Faculty of Charles University, for example, had been Communists. The universities were littered with meaningless institutions that existed on virtually nothing, like fungi; they were already almost dead, but it was nearly impossible to kill them.

Everywhere one looked was decay and environmental degradation. A sickening brown air pollution covered cities with a nasty, sour smell. Consumer goods were flimsy and ugly. Horrid 1970s-type attempts at modern design in the form of brutalist, "modern socialist" architecture would appear among dirty, rundown buildings still bearing bullet scars from the war. Some Communist architecture, including Stalin-era state structures, can have aesthetic qualities, but most of what was built in Eastern Europe during the Cold War suggests an aggressive assault on the senses, on classical form and harmony, on the very idea of beauty. It was a demonstration of power over the sensorium, leading to cynicism and nihilism. A Slovak friend who had been imprisoned for his religious beliefs said the Communist regime in Czechoslovakia had "killed beauty, emotions, and creativity." Millions lived in high-rise tenements that looked virtually the same from Hanoi to Havana.

Whatever the law did not explicitly permit was assumed to be illegal. The creaky, Napoleonic continental legal systems of the region had easily accommodated totalitarian rule, and continued to put the state first after its retreat. Societies were managed by state ministries imposing inflexible bureaucratic rules. The corridors of these institutions were tomb-quiet, with tall, padded doors behind which officials sat in largely empty rooms, frigid in wintertime. It all seemed like a Kafka novel.

The social mood was dark and subdued. Eastern Europeans still speak of a feeling of meaninglessness and hopelessness under communism, of sad faces everywhere, of people walking with their heads down. This mood persists among many today. Popular music was melancholy and fatalistic. Neighborhoods were quiet and empty; people seemed to move slowly, cautiously, as if to avoid calling attention to themselves. Few seemed to care about their health. There was a modesty and deference about them; the overbearing state seemed to have squeezed the ego and life out of people, dried them out. Constant surveillance, either by state apparatuses or by other citizens snooping on the state's behalf, weighed heavily on the human personality, sometimes distorting it permanently. It destroyed the ability to speak directly, perhaps even to think without paranoid and twisted mental maneuvers. Questions were not answered directly, and letters often not answered at all, as the eventual destination of the written reply was unknown, and it could become evidence for a future accuser.

Decades of communism robbed people of their panache, of any healthy self-confidence. They felt that coercion had ruined them. Perhaps worse, they felt weak because they had not been faced with the moral challenges of a free society, and inferior because they had not been afforded the opportunity to succeed or to fail. Only the former apparatchiks seemed to have any optimism, many of them having morphed from corrupt Communist bureaucrats to managers of American and European development projects, or privatizing entrepreneurs. But among most who had adhered to principles, who refused to lie and cheat, a mood of depression and exhaustion had settled like fog as they took stock of the "mentality problems" that were the legacy of communism, an impediment to reform and the building of a "normal" society.

Pondering this mood of sclerotic caution and regret, I contrasted it with my own coming of age in America in the 1960s. I recalled the exuberance of the demonstrations for civil rights and against the Vietnam War that I had joined as a teenager; the passionate jazz and popular hard-rock music; the feeling of personal power in America, the power of positive ideas and hope, of defiance, iconoclasm, and moral rage freely expressed. As a college student I was eventually put off by the excesses and the utopianism of the protest era. What remained with me was something more deeply rooted in the American tradition: a feeling that individual citizens had the power and the right to question and confront authorities—not only law enforcement and governmental officials, but intellectual and moral authorities as well. It was a sense that the individual had moral standing, a feeling of personal freedom and dignity. I became aware of my refusal to defer as something I had taken from the political character of my society. Rebellion, and an awareness of the contrast between freedom and tyranny, was in our DNA. America seemed to keep up a "permanent revolution" for freedom.

The people in the post-Communist societies needed to be liberated both politically and psychologically. Respect for human rights, as I understood it experientially, would allow those people to enjoy freedom—not just the absence of coercion, but freedom as a shared sense of the value of the individual person. It would bring creativity into rigid bureaucratic institutions, and give more people a chance to fulfill their potential. Freedom and human rights would allow the people of Eastern Europe finally to take control of their own lives, their destinies, and their societies.

Whereas I had been able to enjoy freedom and human rights without having to define them, my Eastern European colleagues at the Institute for Human Sciences in Vienna had been denied human rights but were able to define what they lacked. The situation reminded me of Plato's paradoxical observation, in the *Symposium*, that lovers love what they lack. I had enjoyed respect for my human rights, but they *loved* human rights, and they understood that the courage of independent thinking was essential. The Eastern European experts on the higher education committee made fun of "political correctness" in the West, comparing it to the suffocating ideological pressures of communism. The late Hungarian sociologist Elemér Hankiss, who at the time was trying to remove propaganda from the Hungarian state television network, joked that they had had "plenty of PC in the CP" (Communist Party).

Freedom enables us to learn moral lessons. My freedom, even as a child, had sometimes forced me to confront my own weaknesses and failures. Freedom could be bright and hopeful, or dark with uncertainty and fear. How I dealt with a multitude of choices and possibilities had revealed good things and also flaws in my character. Freedom permits individuals and societies to know the painful truth about themselves, and perhaps to change. Like a free personality, American society reflected both the moral virtues and the faults of its citizens, and it allowed a fair fight between the good and the bad. My Eastern European colleagues had suffered fear, restriction and deprivation, but what they resented most about the nondemocratic, collectivist political system was how limits on freedom either prevented individuals from realizing their potential or inflated their possibilities. The state had manipulated the natural ecology of virtue based on individual merit and moral choice, and the framework of political values imposed from above had deformed the development of personal character.

In my mind, the opposite of the arrogant and corrupt collectivism that had ruined Russia and her captive nations was a society based on human rights. The transcendent principles of human rights would be like the Law for the Israelites as they gazed across the River Jordan at the Promised Land. It was not a promise of utopia, but a set of rules to guide individuals and societies toward success in moral terms, through free choice and deliberate action. Human rights would put the destiny of oppressed people in their own hands.

The Helsinki Human Rights Community

In 1993, I became the executive director of the International Helsinki Federation for Human Rights (IHF), and I have since worked closely alongside human rights advocates from throughout the former Soviet Union and Eastern Europe, in North Africa and the Middle East, and in a few other countries like Cuba, Japan, Iran, Pakistan and the Republic of Korea. The IHF, founded in 1982 on a model envisioned by the Soviet dissident physicist Andrei Sakharov, had won international acclaim for its work in supporting "Helsinki committees" and political prisoners behind the Iron Curtain, indirectly hastening its fall. On my first visit to the office in Vienna's 8th District, I met the IHF's three employees in a rundown, ninety-square-meter apartment leased by a former Czech dissident. In the following years, the IHF was able to build itself out with the project support of the European Union and other donors, and eventually grew to encompass NGOs from over forty countries. In 2007, it fell victim to a financial crime and was forced into bankruptcy after twenty-five years of existence. During my fourteen-year tenure, we dealt, inter alia, with the wars in Bosnia-Herzegovina, Croatia and Kosovo; with two wars in

Chechnya; with the rise of Vladimir Putin's repressive Russia; with the harsh dictatorship in Belarus; and with the struggles of local activists to monitor and promote human rights in the Caucasus and Central Asia.

The IHF was a bubble of clarity in the intensifying chaos of human rights politics sweeping the world in the early 1990s. As a diverse, international community of stubborn activists with a mandate to harmonize their approaches and projects, it was certainly not without its problems. Composed of local civil society organizations, and governed by them, the IHF was often pushed from independent human rights work toward partisan political engagement. A number of its associated human rights groups were really fronts for political parties using human rights to advance their objective of deposing or protecting those in power. Principled human rights defenders were forced into political postures by deteriorating conditions in their countries. Others represented particular ethnic interests and were not, in fact, committed to universal human rights. While the older groups in the IHF were clearly driven by principles, some newer ones were more political and attached themselves to human rights to gain legitimacy and funding.

The older human rights communities in Russia and Eastern Europe were largely composed of people who had made huge sacrifices for human rights, and were still doing so; self-interested dilettantes would never join them. Those Soviet-era human rights organizations were socially marginalized, often seen as irritants in the new democracies that did not expect scrutiny about human rights after the end of totalitarian rule. The activists in the dissident human rights organizations had obviously withstood strong pressures for publicly criticizing their governments and their contemporaries, and for defending victims. These people had little to lose except their principles— their most cherished possession, which they would not relinquish. Many faced physical danger. In the course of my work in human rights, six of my acquaintances, colleagues and friends have been murdered because of their human rights and political engagement, including one, a Chechen, gunned down on the street in Vienna.

What made the Helsinki Federation a unique family of human rights activists was its almost complete absence of doctrinal human rights dispute. Around the same period, formations like Amnesty International were ridden with internal, ideological arguments about expanding their mandates to focus more on economic and social rights, which had been given a strong boost by the international community and were also promoted by a number of powerful philanthropies like the Ford Foundation. The IHF members were of a diverse range of political persuasions. There were former Communists and young neo-Marxists who sought to preserve what they felt were the humanistic ideals of socialism. We had hard-core classical liberals who thought governments were inherently obstacles to individual rights and civil society. We had European conservatives and leftists. One member was an anarchist. They were from vastly divergent class and economic backgrounds, including some millionaires along with many living in pathetic poverty.

All the same, I cannot recall a single debate about politics in the sense of questions about social justice, taxation, wealth redistribution, or the like; people kept their political views separate from their work in human rights. The reason the Helsinki Federation did not suffer polarizing ideological debates is because its members focused almost exclusively on civil and political rights—on matters of principle, not politics. There was no rule or policy against taking up economic or social issues, but no one was interested in doing so, and there were no debates about them. Most of the members of the IHF did not monitor or advocate for compliance with economic and social rights standards, although some took up such issues on occasion in order to gain the favor of constituents or to impress donors, including some U.S.-based foundations. But most of the colleagues, having lived under communism, considered economic and social rights to be an ideological fraud that had been used by the Communists to justify and obscure repression. It was remarkable, in view of the fact that people in post-Communist societies had seen their social benefits dramatically reduced; they were deprived of economic and social rights they had previously enjoyed, and impoverished by the "social costs" of the transition to democracy. But the IHF colleagues nevertheless saw the realization of individual, civil, political rights as the key challenge in their societies, and focused on issues like censorship, unfair elections, arbitrary arrests, unfair trials, interference in religious organizations and other civil society structures, and legal discrimination against members of minority groups. For the same reason that we avoided partisan, ideological issues, we found unity in our consensus about the centrality and the indispensability of civil and political rights.

We understood tacitly that discussion about the allocation of resources, and about group rights, was political; that politics and human rights were different, and should not be mixed. Economic and social rights were different from civil and political rights in form and in substance. Not only did they reflect partisan positions, but they did not function in the same way as freedom rights. Human rights defenders should focus on the problem of freedom, not become social workers attending to the boundless needs of citizens. Unlike civil and political rights, economic and social rights took time to implement, and required bureaucracies and regulations. They were subject to a huge range of conditions, and to relative definitions and compromise. But human rights, according to their defenders in the IHF, could not be compromised. There were no excuses for violating them.

Real human rights problems could be remedied in straightforward actions, by changing repressive policies. Torture could be ended swiftly by government decrees and by well-publicized litigation and prosecution. Censorship could end in a very short time if governments and courts would stop censoring and intimidating citizens and stop prosecuting thought crimes. While organizing a free and fair election was a complex process, the main challenge was simple: keep politics out of it. The most important human rights issues were matters of urgency. Addressing them was not about finding compromises and gradually implementing long-term solutions, but about the clear-cut application of principle, by a government or a court, with measurable outcomes.

Human rights purism was respected at the IHF. One of the most intellectually astute members of the organization calmly explained during a meeting that there was no such thing as women's rights. This was understood as a statement of principle consistent with the idea of human rights applying equally to all human beings. I don't recall anyone recoiling in horror; everyone trusted the speaker's commitment to individual rights, including those of females. The IHF gave special attention to the members of vulnerable groups whose rights were often trampled, and thus drew attention to how the human rights of women needed to be protected in particular ways. The distinctions upheld by the human rights activists in the IHF showed that the most important human rights are the simplest to understand and to enforce, and those rights are relevant to all people everywhere.

The acceptance of rational rules that protect everyone's basic rights was understood to be the foundation of freedom in society, and the vision of freedom gave hope and life to human rights work. Freedom would allow citizens to build fair and just societies, if they had the strength and will to do so; it was the first and most important prerequisite. Freedom was possible, but it was not utopia. In accepting the legitimacy of civil society, one had to take the bad along with the good. Freedom was also not self-sustaining; it needed to be actively maintained. Threats to freedom would have to be continually monitored, and this required an engaged, independent civil society.

Human rights, oriented toward freedom, was not an overly complex or technical issue. The call for human rights, while clearly not religious, evoked the spirit of prophets who cut through the obfuscations of rulers, demanding truth and fidelity to the law. Like monotheism, human rights made each of us subject to the discipline of transcendent rules, and equal before them. Among our clients were people whose political and moral views we abhorred, and we often had to put our own opinions in a box, segregated from our obligation to respect the human rights of all. The members of the human rights community were like orphans who had run away from their national identities and loyalties, and their own sensibilities, and had found a home in human rights. Uli Fischer, a former member of the German federal parliament and a leader in the IHF, said that human rights defenders needed to be more loyal to one another than to their own governments. The basic freedom rights, our moral roadmap, presented a clear and accessible surface, but like the deceptive simplicity of Old Testament stories, they had deep human implications underneath.

Moral Challenges to Human Rights

The moral equality of all human beings, and their capacity for reason and choice, is the basis of the universality of human rights. Nationalism and the pull of ethnic and religious identities and loyalties acted as a centrifugal force against the ethos and unity of the IHF, especially when ethnic war erupted in the Balkans and later when NATO bombed Serbia. The ethnic nationalism driving Serbian aggression and violence in Bosnia-Herzegovina, and also present among Croats, Bosniaks and Kosovars, was condemned by human rights communities, but the chauvinistic hostility and victimhood that Tito had forcefully held in check raised its ugly head even among them. Cultural relativism has always posed an intractable challenge to campaigns for universal human rights. Ever since international pressure began to be exerted to respect the Universal Declaration of Human Rights, various regimes have used cultural exceptionalism to argue for special approaches to human rights that exempt them from honoring its principles.

The ethnic nationalism that surfaced in Europe in the early 1990s, and has recently emerged yet again, brooked no notion of individual rights to be respected in a pluralistic civil society. The nation loomed as the ultimate social fact and reality, and individuals had a meaningful existence only as parts of the whole. The unity of the nation had to be seamless and absolute, like that of an organism. History (generally infused with myths), language, customs, traditions, and attachment to clans and ancestral homes had compelling sentimental power, while individual human rights was dismissed as either a weak cosmopolitan illusion, a kind of sickness, or a trick used by foreigners to weaken and destroy the nation. Ethnic nationalism dehumanized outsiders and legitimized violence against them. It was predatory and heartless, seeking domination, lacking empathy for any who were not kin. Moving forward, it has energy and vitality in part because it is devoid of self-reflection or doubt. Indeed, it presents itself as an "unstoppable force of divine or historical inevitability."[1] While the Helsinki movement sought to limit the power of the state, ethnic nationalism was driven by the "will to power" glorified by Nietzsche.

The former Soviet Union, and especially Russia, was churning with ethnic nationalism that had been largely kept in check by the deep freeze of Soviet ideology. In late 1993, a few months after joining the IHF, I went to St. Petersburg to speak with civil society experts about the rise of the "Red-Brown" movement, a toxic brew of Russian nationalism and Soviet/Stalinist nostalgia, imbued with racist, fascist beliefs. The atmosphere of violence was palpable. NGO monitors and ethnic minorities were regularly being threatened by Russian chauvinists. Anti-Semitic literature was abundant on the streets. The Orthodox Church was emerging as a source of xenophobia and paranoia. Observing mass in several crowded churches, I felt that the priests conveyed a mood of fear and anguish, even aggression. In the dead of winter, the city was in a dreadful state, its people visibly destitute, its canals polluted with trash including the rusting bodies of wrecked automobiles. If Eastern Europe seemed Kakfaesque, this was like a Dostoevsky novel. In the chaos of the early 1990s, different forces were pulling Russians in many directions. The hatred of minorities and the authoritarianism of the violent, Slavophile Red-Browns posed a threat to international human rights standards, because it denied the very principles behind them.

During those years, the political mobilization of the Serbs under Slobodan Milosevic was based on the idea that different national groups should not cohabit in the same state.[2] It is an idea that might sound reasonable to those who are ignorant of the chauvinism and aggression at its heart. Virtually all societies are pluralistic, and ethnic partitions always threaten the rights of minorities. A campaign of ethnic cleansing had started in multiethnic former Yugoslav republics. The IHF, still pursuing an understanding of the Red-Brown issue and its relation to the war against the independence of Chechnya, soon encountered its international dimensions.

In January 1995, a meeting was organized in Moscow to gather information about the Chechen situation. IHF members and associates from Serbia, Croatia and elsewhere in the Balkans took part, but others, from political circles, were invited by Russian officials, and it became clear that different agendas were in play. A number of Russian liberals spoke movingly about the brutal war against Chechen independence, expressing grief and a sense of responsibility. Among them was Sergei Grigoryants, one of Russia's most forceful and fearless internal critics. During the conference, his son Timofei was run down and killed on the street under suspicious circumstances; Grigoryants had recently received anonymous threats. But when the Serbian militant Vuk Draskovic appeared on the speakers' list, it became clear that the meeting had been hijacked by Russian nationalists.

Draskovic had organized a violent Serb paramilitary group operating in Croatia. In 1990, he had declared all Muslims to be genetically corrupt, and had said that even if half of all Serbs died defeating the Muslims in the Balkans, it would ensure the future for the other half.[3] He spoke in a lilting Russian that charmed his hosts, posing as the true friend of Russia in the Balkans. He spoke mainly about the need for a "strong, democratic Russia" and a "strong, democratic Serbia." It was the voice of power and violence, shrouded in a smooth yet bullying logic of ethnic and national unity. The speech was seductive in its merciless simplicity; it embodied a kind of premodern, irrational force, free of ambiguity. Our Croatian colleague walked out. On the way back to Vienna, I overheard another conference participant, a Slovak official, telling a colleague that the conference had consisted of "a bunch of Jews trying to overthrow the Russian government."

These events of more than twenty years ago were precursors of large-scale violence that led to the deaths of hundreds of thousands of people, largely civilians, in Chechnya, in the Balkans and elsewhere. Today, strong nationalist movements are active in numerous European countries and find support from a significant number of Americans. These movements invoke "globalism" as a threat to national interests and to the nation's citizens. As liberal democracies flounder, China is in the grip of a nationalist regime with aspirations for global leadership. In this situation, we must ask ourselves some questions:

Can an idea of human rights gutted of its core meaning—the protection of individual freedom—be an antidote to the metastasis of ethnic nationalist and neofascist ideas? Can a concept of human rights that focuses on groups and differences offer a vision of universal brotherhood against ethnonationalist claims and the politics of groupthink, as well as repressive states? Can a concept of human rights that morally equates the protection of fundamental freedoms with trivial government services move our spirits to resist profound threats to our liberties?

I fear the answer to all these questions is no. Human rights, detached from their roots in natural law and natural rights, have been transformed from moral principles that affirm our freedom into beliefs about what people need from governments, beliefs that undermine the essential moral agency of the person and encourage dependency on governments and global bureaucracies. As a consequence, human rights have lost much of the moral authority embodied in their founding mandate: the urgent protection of individual freedom and the principled criticism of coercive states. What is most concerning is that human rights in their present ideological and legal form—human rights without freedom, and even against freedom—could provide a moral framework for the neofascism that is emerging as a dominant political force.

There are strong signs that this is already happening, as will be documented in the second half of this book. Authoritarian regimes are on the rise, putting the rights of the state above the individual, and repressing political, religious and ethnic minorities. These regimes pose far greater challenges to liberal democracy than those of the early 1990s. Increasingly, they are doing so under the banner of "human rights," which has become an emblem of the *status quo ante* rather than a beacon of emancipation. At the same time, liberal democracies are restricting basic freedoms in the name of "human rights." Even in liberal democracies, people are being fined or jailed for what they say or write, as a "politically correct" agenda of "tolerance" takes precedence over freedom of speech. The number of states that deprive their citizens of basic freedoms is climbing each year. Powerful authoritarian states and theocracies, essentially fascist and nationalist in orientation, openly vilify the notion of natural, universal human rights, and some are able to manipulate global politics through their economic power. We also face extremist movements whose barbarism is aimed at frightening free peoples into submission or accommodation. Islamic states, which do not accept the idea of individual human rights, often dominate processes in the United Nations. Independent civil society monitoring organizations are essential to protecting human rights, but such groups are being thwarted or banned in many countries, and the local nongovernmental human rights community is under increasing pressure. The expected transition to human rights and democracy has stalled in most of the formerly Communist Soviet republics and has regressed in some of them.

What has changed in the confrontation between free and unfree states is that human rights, in the sense of respect for individual freedom, has ceased to be a criterion for distinctions between free societies and tyrannies, or a test of the moral legitimacy of governments. The Communist totalitarian states of the past were understood to violate human rights, and the ideal of human rights gave their citizens a clear alternative and goal. The dangers of collective economic and social rights and the association of those rights with dictatorships were clear. But that is no longer the case. The idea of human rights is being twisted into something that no longer inspires oppressed peoples with the call for individual freedom and universal moral equality. It is being co-opted as the moral justification for strong states to restrict freedom in return for security. Russia, China and the members of the Organization for Islamic Cooperation (OIC) are not on the defensive about human rights, but instead are reshaping it into a rationale for oppression. Even North Korea—where around 200,000 innocent people are confined in brutal concentration camps and where political prisoners are sometimes burned alive—now brags about honoring human rights and has been praised on that score.

Authoritarian and dictatorial nations are working together to establish a new vision of human rights centered on "security." In this vision, basic freedoms are seriously compromised or do not exist; critics are often labeled "terrorists." The state imposes social peace, and the prerogatives of the state are paramount. There is no positive dynamic pointing toward freedom for literally billions of people living in China, Russia, Belarus, Uzbekistan, Cuba, North Korea, Iran, Turkey, the Middle Eastern sultanates, and many other countries, including war-ridden, destitute African states. Dictatorships and authoritarian governments are feeling flush; a palpable mood of cynicism, indifference and appeasement hangs over human rights. It is liberal democracies, which generally take human rights principles and international legal obligations seriously, that are on the defensive. Yet their leaders and representatives no longer have the capacity, or the will, to defend the core human rights guaranteeing freedom.

The idea of human rights that emerged from the Enlightenment provided the foundation for freedom in liberal democracies—in states that put a premium on restraining their own power. These states formed the most peaceful, humane governments in history, governments under which free people have been able to fulfill their own potential, and contribute to the public good, in unprecedented measure. The revolutionary and emancipative idea of human rights has animated the growth of democracy around the world and inspired an international freedom movement to confront tyrants from the moral high ground of universal values.

But as the concept of human rights is ever more corrupted, the future of liberty and peace is increasingly in question. Neglecting or betraying the central meaning of human rights, the international community is drifting away from the obligation to protect freedom, and toward a notion of human rights that is compatible with the *denial* of freedom. Few experts or activists doubt that the current international human rights system is dysfunctional, but even fewer recognize that the failure to guard human rights and the weakness of our response to ideological challenges to human rights are consequences of a muddled way of *defining* human rights. If our concept of human rights is allowed to erode, the result will be the triumph of a collectivist doctrine that betrays the ideals of universal individual rights. The prevailing discourse and practice in human rights are enabling this to happen.

This book is a critique of the contemporary approach to human rights—of its unmooring from the natural rights tradition, and of the politicized focus on economic and social rights. International human rights has become a technocratic field, yet one that is polluted with leftist political clichés. It needs to be simplified and depoliticized, and it needs to be reanimated by its foundational beliefs and by an authentic call for freedom.

PART I

What Happened to Human Rights

CHAPTER 1

The Achilles' Heel of International Human Rights

The idea of universal human rights emerged from within the philosophical tradition of natural law and natural rights, which formed around the principle that the innate rights of individual human beings are prior to and above the laws of states. Detached from that tradition, the concept of human rights falls apart. It becomes a hollow shell, susceptible to invasion by contradictory notions, and that is what has happened in the international human rights system.

The foundation of that system is the Universal Declaration of Human Rights, which diverges from the principles of natural rights by mixing in rights of a political character that require positive state action. Its contents reflect accommodation with totalitarian states and the influence of the progressive political tradition, devaluing human rights in favor of creating a fair and efficient planned society, and emphasizing collective rather than individual rights. Fundamental rights were originally conceived as rights that cannot be impinged upon by other considerations. But if human rights are essentially no different from other kinds of rights, then they can be subject to conditions like other rights. They are no longer sacrosanct. The Universal Declaration politicized the meaning of human rights, calling their distinctive character into question while reifying state-granted rights based on ideological values.

Reason, Freedom, Natural Rights and the State

Reasoning from the natural law tradition established that human rights are different from other kinds of rights. Natural law refers to an "objective moral standard independent of human conventions."[1] Socrates taught that laws contravening nature should not be obeyed, but the idea of natural law really took shape with the Stoics, the philosophical school started by Zeno in about 300 B.C. The Stoics distinguished the law of nature from conventional laws promulgated by governments, and in so doing they arrived at basic elements of liberalism and the principles of fundamental human rights. According to Heinrich Rommen, a German lawyer who opposed the Nazis in the 1930s, the Stoics grasped "the rights of man and the idea of mankind."[2] They understood the principle of universalism, seeing universal commonalities in human nature beneath disparate religious values and cultural traditions. While human law reflects and serves diverse political interests, individuals are all naturally equal and entitled to natural freedom.

In the Stoic view, natural law provided a fixed and transcendent moral standard to constrain the arbitrary laws of governments.[3] Human rights based on natural law are not created or granted by governments; instead, they are to offer protection from state power, and are to be honored by governments. They are not part of the positive law made by governments and legislatures, nor of the same nature as rights granted by states.

The distinction between natural and conventional law entered into Roman law as *ius naturale* versus *ius civile*. The laws created by men were seen as distinct from sacred laws rooted in the natural order. Cicero wrote in *The Republic* (III:33) that sound civil law had to be based on natural law consistent with human nature, and that natural law is universal because human nature is universal.

> We cannot be exempted from this law by any decree of the Senate or the people; nor do we need anyone else to expound or explain it. There will not be one such law in Rome and another in Athens, one now and another in the future, but all peoples at all times will be embraced by a single and eternal and unchangeable law ....[4]

The author of natural law is God, the "lord and master of us all." Cicero won a court case by arguing that a particular law was contrary to natural law, and thus he established a precedent as the prototypical human rights lawyer.

Natural law as understood by the Enlightenment philosophers was not the same thing as sacred law, but inhabited the moral space it had formerly occupied. Rommen clarified the distinction between natural law and sacred law this way: "The idea of natural law emerged along with the realization that not all law was sacred and with the recognition of cultural diversity."[5] In Nazi Germany, Rommen had seen how positive law, the law of governments and legislatures, could be perverted to legitimize atrocities when driven only by political will, unconstrained by reference to fixed moral principles. Natural law is prior to civil law and puts limits on it—limits grounded in reason. It protects what is vital to human nature from harm by society and the state. In the natural law tradition, states may not pass legislation that infringes on the freedom and dignity of the individual, and rulers are subject to the same positive laws as other citizens.

Natural law is the foundation for the idea of human rights. Universal human rights have their basis in a common human nature, not in any particular culture or society. Natural law is the basis for rational judgments about what is and is not a human right. If we do not approach human rights from this perspective, the idea has neither logical boundaries nor any compelling basis for respect. But very few actors in the international human rights community at present appear to understand or be guided by the notion of natural law and natural rights. In about twenty-five years of working in international human rights, I have heard virtually no references to natural law or natural rights in the hundreds of seminars, conferences and briefings I have attended. The foundation of human rights in natural law has been eroded by ignorance or torn away by opposition. In its place are international standards and laws purporting to be concerned with universal human attributes but actually reflecting specific ideologies and time-bound geopolitics.

True human rights, in order to be firmly respected on a principled basis, must be understood to exist as *natural* rights, intrinsic to human beings.[6] These rights are "discernable by reason," which is transcultural and transhistorical. The ability to reason unites mankind, and reason is at the core of our common human nature. Natural rights are universal in their rationality, providing logical grounds for respecting the freedom and dignity of others, not as a matter of faith or dogma but as "principles of practical reason."[7] This does not imply that such principles are universally known, however, because reason is not universally respected.[8]

If we are to regain respect for authentic, universal human rights as distinct from those established by particular political communities, we must respect the idea of natural law as the source of human rights, existing prior to positive law and setting moral limits on state power. As societies have become secularized and have sought a rational foundation for ethics, natural law has assumed the place of sacred law, retaining a sense of the transcendent character of what is universally innate to human beings. Governments must honor human rights based on natural law if they are to respect human dignity and allow individuals to fulfill their human potential—if they are to respect the sacredness of personality and the sanctity of life, the highest teachings of our civilization.

The State's Obligation of Restraint

True human rights compel governments not to infringe on individual freedom; they do not require positive actions to change society. John Locke (1632–1704), considered to be the father of classical liberalism, showed that the primary obligation of governments was to reject the arbitrary exercise of power and to respect natural rights. He understood respect for natural rights as indispensable to peaceful and secure societies. Locke saw the main challenge of modern societies, and of the international community, as the tolerance of diversity. With the end of monarchical absolutism and the growing social and religious diversification in societies, a new social order required laws consistent with pluralism. (In fact, the challenge of *all* societies is diversity, because all cultures are pluralistic and dynamic, despite claims to the contrary.) Respecting rights in the situation of diversity called for protecting adherents to minority religious and political ideas from tyrannical rulers who aimed to suppress any possible threats to their power. The alternative to tolerance was oppression, bloodshed and endless chaos. Pluralism became an urgent challenge in premodern Europe, and it had to be addressed in a rational way. What would be the features of a state that allowed all to live in dignity and to "pursue happiness"?

In the tradition of empirical philosophy, seeking practical ideas based on observed reality, Locke found the main natural rights to be life, liberty and property. The state must not arbitrarily take life, because man by nature has a right to life. This means more than a right to be alive; it means a right to make of one's life what one chooses.[9] It means the right to a free life, because a life under coercion is not one's own. Since the right to life depends on the state to preserve law and order, some freedoms must be traded for the service of protection from criminals and invaders. But beyond this, governments should leave people free to take care of themselves. In the state of individual freedom from oppression by government, property rights have a central place, for property reflects what one has made of one's life. If governments or criminals can arbitrarily take an individual's property, then the freedom to acquire it means nothing, and the effort and ingenuity exercised to acquire it mean nothing. Brute force would become morally equal to intelligence and perseverance.

The rules to protect liberty are primarily rules about what states *should not* do with respect to the individual's choices, dignity or security. All of the early human rights declarations were about such "negative liberties," beginning with the Magna Carta of 1215, which Lord Denning described as "the foundation of the freedom of the individual against the arbitrary authority of the despot."[10] Negative liberties are not hard to define, to measure or to enforce. The major historical human rights charters were simple, and they emphasized the virtue of simplicity. The preamble to the French Declaration of the Rights of Man and of the Citizen (1789), for example, refers to its "simple and incontestable principles." Bills of rights need to be simple and accessible so that citizens can know and understand their rights.

Today, human rights law has all the clarity of a tax code, observes Jacob Mchangama, a Danish human rights lawyer. The average person needs the mediation of experts to understand human rights, and experts often disagree. This complexity owes largely to the mixing of human rights with positive law, with schemes to "enable freedom" by state intervention, through the regulation of economic, social and cultural life. The result is a system whereby individuals need to engage with complex and remote bureaucracies in order to make claims against the state for their basic liberties.

My experience in defending human rights against authoritarian governments has confirmed for me that violations of authentic human rights—of natural rights—are obvious, and so are their solutions. If a government is interfering in the work of a church or a club, the problem can be solved if it ceases to do so. If a government does not protect the equal rights of members of a certain religion, it can change its policy and start treating them equally.

If a government is censoring ideas and information, or using torture, it can simply stop engaging in those practices. The guarantee of negative liberties does not mean passivity on the part of the state, for positive law and regulations are required in order that states treat all individuals equally. Training and monitoring are needed to ensure that torture is not used. Apologists for the extension of human rights as positive rights often adduce this kind of state action as a ploy to blur the distinction between negative and positive liberties. But simple common sense tells us that what states must do in order to respect fundamental rights is mainly to refrain from interfering with individual freedom and civil society. The first priority of a liberal state is to ensure the rights of its citizens against its own power.

The Individual Human Right to Freedom

The *subject* of human rights is the individual person; only individual humans can have human rights. The rational foundation for this understanding draws upon Aristotle's analysis of the nature of man in the *Nicomachean Ethics* (350 B.C.). Aristotle said that in order to understand what is good for man and for communities, we must first understand the individual person and what is good for the individual. All individuals have a particular and unique existence; their character and their potential are not fully determined by any group, not even by the family, and in this respect they are free and self-determining. All individuals have the capacity to make sense of the world, to act independently, to appreciate moral ideas and intellectual challenges. While Aristotle concerned himself with the problem of maintaining security and order in society, he also established that individual freedom is necessary to human fulfillment.

Individuals are objectively the basic unit of human life everywhere, so we need to begin with the individual in seeking answers to ethical and political questions about freedom, authority, and the obligations and limits of governments. Individuals are a universal and irreducible human reality; there is nothing less than an individual. Social formations are not universal; some would say they are artificial. Families are defined in various ways in different societies and cultures; so are racial, ethnic, tribal, national, religious and other communities. Members of specific age cohorts do not have the same rights everywhere. Gender is more and more the source of category disputes, with individuals challenging gender categories as well as social traditions.

Categorical identities become more fluid and irrelevant to dignity and rights. Because group identity is arbitrary, the assertion of *individual* human rights makes rational sense. Human rights apply to individuals per se.

The classical concept of human rights is based on core human characteristics found across all cultures. This view is in sharp contrast to any form of tribalism or ethnic nationalism, to any form of coercive collectivism, and to any project of universalizing a political idea. Ethnic or religious or political chauvinism can encourage human rights violations under a suffocating conformism, and may condone aggression against other peoples and against nonconforming members of the society. Communists may say that economic class determines character and outlook, and therefore dictates the rights of particular individuals within states organized to meet collective interests. Nationalists may say that a person is fundamentally an element of an organic "nation," and that human fulfillment is impossible outside the context of one's nation. Extreme ethnic nationalists may believe that individual existence is only an abstraction and that individualism is a threat to the ethnonationalist state. Feminists may emphasize gender as determinative. To think of our core identity as being defined by group affiliations is inherently divisive, but the principle of individual human rights brings us together in mutual respect and freedom.

Although human rights focus on individuals, they have given us an ideal of brotherhood across ethnicities and creeds, political or religious, and across national borders. The idea of universal human rights draws upon the ethical foundation of monotheism—the moral teachings of Jerusalem and the rational philosophy of Athens. The Old Testament tells us that all human beings descended from common parents and are members of a single family; therefore none of us can claim a special birthright. It teaches that we are all subjects of one transcendent God, equal to one another and owing to each other the respect due to an equal. No earthly king can have total dominion over us, for monarchs too are subjects of the same God, a transcendent power beyond human understanding. Political power cannot be absolute; it is intrinsically arbitrary and must be judged against the principles of an eternal moral order. Each human soul, each personality is sacred. It is in our individuality, not in political or social structures, that we find a relationship to ultimate, universal truth. Religions have provided a basis for appreciating the freedom and dignity of individuals, which human rights are to protect, although no religious tradition includes any legal concept of human rights.[11]

Aristotle cannot be considered to have established the idea of human rights, since he shared his contemporaries' expectations that the state should coercively shape the character of citizens. Aristotle did not value freedom above all else, and he had no problem with governments restricting freedom. He was certainly unconvinced of the moral equality of all people, and he held that slavery was consistent with the natural order because some people were slaves by their nature. But he understood that freedom meant the absence of external coercion, as well as the ability to act by the guidance of reason rather than by internal compulsion.[12] The Stoic philosophers likewise considered freedom to include the ability of a person to apply rational self-scrutiny, to bring the passions under control, and to assume responsibility for one's own life.

A society governed by human rights principles is also capable of scrutinizing and critiquing itself, and of organizing its laws in a way that protects the freedom of the individual. Drawing upon the classical tradition of legal naturalism, Immanuel Kant (1724–1804) arguably did more than any other single figure to establish the modern idea of human rights. Kant showed how moral and ethical questions can be solved by reason, and he discovered rules for thinking about ethical problems that have universal application. Like Aristotle, he looked for practical and fair solutions to the moral problems of the individual and society, beginning with the human person—with the individual as a moral agent, capable of reasoning and of making choices based on reason. Kant's definition of freedom followed that of Aristotle: freedom is "independence from being constrained by another's choice."[13] Moral agency cannot be fulfilled without freedom, because without freedom we cannot properly bring our reason to bear on moral questions. A person's freedom of choice based on reason has intrinsic value. Individual freedom requires no utilitarian justification; it serves no purpose higher than itself.

In contemporary human rights discourse, we often hear about the need to establish the "conditions for the enjoyment of freedom." A potentially endless list of unfulfilled "needs" can thus be designated as obstacles to realizing individual freedom, and this list serves as a recipe and a rationale for compelling positive state actions on the basis of international law, burdening human rights with political and economic questions. But the idea of human rights holds that the condition for freedom is the absence of coercion. In his *Groundwork of the Metaphysics of Morals*, Kant wrote that actions can be right only if they are consistent with everyone's freedom. The goal of ethics, and of a state established on an ethical basis, is freedom, "the only original right, a right belonging to every individual by virtue of his humanity."[14]

Because the right to freedom is innate, it is not to be encroached upon by laws; hence the words in the United States Constitution: "Congress shall pass no law...." A bill of rights is a list of freedoms not to be threatened by legislation—of rights that originate in natural law, standing outside and above the positive law of states. Governments should allow their citizens to come together around social policies, in democratic legislative processes. Social policy is for legislatures, but sometimes legislatures pass laws that contravene human rights. For this reason, constitutions, constitutional courts and international standards are needed to protect human rights from overreaching legislatures and from majority rule. Ideally, human rights are sacrosanct and unconditional. They are to form a protective canopy over the individual, guarding a zone of autonomy and freedom. The strongest human rights protections, like the Bill of Rights appended to the Constitution, do not admit any conditions, although courts in fact apply conditions in deciding on rights claims. Under international law, all human rights are limitable except the right to be free from torture. Yet in limiting the exercise of human rights, governments must clearly state the specific circumstances and the reasons why those limitations are justified. Ideally, human rights are a "trump card" in the legal system.

Kant suggested a culture of human rights in which reason and freedom reinforce each other. Human rights are illuminated by reason; we arrive at the need to respect human rights through intellect. This basis for respecting human rights lies within each of us. The moral and natural law is rooted in our common capacity for rationality and moral autonomy. A person is morally good when he or she is able to act on an impersonal principle that is valid for everyone, not driven by passions or self-interest. This detachment from one's own political passions is a fundamental principle in the defense of authentic human rights.

Reason is necessary for recognizing and for implementing human rights, and with freedom comes a duty of the individual citizen to employ reason. Together, reason and human rights create societies where the freedoms of all are honored. Kant foresaw that a liberal democratic society that respects human rights must be one in which individuals employ reason in making moral and political decisions. Freedom is constituted by rights that prevent coercion, and also by the exercise of rational and moral agency. To be free, we must *think*.

Kant thought of human rights as not mainly concerned with security; he found that "rights are more precious than the safety the rights help secure."[15] This is something worth pondering for those living in modern industrial societies where governments have severely infringed on liberties, and increased their own power, in the process of protecting civilians from attack.

Political Neutrality and Individual Responsibility

Being above politics and positive law, human rights are not partisan or ideological. They are not meant to achieve specific social goals or objectives. Authentic human rights are politically "neutral," intended to protect freedom of choice and freedom from coercion and manipulation. Human rights do not establish a particular vision of a good or just society beyond the protection of basic individual freedoms. It was the moral genius of the Enlightenment philosophers to realize that any formula to protect human rights had to work in diverse political milieus. Human rights are politically flexible within the limits defined by preserving individual freedom. They are not supposed to create "social justice," which is defined variously by different people and groups; they do protect the *processes* by which people define and promote social justice as they understand it.

We do not know what will be the *results* of honoring human rights; that depends on the moral qualities of individuals whose rights are protected, whose freedom is respected, and whose activity in concert with others is honored. Human rights are not a matter of utilitarian calculation about what will or will not work to achieve social and political goals. In international human rights conclaves it is common to hear questions about whether respect for human rights will, in a specific situation, result in a more secure or harmonious society, in greater tolerance, or in peace. At a recent meeting of the Organization for Security and Cooperation in Europe (OSCE), for example, an American government delegate suggested that protecting freedom of religion "strengthens peace and stability." That may or may not be so; in some cases protecting human rights leads to conflict. Is strengthening peace and stability why protecting freedom of religion is necessary? If respecting human rights produces undesirable results, should those rights be infringed? Another example: in a social media chat-room, a contact claimed that affirmative-action racial quotas, which violate the principle of equality, are justified because they have been scientifically demonstrated to improve the cognitive performance of students. Even if that were true, is it worth violating a central principle of human rights? What if racial segregation were shown to improve cognition? Would that justify segregation?

Human rights is a formula that protects freedom and places moral responsibility on individuals. It makes moral agency possible, which is an end in itself. What people do with their freedom is up to them. Human rights do not make people good, but they give people and societies the *opportunity* to be good, with freedom and the burden of moral accountability.

The Duty to Protect Human Rights

Classical human rights established that states should respect the freedom of individuals not in order to accomplish social objectives, but because it is their *duty* to do so. A government policy can be changed if it does not produce the results intended, but honoring human rights is a matter of respecting principles, not of achieving specific results. Their motivation is "deontological," from the Greek *deon*, or duty—the ethical motivation to do what is right for its own sake. I have heard many government officials question whether taking action against human rights violations in specific situations would "do any good." Human rights activism is often criticized for being futile or quixotic, a criticism showing that the fundamental duty to respect human rights is neither recognized nor understood. Governments need to respect human rights not for the results that follow, but because doing so is consistent with a universal principle, the principle of freedom.

In the classical human rights vision, the societies of the world are bound together by the common duty to respect individual freedom and prevent tyranny. Kant's vision of human rights led to the conclusion that we all have a stake in one another's freedom, and that international peace and security require respect for shared principles and duties, international monitoring of the conditions of liberty, and global cooperation and pressure to address infringements. Kant envisioned an international human rights system as a politically neutral forum.[16] In *Perpetual Peace*, he proposed a global federation of republican states based on human rights and rule-of-law principles. This has discredited his other ideas among many who wish to preserve national sovereignty against "global governance," and who reject a "cosmopolitan" detachment from national identity. But if we believe in the universal right of all to enjoy the same freedoms and opportunities, and believe that tyranny in any part of the world is an assault on the dignity of people everywhere, we must conclude that an international human rights order that sets out standards and allows sovereign nations to be held to account has value for individual citizens, especially those struggling against oppression. When international human rights standards have been interpreted clearly and in a politically neutral manner, they have served as a point of reference for measuring the legitimacy of governments and identifying oppressive and abusive ones.

Yet today, faith in this system has been severely eroded, and it is not difficult to understand why. The international system of human rights, including international courts like the European Court of Human Rights, has strayed far into the realm of partisan politics. Respect for basic freedoms has become diluted as more and more things—human needs or simply wants—are named human rights. One consequence is a backlash against human rights hubris, and thus a weakening commitment to the very idea of an international human rights system among heirs to the classical liberal tradition. That system has become a tangled bureaucracy where core concepts are distorted by politics and faddish judicial activism. Now we begin our analysis of how this unfortunate situation came about.

The Universal Declaration: Geopolitical Expediency, Ideological Bias

The international human rights system is built on a faulty foundation, one inconsistent with the foundations of the idea of human rights itself. The Universal Declaration of Human Rights (UDHR) of 1948 mingled human rights based on natural law with positive rights granted by states—rights that emerged from specific political traditions. By doing so, it aggrandized positive economic and social rights as human rights intrinsic to human beings, while degrading authentic human rights into nothing more than arbitrary gifts of the state. But the international community did not grant human rights to the people of the world. If we accepted that notion, we would be no more respectful of human rights than Chinese Communists and other state ideologues who claim the prerogative to define human rights to suit their own politics.

Because it includes economic and social rights, the Universal Declaration is a political document, with both virtues and faults. Yet to cast doubt upon its integrity is considered a form of heresy, like criticizing the Ten Commandments. Although dictatorships such as the one in Uzbekistan have been known to abuse citizens for possessing copies of the document, it is virtually everywhere afforded unique moral authority and prestige. The

UDHR is regarded as history's proudest example of forging an international, multicultural, politically pluralistic consensus on the need to protect human dignity. It has defined human rights for the international community and established principles for the self-regulation of sovereign states. It provides a framework for international dialogue on human rights, for the promulgation of legally binding treaties, for monitoring and enforcement mechanisms, and for the human rights work of civil society. It is considered a triumph of Eleanor Roosevelt and other revered personalities. The emergence of the Universal Declaration has assumed an almost miraculous aura—comparable to the Decalogue being handed down by God, except this list was crafted by men from the best human values. Asbjørn Eide, a leading scholar on human rights and an advocate for economic and social rights, wrote that the UDHR marked the start of a "program" of global transformation to allow all people to live in "humane" societies.[17]

If public advocates for international human rights disagree with parts of the UDHR—or, for that matter, with the various UN human rights treaties it spawned—they face the legitimate criticism that they are violating a basic principle of the rule of law by "cherry-picking" among internationally endorsed principles. The UDHR established a way of thinking about human rights that has shaped our contemporary approach to the issue. Tragically, it set processes in train that have led to the disintegration of human rights as a concept. If we are serious about addressing the problems in human rights discourse today, we need to recognize that these problems stem from the UDHR, and stop treating it as a sacred cow, immune from criticism.

A Note on Historical Context

An international scheme for the protection of human rights became a central concern of some members of the world community during World War II, when leaders of the Allied powers sought to define their vision of a peaceful and just world that would follow the expected defeat of Nazi Germany and imperial Japan. Respect for *individual* human rights gained favor as a principal goal of the nascent United Nations Organization, in part due to the failure of the League of Nations to protect collective, minority rights, and the Nazis' cruel exploitation of the principle.[18]

The preamble of the 1945 Charter of the United Nations declared that the founding members were "determined . . . to reaffirm faith in fundamental human rights." Under Chapter IX, they agreed to promote "universal respect for, and observance of, human rights and fundamental freedoms for all without distinction as to race, sex, language, or religion." The project of an international bill of rights started in 1946, with the appointment of an initiating committee by the United Nations Educational, Scientific and Cultural Organization (UNESCO). Ideas about what ought to be included as human rights in such a document were solicited through a survey sent to world leaders. Apparently there was no dominant *a priori* concept of human rights at the outset, or any standard by which concepts would be evaluated. At a later stage, a wide-ranging committee of jurists and social scientists put forth their views on what human rights were, or should be. The guiding principle was inclusion: *Human rights were taken to be what respected leaders and intellectuals from around the world considered them to be.* A multiplicity of approaches to protecting universal human rights would be accommodated.

As a central project of the developing United Nations, the UDHR was produced by an eighteen-member, international Human Rights Commission chaired by Eleanor Roosevelt. It was approved on December 10, 1948, the day subsequently celebrated each year as "Human Rights Day." Given the importance that human rights have assumed in international affairs over the past sixty-nine years, the inception of the UDHR is regarded by internationalists as a turning point in history. But at the time it was a peripheral event during a period of dramatic change and peril. Some comprehensive histories of the postwar period and detailed biographies of top world leaders do not even mention it. The signing of the document did make the front page of the *New York Times*, but not as the top story. The event has assumed its importance in retrospect.

The Universal Declaration is commonly seen to reflect a global moral response to the Holocaust and to assaults on civilians during the Second World War. It is thought to demonstrate that the genocide and mass murder during the war years had convinced world leaders and the international public that respect for human rights must underpin the values of a new international system, indeed, a "New Postwar World."[19] It is probably an exaggeration, however, to say the UDHR was mainly prompted by the shock of the Holocaust. In 1948, the Nuremberg trials were over and a desire to close the books on Nazi crimes was palpable. Few were interested in the horrors known to the survivors. There was little public information or discussion about the Nazi genocide, as both perpetrators and appeasers tried to evade responsibility, while the living victims struggled mainly in silence.[20] As for Stalin's mass murders, they are rarely cited as a motivation for the human rights initiative.

While the UDHR is now typically seen as a response to the bloody and tragic historical events of World War II, descriptions of the document largely ignore its postwar political context and its political *character*. In fact, it was a product of domestic and international politics as much as idealism about human rights. It came into existence during years of intense military and ideological combat. The document was written during a phase of ideological rearmament both by the democratic West and by the forces of Soviet-backed communism. Communist agitation had made Italy unstable; the Communist Party in Italy included two million members. The Communist Party in France made a serious bid for power. Communists seized control of Czechoslovakia in a coup organized by Stalin in February 1948, foreshadowing the future of a Soviet-controlled Eastern Europe. The conflict between the Communist and the Free World was overt and violent; people around the world felt a third world war was imminent. The American president compared dealing with Stalin to dealing with Hitler. A civil war raged between Communists and their opponents in Greece, with both sides getting support from outside states; it ended in 1949, after almost 160,000 had been killed. West Berlin was block-aded by the Soviets, causing a dangerous international crisis and forcing an airlift. The Communist Party of China made strong gains in the Chinese civil war, which claimed six million casualties, mainly civilians, between 1945 and 1949; the capture of one city, Changchun, resulted in about 160,000 civilian deaths. Other conflicts raged, most notably the Arab-Israeli War.

Despite Stalin's atrocities, the aggressive usurpation of power in Central Europe, and threats to democracy posed by Communist parties in Western Europe, the Soviet Union and communism enjoyed heightened global prestige in the immediate postwar years. After all, the Soviet Union had played a crucial role in defeating Nazi Germany, suffering massive civilian casualties in the process. Communists were seen as "liberators" who brought with them a humane vision for the postwar world, as contrasted with the "right-wing" fascism they had vanquished. Conservatives in Europe and the United States found themselves placed on the "fascist" side of an ideological map drawn by Communists and socialists. Movements against colonial rule and colonialism were sweeping the globe, and most of these were not simply about self-determination, but aimed to bring an end to economic inequalities and exploitation and racial discrimination. In a mood of economic optimism, leaders in liberal democracies promised generous benefits to citizens.

The content of the UDHR reflects this global political landscape and the move toward socialism in Western states that occurred during the Great Depression and the immediate postwar years. The document might be seen as a sort of ideological peace treaty in a militarized and fluid international climate, with its combination of Western and Eastern concepts of human rights. The Christian humanist scholar Jacques Maritain, in mapping a human rights standard for UNESCO in 1948, said those differing concepts could be bound together "if we adopt a practical viewpoint and concern ourselves no longer with seeking a basis and philosophical significance of human rights but only in their statement and enumeration."[21] What he seems to have meant is, "Accommodating the Communist view of human rights is simple: just forget about what human rights means." The framers of the UDHR, strongly influenced by a belief that peace could be secured through redistributionist economics, strove for a consensus on the concept of human rights not in a legally binding treaty, but in a set of principles, a "common standard of achievement." At that time, states were unwilling to cede their sovereignty to support a human rights treaty, but virtually all agreed to endorse the lofty aspirational principles contained in the UDHR.

A Political Accommodation

The Universal Declaration accepted by members of the United Nations reflected the political values both of states committed to individual liberty and of Stalin's totalitarian regime, which, it can be argued, had less respect for individual freedom than had Hitler's Germany. Soviet communism recognized no individual human rights or freedoms that could be exercised against the state and that inhered in human existence as such. The Soviet ideology held that the state confers human rights, and no right thus conferred would allow citizens to mount a serious challenge to the state or the Communist Party. People living under Soviet dominion enjoyed no right to choose alternatives in elections, no freedom to form civil organizations, no freedom of speech, no access to independent courts. The Soviet constitution of 1936 recognized collective economic and social rights, which were claimed to benefit the whole society. It did guarantee freedom of religion, in Article 124, but this was never implemented. Citizens lived at the mercy of a single-party state so disrespectful of their right to life that it murdered as many as twenty million people considered to be political opponents by summary or quasi-legal executions, in Gulag camps, or by starvation. Soviet law was seen by state officials as nothing but an instrument of power, to serve the goals of the Communist Party. They regarded this as the proper role of the law. Vladislav Ribnikar, the Yugoslav delegate on the Human Rights Commission and an orthodox Marxist, declared that "in the modern world, the right of the state superseded the so-called rights of the individual, and that real liberty could be reached only by achieving a complete harmony between individual people and the collectivity of the state."[22]

The Universal Declaration was constructed to gain the acquiescence of the Soviet Union, its satellite nations and its many client states in the Third World, by incorporating collective economic and social rights including the right to social security (Article 22); "the right to a standard of living adequate for the health and well-being" of oneself and one's family, "including food, clothing, housing and medical care and necessary social services" (Article 25); and the right to education (Article 26). And the framers of the document insisted that these rights be given full moral equivalence with fundamental civil and political rights.

The inclusive list of human rights in the UDHR thus reflected a philosophical compromise, giving liberals, socialists and Communists what they considered to be human rights. But it also served geopolitical purposes. Western powers needed the Soviet bloc *inside* the new international security architecture; they thus needed them in a global consensus on human rights, which was becoming a primary measure of the legitimacy of states. To bring the Eastern bloc along, it was necessary to put economic and social rights alongside those protecting freedom. Economic and social rights provided these states with an illusion of upholding human rights, *an illusion not only they, but also the rest of the international community needed.* The world powers were exhausted by the most devastating war in history. The progressive parties in the United States and Europe in particular sought peace with Stalin. The inclusion strategy was the way of those who opposed confrontation, and it remains the same in the contemporary world. For example, international structures like the European Union and the Council of Europe, which impose human rights standards on their members, have been expanded to include states that have not complied, as a means to transform them "from within." The expansive interpretation of human rights was a way to avoid violent conflict with the East, and to support long-term processes of gradual internal change within totalitarian states.

The resulting document is thus a bricolage that posits as universal both human rights illuminated by philosophical reflection and human rights that emerged from political traditions and movements. Its authors melded principled and politically neutral freedom rights with particular entitlements said to be essential to enjoying freedom; they fused together "negative" and "positive" liberties. The Universal Declaration thus represents incompatible ideas about the essence of freedom and of human nature. Its authors sought inclusion and consensus, sacrificing moral distinctions that would have been divisive and probably destructive of the process that created the document. While acknowledging practical differences in honoring the different kinds of human rights, they equated those rights morally. In the last interview he gave before his death in February 2013, Stéphane Hessel, a French diplomat and former Resistance hero who participated in negotiations over the UDHR, said it was crafted to satisfy everyone.[23]

As it happened, the Soviet Union and several of its allies abstained from endorsing the document, as did Saudi Arabia, because it called for respecting individual civil and political rights. These were seen as political weapons that had been forged into international human rights standards to serve the political agenda of Western democracies, namely to overthrow Communist regimes. Then as now, civil and political human rights were seen as a form of politics, not as politically neutral rules that protect the freedom of all citizens, including members of minorities.

For some, the content of the Universal Declaration was perhaps a compromise for the sake of a greater good. Indeed, the drafters have been hailed as visionaries for mixing the "rights" touted by totalitarians with the classical freedom rights, and the document itself has been described as possessing an "organic" quality. According to Hessel, "It was agreed that civil and political rights could not be addressed without also addressing economic and social rights," and he credited Mrs. Roosevelt and René Cassin with joining the two kinds of rights "and even declaring them inseparable." Hessel also observed that "this unifying of the preoccupations of the West and the East corresponded to a very particular moment in history, i.e., to those three or four years after the war."[24] Hessel, it may be noted, was an ideological leftist who in his last years gave impetus to the Occupy Wall Street movement with a pamphlet urging revolt against the "international dictatorship of the financial markets."[25] He also bemoaned that the UDHR had not included "environmental rights."

The Influence of Progressivism

Economic and social rights found their way into the international human rights system in part as a result of international realpolitik, by which their inclusion was justified as a condition for international peace and security. But what is more relevant for the subsequent development of human rights is the influence of a positive tradition of social activism that framed itself as promoting human rights through the Universal Declaration. As the historian Samuel Moyn wrote, the document serves as "a template for national welfarism," consistent with the "unprecedented promises" that nation-states were making in the postwar period.[26]

Received opinion held that the catastrophe of World War II had sprung from economic problems. Widespread unemployment and poverty after the First World War had led to political upheaval and the rise of totalitarian regimes, it was believed, and thus the horrors of Nazism became an argument for advancing specific economic policies under the banner of human rights. Particularly in the West, securing economic and social rights came to be regarded as good in itself but also as essential "for the preservation of individual freedom and democracy."[27]

The idea of economic and social rights as human rights to be achieved via positive law embedded itself into the Universal Declaration as a reflection of the progressive political tradition. Progressivism is a broad term that encompasses a range of political doctrines sharing a belief that government can and should intervene heavily in society to achieve more equality and efficiency and to solve social problems. It originated with Plato's hierarchical yet essentially communistic vision for society in *The Republic*.

In the nineteenth century, G.W.F. Hegel, in *The Philosophy of History*, took the position that societies and communities are the true sources of moral and political values; that ethical obligations have their basis in social life. Hegel was deeply skeptical of any notion of universal human rights, and he regarded human rights as "empty abstractions."[28] True freedom could be realized only through the state. Isaiah Berlin, who illuminated the distinction between positive and negative liberties in his influential *Four Essays on Liberty*, wrote that Hegel's notion of positive liberty was "at the heart of many of the nationalist, communist, authoritarian and totalitarian creeds of our day."[29]

Karl Marx had nothing but scorn for the idea of human rights. His clearest words on the subject are found in the essay *On the Jewish Question*, in which he said that the "so-called rights of man" was a bourgeois idea, representing man as "an individual withdrawn behind his private interests and whims and separated from the community," as a citizen and "a member of civil society" but "egoistic and independent."[30] As Zühtü Arslan summed it up, "Marx attacked human rights because he believed they represented a false view of human nature as selfish and egoistical, and of the social structure as consisting of isolated monads separable from and atomically constitutive of the community."[31] This view of individual rights as fundamentally self-seeking persists strongly today. Professor Thomas Cushman observed in a Facebook post that left-wing ideologues regularly insist that individual rights claims are "always about power and domination, rather than freedom."

Unlike the natural rights tradition, which is *philosophical*, progressivism is a *political* tradition, elements of which exist in many mainstream political parties. The progressive tradition is not about *how* the state ought to treat individuals, but about *what* the goals of society should be—about the meaning of "social justice." It asks what the ideal society would look like and how it could be achieved. Progressivism has been described as a reaction to liberalism and a result of declining religious belief: having lost faith in God, progressives put their faith in the ability of the state to create a utopia.[32]

Since the early nineteenth century, the progressive creed has animated various political movements, some following the revolutionary doctrines of Karl Marx, waging campaigns, often violent, on behalf of poorer citizens. In 1848, violent upheavals affected virtually every European country as well as some in Latin America. New urban working classes, emerging middle classes and reformers demanded political reforms from monarchies. The uprisings faltered after a short time but instilled fear in political leaders. The threat of class warfare led Otto von Bismarck, as chancellor of Germany, to institute social legislation to provide for health insurance and unemployment compensation. In 1881, Bismarck prompted Germany's emperor, Wilhelm I, to write in a letter to the parliament that "those who are disabled from work by age and invalidity have a well-grounded claim to care from the state." The German government established the most comprehensive program of social entitlements in the world, to ward off the threat of a Communist revolution and in an attempt to nullify the political attraction of the Social Democratic Party. Those entitlements were called "rights." They were created by legislation that identified various categories of people as bearers of rights, and the government and its bureaus as "duty-bearers." Economic and social rights appeared in the constitutions of the Weimar Republic, Spain, Ireland and numerous other countries.

The ideal of a welfare state with the main goal of solving social problems and the power to do so had grown stronger across Europe and America, but it ran into conflict—especially in the United States—with the liberal principle that the primary obligation of the state is to protect individual freedom. The American Founders, and particularly James Madison in *The Federalist*, saw restraints on state power through the enumeration and separation of powers as key to preventing tyranny and to safeguarding basic liberties. But progressives of all varieties have shared an impatience with individual rights and have associated the protection of those rights with *individualism*, which they oppose.[33] Progressives in the early twentieth century espoused what was essentially a Hegelian notion of positive freedom, and explicitly rejected the idea of natural rights. According to David Bernstein, a legal scholar, they "thought that the very notion of inherent individual rights against the state was a regressive notion with roots in reactionary natural rights ideology."[34] True freedom, they said, was made possible by government action, not by government restraint.

The progressive movement deepened a rupture in American politics over the classical liberalism of the Founders. Ambivalence about natural rights had been building since the early nineteenth century, but it became acute during the presidency of Franklin Delano Roosevelt, who in 1944 urged the passage of a "Second Bill of Rights." In his State of the Union address that year, Roosevelt ruminated about how the war had demonstrated the importance of "interdependence." He made what was essentially a revolutionary proposal to supplement the basic, negative liberties guaranteed by the Constitution with economic and social rights. He famously said: "We have come to a clear realization of the fact that true individual freedom cannot exist without economic security and independence. 'Necessitous men are not free men.' People who are hungry and out of a job are the stuff of which dictatorships are made."[35]

Roosevelt's statement manifests a reductive determinism that made the attainment of freedom dependent on the social programs central to his political agenda. This position contradicted the traditional American view that the real threat to freedom is coercion; it was at odds with the vision of man as a moral agent with moral freedom, suggesting instead that economic conditions mold human character and potential. Roosevelt's vision stood in stark contrast to that of the Enlightenment philosophers who saw humans as independent individuals with the capacity for moral choice and with responsibility for their actions. To Roosevelt, as the statement suggests, people were "stuff" to be formed by their social environment and by the state's largesse, and also "stuff" with which government builds the state.

Roosevelt's view could be seen as calling into question the foundational American quest for liberty. In choosing to revolt against the British Crown to secure basic liberties, the American revolutionaries had risked their security and well-being, which at that time had reached a high standard in the world. The subsequent history of the United States was replete with examples of political freedom being responsibly exercised by disadvantaged and destitute citizens, contrary to what President Roosevelt claimed to be a "self-evident" truth. On the basis of his so-called "economic truths," he outlined an extensive list of rights, including rights to a "decent and remunerative job," a "decent home," "adequate medical care," and a "good education." These benefits could be supplied as "rights" only by taxation and coercion, and the president's speech includes a thinly veiled threat of dire political consequences if they are not provided. Perhaps most importantly, it expresses a view of the individual as not ultimately responsible for moral or political choices. It is the vision of a person whose actions are not the result of rational choice or moral agency, but only reactions to events and conditions. Note that Roosevelt was speaking at a time when the horrific crimes of the Nazis were coming to light, and his words might even be seen as providing an exculpation.

Again, Roosevelt's idea of human rights had its opponents in American politics, and the United States government's approach to the Universal Declaration can be described as a pragmatic effort to smooth over the division. The administration of Harry S. Truman, who had appointed Eleanor Roosevelt to the UN Human Rights Commission, solidly supported the inclusion of economic and social rights in the document. Truman's views are clear from a speech he gave at Christ Church College, Oxford, after he had left the presidency, in which he stated that "we must declare in a new Magna Carta, in a new Declaration of Independence, that henceforth economic well being and security, that health and education and decent living standards, are among our inalienable rights."[36] The American and other Western diplomats who went along with including economic and social rights sought a middle path within a middle path: these rights would be seen as human rights in the UDHR, but were not fit to be codified into legally binding international obligations. It was a strategy of philosophical appeasement, a vague "third way," but also a holding pattern wherein economic and social rights were seen as human rights, though not of the same kind as civil and political rights. The failure to defend human rights on the basis of natural law and natural rights would exact a terrible price.

The Implications of Economic and Social Rights

The Universal Declaration was drafted mainly by John Humphrey, a Canadian jurist who had been appointed the first director of the UN Division of Human Rights in 1946. That he was personally a socialist could and should have meant nothing, since classical freedom rights are nonpartisan and can be embraced by people with a wide range of political views. But the most careful academic analysts have shown that Humphrey's language—the language that would end up in the document—mirrored what the Soviet Union tried to insert, affirming a "state as provider" model of human rights.[37]

In his book *Human Rights and the United Nations*, Humphrey claimed that he had not been influenced by any particular view of human rights, but simply tried to "include all the rights mentioned in various national constitutions and in various suggestions for an International Bill of Human Rights." But he also wrote, "The best of the texts from which I worked was the one prepared by the American Law Institute, and I borrowed freely from it."[38] The American Law Institute promoted a "relational" approach to human rights, and Humphrey evidently "drew extensively" on ideas submitted by the organization.[39] In this view, human rights were not narrowly a matter of the relation between the individual and the state, but were also to govern horizontal relationships in civil society, providing a comprehensive moral frame extending into the economic and social spheres.

Another important influence was the work of a "Conference of Philosophers," or "Committee on the Philosophic Principles of the Rights of Man," convened by UNESCO to provide input for the Universal Declaration. The philosophers' recommendations included both freedom rights and economic and social rights.[40]

It seems that the strongest influence on the content of the document was the work of Hersch Lauterpacht, a brilliant legal scholar and prominent expert on international law. Humphrey admired Lauterpacht and had collaborated with him on joint publications. Lauterpacht had been commissioned by the American Jewish Committee in 1942 to draft an international bill of rights, which he finished in 1944. His book *An International Bill of the Rights of Man* shows with remarkable erudition how natural rights must lie at the foundation of an international human rights treaty. But he included economic and social rights in a model international bill of rights presented in the book. Such a bill "must recognize the connection between political freedom and economic freedom, between legal equality and economic and social equality of opportunity," he wrote in explaining their inclusion. "That connection has been gradually admitted since the French Revolution," he added, saying that human rights "should safeguard man from undeserved want generally" and should "assure to him the right to work, to education, and to social security."[41] Political freedom was "incomplete" without "economic freedom," said Lauterpacht. He equated entitlements with freedom, which meant that "economic freedom of the many…can in many respects be achieved only by putting economic restraints upon the few."[42] The case for economic and social rights as human rights was argued not in terms of natural law or natural rights, but on the grounds of history: these rights had become the norm, and thus existed as universals. Lauterpacht sidestepped the central question of whether or not we can classify entitlements granted by governments as innate, natural, universal human rights that exist in a transcendent moral realm. "It is idle speculation," he asserted, "if positive action on the part of the State is the consequence of any inherent natural rights, or whether it is an obligation of the State implied in the fact of social solidarity and independent of any individualistic doctrine of society. The result is the same."[43]

Here was perhaps the seminal logical lapse that would corrupt international human rights. The very idea of human rights that was subsequently adopted by the international community and the human rights community was fundamentally unsound.

First, it suggested the existence of *collective* human rights, which is a logical contradiction. Human rights are by nature rights belonging to individuals. Groups, nations, states and other collectivities do not and cannot have human rights because they are not humans. They do not possess moral agency; they cannot make decisions, have beliefs, or engage in reasoning.[44] But economic and social rights, as they appeared in the UDHR and in subsequent human rights documents, are framed as the claims of groups. Individual rights apply universally and are relevant to every human being, while economic and social rights apply to those in particular situations of need, addressing interests of some groups that inevitably conflict with those of others.

Rather than promoting a brotherhood of man, these collective rights have produced a human rights tribalism and identity politics on the international level. New UN human rights treaties protecting the elderly and "peasants' rights" are under consideration. The UN human rights system includes an array of over thirty special investigative and reporting mandates, many of which deal with issues that have nothing to do with human rights at all, such as sovereign debt, yet these institutions occupy resources and time, serving as platforms for political propaganda and crowding out the issue of freedom. Human rights proliferation has encouraged the belief that all groups that are in some way disadvantaged in society must have their own human rights treaty mandating government entitlements. Economic and social rights have opened a moral and legal space to justify discrimination in the name of an engineered equality, for example with racial and gender quotas in international human rights legislation.

Second, economic and social rights do not protect individual freedom and moral autonomy, but instead are meant to enhance well-being. They are associated largely with political systems in which restrictions of individual freedom are regarded as necessary and are often morally rationalized. The presence of economic and social rights in the UDHR has encouraged the notion that human rights, and freedom itself, are dependent upon state programs rather than government restraint. Freedom, as per Hegel's view, has been made into a product of the state, unattainable without specific state actions.

The goods provided by economic and social rights are not universally understood, but are relative to time and place. Positive state actions require time to be developed and to take effect, so a delay or failure in implementing those rights may be understood and forgiven. This understanding creates mental space to think of *all* human rights as requiring time to implement, and thus it diminishes the urgency of removing impediments to freedom and suggests that honoring basic freedoms is more complicated than it actually is; that such rights can be subjected to compromise and adjudication.[45] Because economic and social rights are realized only with adequate national resources and through gradual development, the presence of these rights in the international system has given the impression that authentic human rights also require time and funding. The republics of Central Asia became independent with the dissolution of the Soviet Union decades ago, yet their representatives in international forums still beg for time to eradicate torture, to respect the rights of free and independent media, and to hold free and fair elections. Often these pleas are accompanied by requests for more financial assistance and training.

When an "adequate standard of living" is declared to be a universal human right, anything deemed necessary to an adequate standard of living must be guaranteed as a matter of logic. And so there's a proliferation of new human rights—to water, sanitation, clear air, *ad infinitum*—portending a global community in which a huge spectrum of activity is regulated by human rights law. The clear, sharp focus of human rights has been dissolved in an amorphous stew of what is considered prerequisite for the good life.

The third contradiction is that economic and social rights are aimed at achieving specific social objectives; they are thus utilitarian or pragmatic, by contrast with rights that are to be honored on the basis of a universal principle. Social policy is concerned with achieving results, but human rights cannot be about specific results, for that would amount to a political program. Social policy can accommodate a pragmatic approach, whereby some undesirable outcomes may be tolerated for the sake of a larger good. But human rights are ends in and of themselves, not to be traded off in deference to other objectives. In fact, protecting human rights can and does lead to some undesirable outcomes by allowing individuals to exercise free will in a self-determining civil society. The Ku Klux Klan is free to be a racist, anti-Semitic association if it does not advocate violence. It is up to civil society to counteract such moral failings. The protection of human rights should not be dependent on calculations of whether it delivers what is thought to be good. If the human right to be free from torture were subjected to a pragmatic calculus, torture would be permitted when it served some good purpose. Thankfully, there is a firm sense among law-abiding governments that torture is universally a violation of human rights. But the pragmatism inherent in economic and social rights is a threat to the unconditional character of the human rights that protect fundamental freedoms.

The recognition of economic and social rights leads to indulgence of oppression within the human rights framework. For instance, a human rights activist involved in urging governments to improve the availability of palliative care had extensive cooperation from dictatorial regimes, and he said it was a relief to be free of confrontation in civil and political human rights work. But the cooperative process with a human rights organization on the subject of medical reform would likely be ostentatiously put on exhibit by abusive governments as proof that they respect human rights and that criticisms on that score are unfounded. By the same token, campaigns to promote economic and social rights sometimes make liberal democracies, where citizens enjoy freedom and political choice, appear no better than dictatorships. When the UN special rapporteur on the "right to food" investigated Canada, for example, he found that food prices were higher in the more remote regions and that many Canadians made use of food banks. The media painted Canada as a country where elites willfully deprived others of nourishment.

Economic and social rights blur the distinction between tyrannies and free states, a fundamental standard by which the legitimacy of regimes should be judged. It is perhaps in reaction to this error that some activists have focused only on governments they consider dictatorial, ignoring the situation of many citizens in liberal democracies whose human rights are violated.[46] In this way, economic and social rights have pushed authentic human rights into the political realm, compromising the political neutrality essential to their protection.

At the same time, political issues have been moved into the realm of international law by the elevation of economic and social rights. The goals of social policy are intrinsically political; they are matters of dispute in society, best decided by democratic processes. But economic and social rights provide a legal basis for citizens to make claims against the state for services (or a "share of material goods")[47] that states are obligated to provide.

Thus, international human rights have been politicized. Frank Holman, who was then the president of the American Bar Association, predicted in 1948 that the United Nations human rights system "would promote state socialism, if not communism, around the world." He and others feared for the sovereignty of the United States if it accepted the international human rights system, as they thought it might impose a particular economic regime on the country in the name of human rights.[48] These fears have not been realized, but there is no disputing that economic proposals with a distinctly ideological basis are actively promoted under the flag of the United Nations. As will be seen in more detail below, the UN human rights system is *increasingly* politicized and ideologically slanted.

The Universal Declaration's inclusion of economic and social rights thus did much more than provide totalitarian states with a place under the moral tent of human rights and integrate them into the ethical dimension of the United Nations. It did more than confer moral respectability on brutal dictatorships. The Soviet bloc had used human rights, or their interpretation of human rights, as a "weapon," according to Stéphane Hessel. Subsequent generations of ideologues would follow suit, with varying degrees of transparency, while also claiming that civil and political rights were nothing but ideological weapons. In the United Nations, the definition of human rights could be bent to accommodate both political expediency and ideological politics.

As Hessel noted, the UDHR also embodied the notion of the *indivisibility* of human rights—the idea that citizens of a society without social rights cannot by definition enjoy freedom, and vice versa. As we will see, "indivisibility" does not stand up as a legal principle when one looks carefully at relationships between different kinds of rights and how they support or conflict with one another. In essence, it is a slogan generally used to promote leftist economics or anti-Western politics. Although "indivisibility" did not emerge as a political human rights strategy until the early 1950s,[49] an astute observer of UN human rights politics would later note that "[t]he Declaration had given authoritative expression to the fact that human rights are indivisible. . . . It is the synthesis of classical and social rights which, perhaps more than anything else, has given the Declaration its universal appeal."[50] Social rights were not only embedded next to freedom rights and locked with them in a poisonous embrace; they were equated with those rights. Indivisibility would become another political tool for expanding human rights discourse in order to advance the status of marginalized people and their "suppressed narratives."[51]

The Universal Declaration did not provide a clear path forward for human rights, but created paths leading in various directions. It opened human rights law to political agendas. The historian Mark Mazower described the mix of rights and politics in the document as a victory over formalists who tried to insist on the inclusion only of rights that could be precisely defined and simply enforced. Aside from the geopolitical expediency of including economic and social rights, the declaration reflects the view that "moral aspirations might come themselves to be regarded as a source of law." Its ambiguities as an "aspirational document" were an invitation to activist interpretations that serve an "ongoing effort to assert the power of law over politics."[52] In declaring specific political values to be human rights, the UDHR paved the way for the postmodern school of critical legal theory, which maintains that the law is nothing more than a reflection of power relationships and is designed to serve political interests.

In fact, the growing quasi-legal machinery of international economic and social rights is transparently driven by ideological motives, toward political ends. The distinction between ideology and human rights is overwhelmingly disregarded by the international human rights community. Most activists evidently do not even recognize a distinction. Political consensus and pragmatism are considered legitimate sources of human rights, despite the fact that majoritarian democratic politics often lead to violations of human rights. For example, William F. Schulz, who led the American chapter of Amnesty International, said that sources of human rights included political thought and action, religion, natural rights and philosophical pragmatism. According to Schulz and colleagues in a publication of the Center for American Progress,

> Progressives throughout time have drawn on all four sources in their defense of human rights, although they have sometimes expressed criticism of religious and natural rights traditions as insufficient grounds for protecting the full range of political, social, and economic rights and instead favored a pragmatic defense of human rights grounded in political consensus as more enduring.[53]

Democratic consensus is essential to evaluating the "moral and practical worth of ideas." A "pragmatic" mixing of leftist political ideology and natural rights has, indeed, become second nature in the international community.

Some activists and other members of the human rights community understand the contradiction between economic and social rights and human rights, but will not defend a critical position that places them against international law and public opinion, and out of favor in international institutions; a position that generally—and unfairly—tars its adherents as "right wing" and unconcerned about poverty, injustice, and the wide range of other problems like environmental degradation and climate change that are purported to be proper subjects of human rights legislation. To admit the deep contradiction between economic and social rights and human rights places one in an untenable position, unable to work with a large and expanding range of human rights issues in the international system. The intellectual corruption of international human rights is something better left "under the rug" if activists want to preserve the good things about human rights law, of which there are many.

The vast majority of human rights activists and lawyers, international civil servants, legal scholars and philosophers have tried to find ways to classify economic and social rights as human rights, in part to defend the flawed international system of human rights, and in part for ideological or pragmatic reasons, but it is intellectually dishonest to do so. Critics of economic and social rights typically speak of their weaknesses as human rights: the fact that they are vague and not justiciable. Some rightly point out that supposed economic and social rights impinge on democratic processes, placing courts in the position of making laws. Others have noted that they do not address "paramount" questions.[54] But most of those who have cautioned against equating civil and political rights with economic and social rights have usually argued that the latter *are* human rights, but of a different kind than civil and political rights; that they are "second generation" rights that need to be treated differently, and perhaps are of secondary importance. The position of Human Rights Watch, a leading American NGO, seems to be pragmatic: to work with economic and social rights when they can be the basis for extracting concrete benefits that people need. The human rights organizations that have followed this practice have drifted toward becoming social welfare lobbies, addressing a vast range of social problems with no firm criteria for setting priorities.

The defenders of economic and social rights downplay or discount altogether the difference between negative liberties and positive rights. A philosophy professor at a leading British university informed me that over the past twenty years, no philosopher of human rights has conceded that there is any fundamental difference between human rights that require restraint on the part of states and those that require positive actions. The mixing of human rights with economic and social rights is often defended with the trivial argument that state actions are also necessary to achieve negative liberties, such as freedom from torture, or the right to a fair trial. Another argument is that the achievement of human rights too is a process, involving compromises. The effort to prove that these kinds of rights are the same has the effect of burdening human rights with the difficulties of economic and social rights.

The inclusion of economic and social rights in the Universal Declaration has been the Achilles' heel of international human rights, the weak point that has allowed the fundamental human right of freedom to be demoted and trampled. In the majoritarian international system, social-democratic goals now called human rights can give way to repression in the name of human rights. The UDHR provides a flawed conceptual foundation for the international human rights system. And despite the pragmaticism involved in drafting the document, the resulting approach to human rights cannot be called truly pragmatic, for that would involve testing ideas and strategies to see if they are correct. The flaws in the declaration have become more apparent as international human rights law and practice developed, yet this has not led to any serious rethinking of its construction.

CHAPTER 2

The Concept of Human Rights
during the Cold War

The mix of human rights with economic and social rights in the Universal Declaration of Human Rights created a permanent contradiction in the way the international community would conceive of human rights. In the United Nations, states debated how to treat two kinds of human rights, and while there were practical questions about the implementation of economic and social rights, few questioned their ontological status. Instead, their putative indivisibility from freedom rights became the basis for notions like the "right to development." Meanwhile, Soviet dissidents, isolated both from the natural rights philosophical tradition and from the politicized human rights promoted in the United Nations, rediscovered the principles of classical freedom rights through their experiences with totalitarianism, by their moral values and their reason. Totalitarianism stood as concrete proof that economic and social rights are incompatible with authentic human rights.

To an extent, the Cold War was a conflict over the meaning of human rights. The stark contrast between the totalitarian denial of freedom and the liberalism of the West offered clarity. In his inaugural address in 1961, President John F. Kennedy proclaimed that "the same revolutionary beliefs for which our forebears fought are still at issue around the globe—the belief that the rights of man come not from the generosity of the state, but from the hand of God." In the ideological conflict with Soviet and Chinese totalitarianism, Kennedy promised, the United States would defend human rights as rooted in natural rights. He continued: "Let every nation know, whether it wishes us well or ill, that we shall pay any price, bear any burden, meet any hardship, support any friend, oppose any foe, in order to assure the survival and the success of liberty."

The new president thus reiterated the American Founders' belief that the natural right to freedom was God-given and could neither be established nor be taken away by the laws of men. Kennedy, the leader of the Democratic Party, was a champion of such things as government housing and public education, and had worked for more government services for his mainly poor constituents while a member of Congress, yet he believed nevertheless that human rights meant the right to freedom. He called the Soviet Union a "slave state."

An international human rights community emerged to campaign for freedom—freedom from totalitarian control and brutality, and freedom from repression by authoritarian dictators who defended their policies, often with the support of the United States, as necessary to thwart the rise of communism. American civil rights activists were generally in accord with the people campaigning for the rights of citizens behind the Iron Curtain, though some advocated including concepts of social justice or "economic justice" in the civil rights agenda. Social-democratic welfare programs flourished in the Free World, including the United States, being fueled by the success of capitalist economies in providing the highest living standards known to man. The most ambitious social assistance programs yet conceived, such as the "War on Poverty" of the 1960s, redistributed wealth on a massive scale. But these programs were not compelled by "human rights" obligations. The central human rights concerns in Western societies, at the domestic and international levels, were equality of opportunity and basic freedoms. Thus the concept of human rights as freedoms based on natural rights retained some of its basic shape and content during the Cold War, despite the smorgasbord of human rights ideas offered up in the Universal Declaration.

Economic and social rights remained an intellectually marginal concept, generally viewed as an ideological weapon or an element of social-democratic political rhetoric. Scholars and human rights activists in the West pointed to the brutality of the Soviet and Chinese regimes and the deprivations suffered by their subjects as evidence that the idea of economic and social rights as human rights was bankrupt, and that freedom was more important than the provision of material security by the state. After all, the Germans gunned down by border guards as they tried to escape from East Berlin were seeking freedom, despite the economic and social rights to which they were entitled in East Germany. Virtually no one defected to the Communist states. Behind the Iron Curtain, the most principled members of the dissident human rights movement emphasized their commitment only to basic political freedoms.

Regional Conventions on Human Rights

The Universal Declaration was a nonbinding statement of principles, but regional conventions were soon formulated to set standards and mechanisms for enforcing the protection of human rights. Two of these regional treaties, the European and the American, focused exclusively on freedom rights, though for reasons of expediency rather than from a principled commitment to a clear idea of human rights. In fact, both of these conventions were constructed to suggest the eventual addition of economic and social rights.

European nations, largely at the behest of Winston Churchill and other conservatives, formed themselves into a community sharing fundamental human rights principles based on natural law and on the civil law tradition—on freedom rights. The European Convention on Human Rights (ECHR) was drafted in 1950 and came into force in 1953, with the explicit purpose of being a bulwark against totalitarianism and a specific defense against communism. The ECHR includes a list of human rights that were proposed by Pierre-Henri Teitgen, a French former Resistance fighter. The treaty protects the right to life (art. 2), prohibits torture (art. 3), prohibits slavery and forced labor (art. 4), guarantees the right to liberty and security (art. 5) and the right to a fair trial (art. 6), guarantees that no one shall be punished except for criminal offenses (art. 7), and protects the right to respect for private and family life (art. 8). It protects freedom of thought and religion (art. 9), freedom of expression (10) and of association (11), the right to marry (12) and the right to effective remedies (13), and it prohibits discrimination (14).

The European Convention drew upon the natural rights listed in the Universal Declaration but excluded the economic and social rights. The document, "scrupulously drafted and rigorously defined, provides no comfort for socialist conceptions of social or economic justice," as Jesse Norman and Peter Oborne remark. "It is implicitly skeptical about the power of the state."[1]

The report containing the recommendation about what rights to include said that its drafters unanimously agreed that "for the moment, only those essential rights and freedoms could be guaranteed which are, today, defined and accepted after long usage, by democratic regimes. These rights and freedoms are the common denominator of our political institutions," and while social rights might be recognized in the future, "everyone will understand that it is necessary to begin at the beginning."[2] Yet standing behind the European Convention was the Universal Declaration with its morally ambivalent mix of human rights and entitlements. Indeed, the preambular to the convention (par. 6) calls it the "first steps for the collective enforcement of the Rights stated in the Universal Declaration." But the framers of the convention were interested in efficiency, and they were working in a relatively homogeneous cultural environment where a consensus about basic rights would be fairly simple to achieve.

Some critics regard the European Convention as a retrograde step and as essentially an attack on communism, reflecting Cold War ideology.[3] But those who complain of its putative liberal bias have tried to insert their own ideological and political goals. At first this agenda would rely on expansive interpretations of the convention by activist judges on the European Court of Human Rights. Then, in 1961, the Council of Europe adopted the European Social Charter, which guaranteed a wide range of economic and social rights.

The story of the American Convention on Human Rights is similar, reflecting an effort to hold the concept of human rights to a relatively narrow meaning rooted in natural rights, but also the influence of political forces trying to insert ideology into human rights covenants. The American Convention, signed in 1969 by a dozen countries and later by several more, included twenty-three articles protecting basic civil and political rights, but its preamble portends a complete cave-in to the statist claim that freedom is contingent on specific social policies. It says that "in accordance with the Universal Declaration of Human Rights, the ideal of free men enjoying freedom from fear and want can be achieved only if conditions are created whereby everyone may enjoy his economic, social, and cultural rights, as well as his civil and political rights." Chapter III of the convention, consisting of one article on "Progressive Development," committed the states parties to "adopt measures...of an economic and technical nature" toward achieving the "full realization" of economic, social and cultural rights implicit in the Charter of the Organization of American States. The states parties to the American Convention later adopted the additional "Protocol of San Salvador," concerning economic, social and cultural rights.

The African Charter on Human and Peoples' Rights got to this point more directly; indeed, its very title suggests a collectivist distinction between human rights and "peoples' rights." Adopted in 1981 and entering into force in 1986, it includes guarantees of classical human rights, and of economic and social rights relating to property, work, health and education (Articles 14–17). The charter also includes the "right to national and international peace" in Article 23, which commits states parties to ensuring that "their territories shall not be used as bases for subversive or terrorist activities against the people of any other State Party to the present Charter." Article 24 states that "All peoples shall have the right to a general satisfactory environment favourable to their development."

Two Global Treaties: Separate but Equal Human Rights

Beginning in the early 1950s, in the Third Committee of the UN General Assembly, dealing with social, humanitarian and cultural affairs, and in the Human Rights Commission, a complex debate took place on the question of promulgating legally binding international legislation to guarantee the rights enumerated in the Universal Declaration. (The UN had already adopted the Convention on the Prevention and Punishment of the Crime of Genocide, which came into force in 1948.) In 1952, Resolution 543 (VI) was approved, reflecting a decision to create two separate treaties for two different kinds of rights. The International Covenant on Civil and Political Rights (ICCPR) and the International Covenant on Economic, Social and Cultural Rights (ICESCR) finally emerged for signature and ratification by members of the United Nations in 1966. Along with the UDHR, these two covenants would be regarded as the International Bill of Human Rights.

The decision for two separate treaties followed a lively debate about differences between the two categories of rights. It was not a debate about whether or not economic and social rights are authentic human rights; the historical record shows few questions by UN delegates raising ontological issues. The United Kingdom, India and Pakistan did raise serious concerns about the status of economic and social rights. During one debate, for example, a Pakistani diplomat said that "the concept of fundamental human rights should not be extended to include economic and social rights...since such an extension of the meaning of the term both weakened and confused it. Fundamental human rights are fundamental human rights."[4] But the discussion quickly moved away from philosophical questions, leaving them unresolved and obscured in a cloud of political rhetoric, and went on to questions about how to deal with rights that had been affirmed by the Universal Declaration.

States felt a powerful obligation not to take any decision that would discredit the UDHR, which had essentially presented them with an "all or nothing" package. The "moral authority" of the declaration was at stake, said a Cuban delegate. There was also concern not to establish international laws that would suggest any hierarchy of rights in the declaration; they all had to be treated "equally," without the implication of any moral distinctions or priorities. Of course, political factors played a role: the Soviet Union continually accused Western, liberal democracies of indifference to problems of poverty and workers' rights, and to issues of colonialism. The U.S. delegation supported combining all the rights set forth in the Universal Declaration in one treaty, for the political reason of not wishing to be seen as opposing or diminishing economic and social rights. Mrs. Roosevelt candidly admitted the concern that the United States "not again be completely against the majority."[5] But the U.S. Senate was almost certain to reject a treaty containing economic and social rights, so domestic politics drove the United States toward a two-treaty solution.

The reservations expressed about economic and social rights in the debates were virtually all technical. To a large extent, economic and social human rights had been normalized within the paradigm of the UDHR; the paradigm was not debated, only the technical details.[6] The international community had embarked on the rationalization of human rights, so that technicians took over where the philosophers were thought to have finished their job. A set of now-familiar concerns were raised, including the "justiciability" of economic and social rights; the fact that such rights require long-term processes to work; whether an individual complaint mechanism made sense with respect to such rights; and the need for clear and definitive language in any treaty, unlike the vague terms that described economic and social rights.

The decision for two treaties was itself largely motivated by technical concerns and the pragmatic issue of eventual ratification. It was indeed the case that combining both kinds of rights within a single treaty would make passage more problematic, in both democratic and totalitarian states. United, all rights might fall; divided, each set could stand. Since the Communist states had fought for a single treaty to preserve the equal status of economic and social rights with civil and political rights, some observers regarded the two-treaty decision as a victory for liberal democracies that put a higher priority on civil and political rights. But like the decision to include economic and social rights in the UDHR, the two-treaty solution was really a pragmatic compromise.

The treaty debate introduced a process by which Third World, postcolonial states began to claim development assistance as a right: if they took on legally binding international obligations to meet the requirements of economic and social rights, they would need financial help. At the time of the decision in 1952 to create two separate treaties, proponents of economic and social rights began to emphasize the "indivisibility" of human rights, which provided a basis to argue for conditioning freedom on economic progress. Third World states began to claim that without financial help to honor economic and social rights, they could not be expected to give their citizens civil and political rights, as these were all indivisibly connected.[7] Indivisibility was the "covering language" to accommodate the losing side in the battle over single or parallel covenants. And as much as any other concept, it has depleted meaning and efficacy from human rights.

The International Covenant on Economic, Social and Cultural Rights (ICESCR), adopted in 1966 and entering into force ten years later, includes thirty-one articles. It begins, in Article 1, with a declaration that "All peoples have the right to self-determination," setting the tone for its collectivist orientation. Article 2 affirms that economic and social rights are to be "progressively" realized. Developing countries are given leave not to guarantee such rights to non-nationals—a stark departure from the principles of equality and universality.

Some of the rights set forth in the covenant are, in fact, civil and political rights. Article 6 recognizes the "right to work, which includes the right of everyone to the opportunity to gain his living by work which he freely chooses or accepts." The right to form trade unions, in Article 8, is a right to association, a fundamental freedom right protected by the International Covenant on Civil and Political Rights (Article 22). The protection of family life, in Article 10 of the ICESCR, means freedom from interference and coercion. Article 15 speaks of the right to take part in cultural life and enjoy the benefits of scientific progress, also essentially a matter of freedom, and redundant in terms of civil and political rights.

Then we get to the welfare-state entitlements. The covenant mandates "vocational guidance and training programmes," "fair wages," a "decent standard of living," "safe and healthy working conditions," with "equal opportunity for everyone to be promoted in his employment to an appropriate higher level, subject to no considerations other than those of seniority and competence," and "rest and leisure," including "periodic holidays with pay, as well as remuneration for public holidays." The states parties recognize "the right of everyone to an adequate standard of living, including adequate food, clothing and housing, and to the continuous improvement of living conditions," and are legally obligated to "improve methods of production, conservation and distribution of food."

The ICESCR built out on the platform provided by the Universal Declaration and confirmed its wide-ranging political aims. According to Asbjørn Eide, the expert on economic and social rights, the International Bill of Human Rights (the UDHR and the two covenants) was "not drafted to codify a particular set of philosophical assumptions prevalent in the eighteenth century but to develop a comprehensive system of rights which could constitute solutions to important moral and political problems." To deny any of the rights enshrined in these documents implies a rejection of the UDHR "as the source of the validity of the rights they refer to," and without this point of reference, says Eide, there is only "subjective opinions."[8] In this view, any international law is beyond questioning and cannot be judged against any transcendent standard. Positive law justifies all human rights. While some had suggested that natural law still held sway in a system that combined natural and positive rights, Eide suggests that the idea of natural rights was erased by political will.

To buy into the rights enumerated in the ICESCR drives one deep into the technical world of social policy, for the covenant challenges the international community to build a global program of economic regulation. To determine if food supply is "adequate," for example, requires analysis of what types of food are available, where they are available, if they are acceptable to populations, if they are nutritious, if food is safe and of good quality in terms of taste and texture.[9] Now that individuals can lodge complaints about violations of the covenant, perhaps it is to be expected that the UN Committee on Economic, Social and Cultural Rights will rule on a complaint about bad-tasting food. The right to an "adequate" food supply, moreover, brings various other requirements with it, as Eide noted:

> the stability of the food supply and access to food presupposes environmental sustainability, implying that there is a judicious public and community management of natural resources which have a bearing on the food supply, as well as economic and social sustainability in terms of conditions and mechanisms securing food access. Economic and social sustainability concern a just income distribution and effective markets, together with various public and informal support and safety nets.[10]

Likewise, the "right to housing" has numerous parameters. They include, inter alia, facilities essential for health, security, comfort, nutrition, food storage and refuse disposal. There must be legal security in housing. It must be affordable, and located with access to employment options, health-care services and child-care centers.[11]

The most ambitious, and the most vague, of the rights protected by the ICESCR is the "right to an adequate standard of living." The citizens of states parties to the treaty have the right not simply to the basic necessities of food, clothing and housing, but to have these things "under conditions which enable everyone to participate in the everyday life of society. Everyone shall be able, without shame and without unreasonable obstacles, to be a full participant in ordinary, everyday interaction with other people."[12]

Only a state that intrudes deeply into the economic and social life of a society and that severely limits individual liberties could claim to guarantee such standards. Yet liberal democratic states, seeking to avoid the charge of indifference to the poverty that has plagued citizens of Third World countries, rarely criticized the concept of economic and social rights as human rights, sticking largely to the issue of justiciability when they voiced concerns. Many signed the ICESCR, including the United States under President Jimmy Carter.

An Era of Human Rights Revisionism

Soon after the International Covenant on Economic, Social and Cultural Rights had been adopted, human rights in the United Nations began to serve as the vehicle by which poor countries and those that had thrown off colonial rule placed their demands at the foot of the First World. And human rights increasingly became a weapon for ideological attacks by the Communist Second World against the West.

This dynamic was visible at the International Conference on Human Rights held in Tehran in 1968. The meeting was dominated by an array of international tensions, especially the Arab-Israeli "Six-Day" War of the previous year. The Tehran conference had serious consequences for the idea of human rights, expanding it "to cover nearly every concern of the Global South."[13] It was here that an overtly ideological concept of human rights gained a firm foothold on the platform of international legitimacy. Neither the Proclamation nor the Final Act of the conference dealt in any serious way with protecting freedoms. Instead, they strongly promoted placing economic, social and cultural rights and the "right to development" at the center of the United Nations human rights agenda. The Iranian delegation insisted that "the promotion of human rights was directly related to economic and social progress."[14]

Similar language appeared in the Final Act, which asserted "a profound inter-connection between the realization of human rights and economic development" (Article 17). In essence, human rights were being held hostage to international aid. The document called upon developed countries to "transfer adequate development resources to the developing countries," and for a "global development strategy." The Tehran meeting revealed how the concept of the "indivisibility" of freedom rights and economic and social rights would become a lever to pressure wealthy free states for international transfers in the name of "development," as well as a tactical tool for blunting criticism of repression. The Proclamation of the conference claimed that, "Since human rights and fundamental freedoms are indivisible, the full realization of civil and political rights without the enjoyment of economic, social and cultural rights is impossible" (par. 13). In other words, if you want us to grant our subjects freedom, you must pay.

This claim would later reappear in a UN resolution that would prove to be of major import, though of highly dubious value. In 1977, the UN General Assembly passed Resolution 32/130, called "Alternative approaches and ways and means within the United Nations for improving the effective enjoyment of human rights and fundamental freedoms." Like the protocol of the Tehran meeting, it proclaimed that "the full realization of civil and political rights without the enjoyment of economic, social and cultural rights is impossible." A trenchant analysis from that period by Moses Moskowitz, a legal scholar, noted that the resolution passed with "patently ideological and political support."[15] Indeed, it called for a "new international economic order" of global wealth redistribution. The UN's human rights scheme had revealed its potential for absolving states of their responsibility to protect human rights, and for shifting that responsibility onto other states, sending them on a guilt-trip that many were only too eager to take. The resolution made it possible "for any developing country to defend itself against charges of human rights violations by replying that it hadn't received adequate foreign aid."[16]

Some states that put a high priority on economic and social rights disparaged arguments for individual freedom as aggressive calls for regime change. During the debate, as recounted by Moskowitz, the hardline Communist German Democratic Republic (East German) delegation warned that "any outside attempts to 'misuse' the human rights issue to isolate the individual from society and to bring him into conflict with the State, were essentially directed at undermining the sovereignty of states." This is a position held today by states that brag about their social programs and are praised for their supposed compliance with economic and social rights, but thwart attempts to monitor and campaign for civil and political rights, claiming that such efforts create conflict and amount to attacks on their sovereignty. In a sense, the East Germans were correct: Respecting human rights can and does lead to conflicts between citizens and the state when governments trample on natural rights and freedoms. That's how it's supposed to work. Human rights defenders accept the fact that insisting on freedom can lead to conflict within societies, and sometimes between states.

The doctrine of the "indivisibility of human rights" gathered steam with Resolution 32/130, becoming not just an instrument to extract more financial transfers, but also a means to blunt criticism of human rights violations. Notably, states that honor freedom rights *did not vote against the resolution,* but merely abstained. It passed with the support of 123 states, with none voting against—a sign of the failure to defend a clear concept of human rights. Since then, the "right to development," which the American diplomat Morris Abram famously panned as "an empty vessel into which vague hopes and inchoate expectations can be poured," has become almost omnipresent in UN human rights bodies.

President Carter attempted to place human rights at the center of United States foreign policy, declaring in his inaugural address in 1977 that "our commitment to human rights must be absolute." In a sense, his approach was revolutionary: he would orient the policies of the most powerful government in the world toward a principle for its own sake, and not subordinate human rights to the achievement of other objectives. On its face, the policy appeared virtuous, embracing the protection of human rights as a primary duty, not just one factor in international relations or a utilitarian program mixed in with a range of other goals. The human rights violations of both friends and enemies would be criticized; the U.S. government would thus assume the nonpartisan, depoliticized posture of an independent human rights group. But contrary to the rationalism of classical human rights, Carter's interpretation was an expansive political moralism, indeed, a social gospel, framing numerous social problems as human rights problems. The failure of Carter's efforts demonstrated that such an approach to foreign policy cannot be consistent with the responsibilities of a government, the highest of which is to protect the rights and security of its citizens. President Carter had failed to see the forest for the trees. In the struggle against Soviet totalitarianism, his human rights policy paradoxically threatened the freedom of the citizens he was obligated first and foremost to protect, and, by weakening the United States, it threatened freedom everywhere.

The most salient criticism of the conceptual rot infecting human rights in UN circles came during the administration of President Ronald Reagan, when American officials forthrightly denounced the idea of economic and social rights—not just for their lack of justiciability, but as unfit to be called human rights at all. Reagan's officials were concerned that the entire idea of human rights had been corrupted by left-wing politics. The U.S. State Department ceased reporting on violations of economic and social rights.[17] Reagan's ambassador to the United Nations, Jeane Kirkpatrick (a former political science professor), dismissed economic and social rights as a "letter to Santa Claus." And the administration called out regimes that used claims of honoring those rights as a way of disguising their restrictions on liberty.

Prohibiting "Hate Speech" and "Incitement"

As the meaning of human rights was being deliberately distorted, authoritarian and totalitarian members of the United Nations promoted legislation that would use the cover of human rights to put restrictions on freedom. Jacob Mchangama, the Danish human rights attorney, has called attention to the Soviet Union's attempts to limit the freedom of speech in Article 19 of the

Universal Declaration by invoking the threat of fascism. Soviet diplomats proposed that "Any advocacy of national, racial, or religious hostility or of national exclusiveness or hatred and contempt, as well as any action establishing a privilege or a discrimination based on distinctions of race, nationality, or religion" should be subject to criminal penalties.[18] Western diplomats on the Human Rights Commission blocked these efforts to constrict freedom of speech and to insert vague language that could be exploited to hobble political opposition. But the Soviet efforts would find success when the nonbinding principles in the UDHR were codified into international law.

As a consequence, the International Covenant on Civil and Political Rights includes a clear restriction on freedom of speech. In Article 20(2), the ICCPR states that "Any advocacy of national, racial or religious hatred that constitutes incitement to discrimination, hostility or violence shall be prohibited by law." Liberal democracies opposed this language, again warning that such vague terminology ("incitement to hostility") would be exploited for political expediency. Mchangama noted that Eleanor Roosevelt found the language "extremely dangerous" and warned against provisions "likely to be exploited by totalitarian States for the purpose of rendering the other articles null and void." She also feared that the provision "would encourage governments to punish all criticism under the guise of protecting against religious or national hostility." But the language was accepted in the Third Committee of the UN, with the support of Soviet bloc states as well as "non-Western countries with very questionable human rights records such as Saudi Arabia, Haiti, Sudan, and Thailand."[19]

"Third-Generation Rights" and Affirmative Discrimination

The term "third-generation human rights" refers to the human rights claims that cannot be categorized as either civil and political rights or economic and social rights. They are generally collective rights, defined around particular groups. Human rights treaties were crafted to protect vulnerable groups, and some included economic and social guarantees obliging states to implement positive law that infringes on fundamental individual rights (as will be discussed further in Chapter 4).

The International Convention on the Elimination of All Forms of Racial Discrimination (CERD), which entered into force in 1969, places serious limitations on freedom of speech. Article 4(a) says that signatories

Shall declare an offence punishable by law all dissemination of ideas based on racial superiority or hatred, incitement to racial discrimination, as well as all acts of violence or incitement to such acts against any race or group of persons of another colour or ethnic origin, and also the provision of any assistance to racist activities, including the financing thereof....

Article 7 obligates the signatories to adopt measures to combat prejudice and promote racial "understanding, tolerance and friendship" through various means, including education and culture, and information media. Mchangama points out that the CERD "makes the state responsible for eliminating discrimination through coercive measures." And he observes, "The idea that deliberate state action—even at the expense of individual liberty—is the principal vehicle for social change and human progress is a hallmark of socialism, fascism, communism, and in some cases, forms of progressivism."[20]

The same can be said about the Convention on the Elimination of All Forms of Discrimination against Women (CEDAW), which came into force in 1981, and includes efforts to control speech and manipulate thought in signatory countries. For example, Article 10 calls for the "elimination of any stereotyped concept of the roles of men and women at all levels and in all forms of education by encouraging coeducation and other types of education which will help to achieve this aim and, in particular, by the revision of textbooks and school programmes and the adaptation of teaching methods."

Both the CERD and CEDAW obligate states parties to institute discriminatory quotas as a means of reversing the effects of past discrimination—contravening the principle of equality, arguably the core value of human rights. Article 2(2) of the CERD commits states parties to

take, in the social, economic, cultural and other fields, special and concrete measures to ensure the adequate development and protection of certain racial groups or individuals belonging to them, for the purpose of guaranteeing them the full and equal enjoyment of human rights and fundamental freedoms. These measures shall in no case entail as a consequence the maintenance of unequal or separate rights for different racial groups after the objectives for which they were taken have been achieved.

Article 4(4) of CEDAW likewise calls for "temporary" measures that violate equality before the law, for the sake of achieving equality of results. It mandates quotas for representatives to international organizations, and it says:

Adoption by States Parties of temporary special measures aimed at accelerating de facto equality between men and women shall not be considered discrimination as defined in the present Convention, but shall in no way entail as a consequence the maintenance of unequal or separate standards; these measures shall be discontinued when the objectives of equality of opportunity and treatment have been achieved.

As a human rights advocate, I consider any law that intentionally mandates sex discrimination to be profoundly wrong as a matter of principle, and deeply distasteful, regardless of how benign the stated purpose may sound. Cathy Fitzpatrick, a veteran human rights activist, noted in a letter to me: "Nothing is more Soviet than gender quotas [which] come straight out of Marxist identity politics. The Soviets used to put women, Estonians, etc. into committees and commissions—what did it really do for their authentic rights? Nothing."

The principle of equality before the law, with equal recognition and protection of rights regardless of gender, ethnicity, religion, age or any other difference, is one that animates almost every human right. Protecting the freedom of individuals to make choices without arbitrary coercion is the main goal of the liberal state. To privilege one group at the expense of another is contrary to the rule of law, and surely not the remedy for stubborn racial and gender discrimination, a complex problem that reduces opportunities for some. A quota that discriminates against part of the population in the service of a dubious social engineering scheme reflects a "legal relativism" in which principles may be interpreted in any way necessary to achieve political objectives. Quotas would be wrong even if they accomplished their social goals, because they would have done so at the expense of equality before the law. When we disrespect equality and freedom by balancing them against other concerns, we undermine human rights as a bulwark against tyranny.[21]

As political agendas were overtaking human rights, little was done about it in official circles or in civil society. But small groups of intellectuals behind the Iron Curtain were taking a purer, more principled approach to human rights. These dissenters possessed a moral clarity that stood in contrast with the clouded vision of the Universal Declaration and its opportunistic exploiters on the international scene.

Soviet Dissenters' View of Human Rights

The human rights discourse that emerged from Soviet and East European dissent was unique and original, yet largely consistent with the Enlightenment philosophers' understanding.[22] Historians debate the political consequences of this movement, in particular its role in precipitating the collapse of the Soviet Union and other Communist governments. The dissident movement was politically marginal inside the Soviet Union; its main political result was to mobilize criticism by Western governments and civil society against the abusive practices of Communist regimes. But civil society movements in Poland and several other Eastern European states had the power to force Communist governments to make concessions, eventually leading to their collapse. Internal human rights dissent was among the forces behind the implosion of Soviet communism, but the influence of its moral critique of the system appears to have been relatively small. The dissenting human rights movement had more significance for the global spread of human rights activism and for the understanding of human rights. Important parts of the human rights ethos that emerged from Soviet dissent were taken up and internalized by international human rights campaigns—but subsequently betrayed by the civil society human rights community in significant ways.

"One can never be sure about the *pensée intime* of people who have the misfortune to live under a dictatorship," wrote Ernest Gellner, who was among the most penetrating analysts of the Soviet era.[23] A habitual opacity is apparent even among still-living veterans of Soviet-era dissidence, a diffuse and highly diverse assortment of dissenting groups and individuals. This mental habit helps explain why the doctrines of those who campaigned for human rights under the Soviet system cannot easily be described. There has also been a tendency toward defensiveness and frustration in dealing with naive members of the Western human rights community. The dissidents, for the most part, did not spell out what they meant by human rights.

Soon after I started as director of the International Helsinki Federation in 1993, I began to think about how the views of the Soviet human rights dissidents, in whose efforts our organization was rooted, should be brought forward as a model for the growing human rights communities in Eastern Europe and Central Asia. The idea of human rights as expressed in international organizations seemed to be coming apart; the human rights movement was being pulled in many directions. I sent a letter by fax to one of the leaders of one of the earliest Russian human rights groups, asking bluntly how they had seen the idea of human rights. The response was a shock: I was harshly accused of implying that they had known nothing about human rights; that they were primitive. My inquiry had apparently been seen as an interrogation or a test. Of course they understood what human rights were; why else would they have acted as they had? What had they struggled and sacrificed for? But my correspondent was still reticent about the objective meaning of human rights.

The Soviet dissident human rights movement had no central intellectual authority and no organizational leadership; it was a spontaneous movement made up of diverse participants. It had no clearly articulated human rights doctrine. Its guiding principles were largely methodological: how to work with human rights, not about what human rights were. Indeed, Yuri Orlov, a physicist and a founder of the Moscow Helsinki Group, described human rights to me as being about *how*, not *what*—as a kind of process liberalism. The activists focused on their own methods, just as they focused on the methods of the state. It was an empirical, scientific, rational approach to the problem of human rights.

Some Soviet dissidents had no concern for human rights and held views antithetical to human rights. The dissident human rights movement consisted of those who worked for the realization of the rights and freedoms of others, doing so from an inclusive, nonideological perspective, referring to international law and political agreements as standards defining state obligations.

Soviet dissidents reinvented human rights for themselves, according to Ludmilla Alexeyeva, who was also a founder of the Moscow Helsinki Group, and has been the Soviet human rights movement's primary "participant-observer." In her book *Soviet Dissent*, written during her exile in the United States, she explained, "Human rights activists did not borrow ideas from the international human rights movement because they were poorly informed about it at the time the movement emerged in the USSR."[24] The dissenting human rights activists had limited or no access to the philosophical and legal literature that informs the classical human rights tradition, or to human rights developments at the international level. Especially in the early years, they had little or no contact with civil society human rights formations in the West. They constructed the meaning of human rights for themselves, in conditions where basic liberties were denied. Their posture has been characterized as one of "moral idealism."[25] Ludmilla Alexeyeva viewed it as being rooted in the Christian idea of freedom and the value of the human personality.

The members of the Soviet human rights movement tended to promote human rights for their own sake, not as a strategy to achieve particular social goals. An analyst writing at the time observed, "Dissent in Soviet society has an existential stance: the inner need of the individual to speak or act in the name of ideals, even when no concrete means exist to realize them," as by a "moral compulsion."[26]

The Exercise of Freedom

To understand how the dissidents thought about human rights, we must look primarily at what they *did* about human rights. Their activism was itself an exercise of their natural human right to freedom—what Kant called the original human right—and thus a validation of that right. Martin Palouš, a philosopher and leader in the Czechoslovak human rights movement Charter 77, said that freedom in its "positive, classical sense" exists in "public acts based on initiative."[27] The dissidents "behaved like free men," said Andrei Amalrik, one of the pioneering human rights dissenters. The members of the Initiative Group for Human Rights, the first Soviet human rights formation, held that social progress meant an increase in freedom.[28] By their actions, the dissidents established the issue of freedom as the problem addressed by human rights.

The predominant emphasis on civil and political rights is indisputable; the dissident human rights scholar Valery Chalidze wrote of the "definitive significance of civil and political rights."[29] Ludmilla Alexeyeva noted that "only in a country where there are political freedoms will citizens be able to effectively defend their material interests."[30] She knew from bitter experience that freedom from material uncertainties did not necessarily lead to the freedom that guaranteed individual choice, and indeed the Soviet system, which claimed to protect economic and social rights, had produced low living standards for all but the party elites. The way to improve living standards was to honor civil and political rights as priorities—a position totally at odds with establishment human rights dogma today.

The Soviet human rights defenders felt the moral duty to defend freedom, the obligation Kant had identified. It was self-evident, to those living under the crushing weight of Soviet rule, that human dignity depends on freedom. The meaning of freedom was found in the defiance of the everyday reality in a totalitarian system that radically restricted choices. The definition of human rights as *negative* liberties was likewise clear—something requiring no justification in legal or political terms. The idea of human rights as freedom, and the association of human rights with state restraint, had *immediacy* under totalitarian rule. That is, the idea of human rights was not filtered through received ideas, frameworks or methods, but was formed by experience; Amalrik, who had predicted the fall of the Soviet Union in 1969, said his analysis had been the product of his experiences, not academic research.[31] We who have never had to live under totalitarianism cannot understand human rights in the same way as those who have been massively deprived of their own rights and have fought for them under those circumstances. We cannot understand human rights in the same way because we have not experienced the denial of our own human rights.

Valery Chalidze defined freedom more specifically than most others, and explicitly associated the human rights principles of the dissident human rights movement with the principles of classical liberalism. In a 1984 publication that followed his exile to the United States, he noted that the movement's struggle for freedom was "limited to advancing freedom of speech, recognition of the rule of law, and due process."[32] But freedom also meant recognizing and acting upon one's own moral autonomy and agency. It meant rejecting determination by social or economic circumstances. "Freedom means accepting responsibility for one's own behavior and future," Chalidze wrote, and it involves "the need to free oneself from the belief in the possibility of a perfect social system."[33] Freedom meant liberation from an oppressive, controlling state, and from utopian illusions. It also meant emancipation from the passions by rational self-control. In a manner reminiscent of Stoic philosophy, the exercise of freedom was seen as a discipline for the individual, and the protection of freedom as a discipline for society, requiring scrupulous political detachment.

Marxist-Leninist doctrine incorporated the word "freedom" in its texts for manipulative political purposes, but qualified its meaning with denunciations of "arbitrary" individual wishes and with reminders of the obligation to conform to the interests of the majority. The violation of human rights in the name of collective interests made it clear that human rights were *individual* rights. But this point was obscured after the fall of the Soviet Union, when some clients of the dissident human rights movement sought collective rights for nationalities and ethnic groups that had been subjugated under the Soviet system. The aspirations of ethnic nationalism were understood and even respected, despite being inconsistent with human rights principles.

The Ukrainian Helsinki Human Rights Group, for example, concerned itself largely with preserving the national and cultural traditions of Ukraine, but it also stressed individual rights. "A Manifesto of the Ukrainian Human Rights Movement" from 1977, in what is a rare explicit reference to classical human rights doctrine, claimed that "the state does not bestow a right on a citizen, but only defends a person's natural right." The law "should provide for the primacy of the individual" and be "the guarantor of the freedom and sovereignty of the individual."[34] Like numerous other national human rights movements, the Ukrainian activists saw no contradiction between the idea of individual rights and a primary concern for preserving Ukrainian national identity. That issue would surface after Soviet rule ended, when new nation-states needed to protect minority rights within their borders.

It is fair to say that most Soviet-era human rights defenders showed little interest in economic and social rights, or rejected the concept altogether, but significant figures in the movement have taken such rights seriously. Valery Chalidze, whose views are clearly liberal in the classical sense, wrote that civil and political rights are universal, while economic, social and cultural rights "depend largely on a particular economic and social system."[35] Economic and social rights belong to the realm of politics; they are to be established by democratic processes on the basis of community values. The strong emphasis on freedom as "negative liberty" and the insistence that human rights should be nonpolitical indicate the priority of civil and political rights, since economic and social rights constrain choices and decisions about the allocation of community property and the distribution of wealth. A state devoted to protecting freedom is intrinsically a weak state, but it requires a strong civil society to channel the forces of self-interest in positive directions. On the other hand, a state that assumes broad responsibility for social welfare can do so only by impinging upon individual freedom and choice. It is by nature a strong state, where the rule of law has been extended far beyond the protection of freedom, into an enlarged realm of positive law.

The dissident human rights community generally left such conclusions in a strategic silence, not openly criticizing economic and social rights but simply ignoring them. Chalidze attributed this silence to ideological "inertia" and to a deep sympathy with the goals of socialism. He wrote that although economic and social rights had been included among those set forth in the 1948 Universal Declaration of Human Rights to "placate" the Soviet Union, and reflected "Soviet propaganda,"[36] they were never a target of significant invective by the Soviet and East European human rights community. Avoiding doctrinal human rights controversies that abutted fundamental political disputes was consistent with the effort to keep human rights advocacy and politics separate.

Human Rights Work as a Scientific Activity

In his *Memoirs*, Andrei Sakharov cited the main principles of the human rights movement as nonviolence, *glasnost*, respect for the law, and "a conscientious attitude toward information."[37] When we examine the intellectual character of the dissident human rights movement, its *scientific* personality is prominent. Sakharov, Alexeyeva, Chalidze and Orlov, as well as figures like Václav Havel and many others, approached human rights as intellectuals, and in numerous cases as trained physical or social scientists, and while they were clearly motivated by moral principles, they approached the question of human rights detached from political passions, and with a primary concern for objective truth. Any serious scientist adheres to an ethos of independence from influence by governments, political parties or movements, religious affiliations, or even the influence of friends or family. A dissident intellectual was someone determined to exercise intellectual freedom even in an environment of "ritualistic ideological automatism."[38]

In the understanding that truth is independent of the state and its politics, human rights work took on a quality of empirical social-scientific research. A human rights violation could be an objective fact, which might be discovered independently of the values and predispositions of an observer, if those were brought under rational control. It is, of course, an element of the idealist tradition that recognizes a distinction between *values* and *facts*; recognizes that politics can influence perceptions but does not constitute reality, and that independent individuals can distance themselves from and transcend politics, class, economics, even religion and culture. Furthermore, to do so was morally necessary in order to defend individual human rights. The *Chronicle of Human Events*, a primary *samizdat* or self-published underground newsletter (started in 1968), had a factual, dispassionate style, with content consisting mainly of dry narratives about events, and little commentary. The unemotional, nonpolitical style was to be replicated in the reports and speeches of human rights groups in the decades following the collapse of communism, though it would later be out of step with the inflammatory demands of egocentric, emotion-laced Internet journalism.

Human rights activity was seen as a moral and intellectual discipline, the discipline of self-depoliticization, and perhaps even a removal of the self from the process. It was an effort to be an accurate mirror of facts. Human rights documentation allowed a society, looking into this mirror, to understand its problems, including how it violated individual rights. For a state to embrace human rights meant a capacity for self-reflection and self-criticism, and the ability to put these processes above chauvinism and the politics of defensive self-interest.

In this regard, the human rights activist could even be considered an "alienated" individualist, distant from communities at all levels, answering only to the rigid demands of empirical science and the moral obligation to honor abstract universal principles, above national and group values and often in conflict with them. The Soviet human rights dissenters were averse to hierarchically organized groups. A human rights "group" was a collection of independent individuals brought together not by political values, but by a commitment to the freedom to hold and act upon such values; it was perhaps not a group at all, but a "seriality."[39] A life of standing apart from one's own state where society and state are seen as one, and of critically judging state actions and social values against abstract standards, can make one an object of ridicule and abuse. Indeed, human rights activists are routinely called traitors. But for the human rights dissidents, this was an "authentic life," a free life "in truth," as opposed to one in which thoughts and actions are understood as expressions of an all-determining collective identity.[40]

Legalism and Nonpartisanship

Closely associated with the scientific ethos of civil society human rights activity was the principle of "legalism," a reverence for law as an objective framework imposing obligations not only on citizens but also on the state. It was a matter of negating what Chalidze described as the "subordination of law to ideology."[41] An overt contempt for the rule of law was embedded in Bolshevist ideology: the rule of law was strenuously dismissed as a fraudulent mask for bourgeois economic and class interests. Communism meant the victory of socialist ideology over any law; the Communist state thus promoted legal nihilism. In this context, human rights activity was a demand to respect and follow laws that were based on the Soviet and various national constitutions, as well as international human rights law. This activity could thus be defended as *legal* activity, breaking no law and instead supporting the application of laws—that is, due process. The dissident human rights community insisted on respect for existing laws by the state and by citizens. In essence, this was an indigenous form of procedural liberalism.

The political stance of most dissident human rights defenders was non-partisan. The insistence on a firm distinction between human rights activity and political activity was a common refrain, and the distinction has been recognized in varying degrees by the post–Cold War human rights movement. Political activity comes with an agenda of assuming power. Human rights activity did not seek "regime change," or even any specific ideological change, but rather a respect for individual rights and freedoms and the rule of law. Charter 77, the Czechoslovak human rights movement, was explicitly not a base for oppositional political activity, and had no program of political reform or any distinct political agenda. Its main philosophical proponent, the Czech philosopher Jan Patočka, who died in 1977 following a ten-hour police interrogation, considered the movement an "apolitical act."[42] There is little evidence of *political* disputes within the dissenting human rights communities; there were disputes about tactics and about human rights principles. Leaders like Sakharov demonstrated their political neutrality, for example by opposing not only Soviet violations of human rights, but also American policies like the war in Vietnam. A philosophy of political neutrality was central to the promotion of human rights, and also a tactic to thwart interrogations in which human rights defenders were accused of political activity.

The dissident human rights movement also mirrored classical human rights principles in regarding the defense of freedom as a moral obligation rather than a utilitarian activity; as an end in itself, not a means to other ends. It was an independent reconstruction of an essentially Kantian human rights doctrine—a moral stance at odds with the demands of funding organizations that have sought to promote human rights activity in the former Soviet Union and Eastern Europe. Funding agencies typically request that work be aimed at distinct "objectives" and "results," but the human rights communities that emerged from Soviet dissent have seen human rights work as its own end.

Human rights meant that the individual's freedom to reason and judge was honored, but the dissident concept of human rights was "empty" of particular visions of a good society.[43] The dissident human rights defenders upheld the rights of all, including varieties of Marxists and czarists who themselves did not believe in civil liberties, and members of ethnonational movements whose concern was only for members of their own group. Human rights activists defended Slavophile, antirationalist, anti-Western extremists. They separated ideology from human rights, in a "big tent" where diverse perspectives and beliefs found common ground in the struggle for civil and political rights. Political diversity was a principle of both the Charter 77 movement and the Soviet dissenting human rights groups. This inclusiveness was, in effect, a laboratory for the universalism of human rights. Deprived of virtually all civil and political rights and living under a system that rejected the very idea of individual rights, the dissident human rights activists discovered concepts with universal application, creating an intellectual structure for doctrine and practice that still animates human rights communities in many societies.

The Helsinki Process and Civil Society

In 1975, after fully twenty years of sporadic negotiations, the Helsinki Accords were signed by European democracies, the United States and Canada, and by the Soviet Union and its satellite states. The Helsinki Accords famously linked human rights with security and economic development in one package. By calling for the recognition of existing borders, the agreement legitimized Soviet dominion over Eastern European states, which the Soviet Union had occupied at the end of World War II. But the accords also committed all signatories, including members of the Eastern bloc, to upholding human rights principles.

The Helsinki Accords focused primarily on classical human rights. Principle VII called for "respect for human rights and fundamental freedoms, including the freedom of choice, religion, or belief." The contradiction between these political commitments and the political reality in Eastern bloc states was stark.

The Helsinki Accords were political agreements, not a legally binding treaty, and all the signatories were pledged to publish the Helsinki Final Act in prominent newspapers. The Soviet authorities complied, and a new phase of human rights activism was inaugurated. Yuri Orlov, Ludmilla Alexeyeva and others founded the Moscow Helsinki Group in 1976. They understood that the Helsinki process had the potential to bring its signatories into dialogue with each other, and with independent civil society actors, about the degree to which the participating states were in compliance with the accords. The responsibilities of civil society in the process were fully consistent with the ethos of human rights work that Soviet dissidents had established. Human rights analysis required measuring the behavior of a state against its own laws and international standards; now that behavior would be tested with respect to principles and standards to which governments had committed themselves by signing the Helsinki Final Act.

The value of human rights activity rested on objectivity; either love or hatred of the state would distort and discredit the results. The members of the Moscow Helsinki Group and Charter 77 in Czechoslovakia saw their mandate as one of *assisting* the state to abide by the Helsinki Final Act, and they also sought dialogue with authorities. The state was incapable of objective human rights analysis that could serve as the basis for reform, since it had an interest in giving its own policies and actions a positive evaluation. The state thus needed an objective analysis by civil society members who were free from its ideological and political influences, and not dependent on the state for their living or for authority and respect.

The Helsinki Final Act conferred international legitimacy on human rights activists who formed independent, critical views of their own government. The independent human rights activists and human rights groups thus came to be associated with civil society *par excellence*. Yet civil society also came under new suspicion as forming, intrinsically, a political opposition. In 1982, just when a number of Helsinki human rights monitoring groups were forming the International Helsinki Federation at a meeting in Bellagio, Italy, the Soviet KGB forced the Moscow Helsinki Group out of existence. But it was ultimately a futile attempt at suppressing individuals, because what had been started by the Moscow Helsinki Group was an idea, a way of thinking about promoting human rights. A civil society movement had been launched, beyond the capacity of any state to fully suppress.

The forces of independent civil society were modest, yet powerful. Karl Schwarzenburg, a former Czech dissident named president of the Helsinki Federation in the 1980s, who later served as an adviser to Václav Havel and the Czech minister of foreign affairs, said that civil society means simply individuals thinking and speaking among themselves and considering issues in an open way, not adhering to dogmas or propaganda. He was speaking to an audience of human rights activists at an event the IHF organized in Minsk in the late 1990s. The post-Communist Lukashenko regime had continued an essentially Soviet policy of repression, and the human rights community in Belarus was under siege. Schwarzenburg advised its members to appreciate the value of their own independence, in spite of their painful frustration in living under what had been called the "last dictatorship in Europe," and to keep their expectations for change under control so as to avoid a crushing disappointment. Civil society meant independent analysis and debate. The message of the speech was simple, yet it embodied much of what had been so morally and politically significant about the Soviet-era human rights movement. To bring freedom to society required free people, and even in a police state it was possible to seek and act upon the truth.

A Fragile Legacy

In 1985, in defiance of the Communist regime, the newly formed International Helsinki Federation organized an "Alternative Cultural Forum" in Budapest, where a number of influential dissident intellectuals took part. In 2005, the Helsinki Federation and the Hungarian Helsinki Committee, led by Ferenc Köszeg, a former editor of *samizdat* literature, held a commemoratory conference, where a number of the original participants spoke. Professor János Kis talked about challenges to the concept of human rights that had been rediscovered and upheld by the dissidents. The dissident human rights movement, he said, "took the side of human rights universalism, but they took it unreflectively, without being challenged to defend their position against relativistic objections." As a consequence, "the anti-communist human rights movements failed to leave after them any tools to deal with the ideological complexities characteristic of the world after communism."[44]

The dissident human rights movement had focused on what Kis termed the "non-controversial core of human rights." Their concept of human rights was something that grew out of their immediate experiences, their common sense, their rational and ethical outlook, and their empirical methods; it had an Aristotelian character. It bore few if any scars of battle over the meaning of human rights. Facing down the forces of repression with their pure idea of human rights, the dissidents had been shielded from the degradation of the idea they were defending.

But the collapse of the Communist regimes in 1989 hastened the disintegration of the idea of human rights. Kis mentioned two major challenges that had emerged with the momentous changes of that year. One was a postmodern challenge to the universality of human rights, a claim that the concept was merely a "local ideology," socially constructed like all other ideologies. This claim gave rise to various collectivist concepts at odds with the principle of individual human rights. The other challenge that Kis referenced was the idea that political action has no moral dimension but is only about power, and therefore human rights activity is nothing more than a strategy to gain power. But he did not mention the embedding of economic and social rights at the deepest level of the international human rights architecture, which made the idea of human rights more vulnerable to assaults from cultural relativism and postmodern cynicism.

Debate about the nature of human rights was alive and vivid during the Cold War, when the idea of economic and social rights could be seen clearly in the context of the totalitarianism of its proponents. At the end of the Cold War, world leaders sought to put this debate to rest—not by resolving never again to violate human rights in the name of the putative benefits of collectivism, but by constructing another grand compromise emphasizing the legitimacy of economic and social rights, by equating them with civil and political rights, by declaring authoritatively that the two kinds of rights are equal, indivisible and interdependent, and by binding them together into a "holistic" conception. The meaning of human rights was officially settled by a proclamation from leading diplomats who gathered in Vienna for the World Conference on Human Rights in 1993, to the applause of most human rights activists.

Debate about what constitutes real human rights was declared closed. Civil society has generally agreed, and its outlook on human rights has become thoroughly ossified. The strategists behind this development considered it a matter of utmost moral urgency, outweighing any of the intellectual difficulties involved and any possible unintended negative consequences. What is worse, the post–Cold War revision of human rights undermined the position of the human rights defenders who had risked their very existence to defend liberty under Soviet totalitarianism. The next chapter examines the new vision of human rights produced at the World Conference, a vision to be ideologically enforced by the United Nations.

CHAPTER 3

Birth of the Post–Cold War Human Rights Dogma

At the World Conference on Human Rights organized by the United Nations and held in Vienna in 1993, the international community put its imprimatur on a vision of human rights that has strongly influenced discourse and practice in the field ever since. Around ten thousand people took part, including official representatives of 171 countries, of whom nine were heads of government. Three thousand members of civil society participated, representing a huge number of NGOs. It was the largest human rights conference that had ever taken place, and the principles agreed upon there have deeply informed the policies of the United Nations, of most national governments, and of civil society.

In December 1990, UN General Assembly Resolution 45/155, par. 1(b) established the conference, in part, "To examine the relation between development and the enjoyment by everyone of economic, social and cultural rights, as well as civil and political rights, recognizing the importance of creating conditions whereby everyone may enjoy these rights as set out in the International Covenants on Human Rights." The meeting would take stock of the major changes that had occurred in the preceding years and their implications for international human rights. But the World Conference was also clearly initiated with the goal of settling the problem of *the meaning of human rights*, and specifically the status of economic and social rights. The Vienna conference was meant to delegitimize and crush opposition to economic and social rights, and many participants saw its purpose as moving the international community toward giving priority to those rights.

The conference delegates embraced the bogus doctrine of the indivisibility of freedom rights and so-called economic and social rights, making it an official UN doctrine. In doing so they watered down protections of basic human rights and deepened the contradictions between different kinds of rights, requiring a balancing effort that seriously encroaches upon freedom. They endorsed the highly questionable notion that non-state actors can violate human rights, which set the stage for the proliferation of human rights at the hands of diplomats and activist judges. They promoted the notion of group rights as opposed to universal individual rights, thus initiating an era of human rights identity politics and tribalism. They fully associated human rights with enforcing "tolerance," which confused two different things and further made human rights into an instrument of a repressive PC agenda. They placed human rights in the hands of an expanding UN bureaucracy, taking the focus off the duty of national governments to guarantee human rights at the constitutional and legislative level, undermining civil society, and feeding fantasies of global governance.

The World Conference saw the United Nations tasked not simply with monitoring and promoting human rights, but with advancing a specific, politicized doctrine of human rights. A post–Cold War human rights dogma was born in Vienna, but it resembles the ideology of the states that did not survive the Cold War. This outcome was not unprecedented. To quote Leo Strauss from another context, "It would not be the first time that a nation, defeated on the battlefield and, as it were, annihilated as a political being, has deprived its conquerors of the most sublime fruit of victory by imposing on them the yoke of its own thought."[1]

The World Conference and Its Political Context

As observed earlier, the Universal Declaration of Human Rights had come into existence following a world war in which millions of civilians perished, during a chaotic and dangerous period when defining and promoting an inclusive idea of human rights was seen as a path toward peace with Communist nations. The concept of human rights was thus reinterpreted to serve the realpolitik demands of integrating totalitarian states into a world organization ostensibly founded with the defense of human rights as one of its main pillars. The 1993 World Conference likewise occurred during a volatile and confusing historical moment, only a few years after the sudden and largely unexpected collapse of Communist regimes in Russia and Eastern Europe. The end of the decades of East-West confrontation that had framed so many debates, institutions and processes resulted in widespread disorientation and the search for new, encompassing ideas by which to understand events and guide actions. Once again, the meaning of human rights was manipulated to provide a sense of order, to appease difficult and even hostile civilian constituents and members of the international community, and to strengthen the United Nations as a bureaucratic institution.

After the Communist regimes fell, bloody ethnic conflicts broke out, astonishing the international community with their violence and calling forth an image of a world unraveling into chaos, no longer held together by the relatively clear force of bipolar tensions. The world community was being whipsawed back and forth between good and bad news, and being confronted with problems for which there was no playbook.

The "transition to democracy" was proving more complicated for Western powers than dealing with sclerotic and predictable Communist dictators. At the same time, Western nations felt flush, anticipating a "peace dividend" from the end of military confrontation with the Soviet Union. Leaders of international organizations, including the European Union and the Council of Europe, saw new, independent states striving to become free-market democracies as soon as possible, and to join those organizations and receive their benefits and assistance. Yet political systems were still unreformed, and there were disputes about whether aspiring members should be made to demonstrate changes, including respect for human rights, or only promise to institute reforms after gaining membership in the influential international forums. Would a quick conferral of membership in these international bodies be the way to go, or would it be better to hold out the prize of membership as an incentive for reform?

The way human rights were conceived had direct bearing on these questions. If human rights were seen as civil and political rights, which could be swiftly implemented by restraint on the part of the state, there would be little tolerance for delays, and little patience with requests for financial assistance to meet the standards. But with economic and social rights regarded as human rights, temporizing came to be expected. Moreover, spending money to create respect for human rights suited both donors from liberal democracies and applicants for whom human rights became a business and a profession.

A "New World Order" loomed. The term had been coined by two world leaders, President George H. W. Bush and Mikhail Gorbachev, who had allowed the Soviet Union to collapse, or more probably had been unable to stop it. Another slogan that for a time dominated discourse about international affairs was "the End of History," from the title of an article and then a book by an obscure American think-tank scholar, Francis Fukuyama. He meant that liberal democracy had proved itself the most successful and preferred political arrangement of the world, and that with the discrediting and virtual end of state socialism, the ideological combat that had defined the modern era was over. But paradoxically, what Fukuyama and the multitudes who bought into the catchphrase had called "the end of history" turned out to be the beginning of a new historical era of violence and instability, especially in the vast post-Soviet space.

Nor did the end of the Cold War result in global political or ideological harmony, with everyone agreeing on the superiority of liberalism and free markets. In fact, the forces of the political left and of the Global South were reenergized. Domestic politics grew more polarized in many countries, and a worldwide campaign arose to combat "neoliberalism," which Fukuyama had thought was the paradigm whose success made it self-evidently agreeable to all. Demands surged for "social justice" and "economic justice" via the redistribution of wealth, both within and between nation-states, particularly between established liberal democracies and developing nations. The fall of Communist regimes liberated a broad, unorganized constellation of political, economic and social movements to assert their demands without the taint of totalitarian repression. Although communism continued in Cuba, China, Vietnam and a few other states, the disintegration of the Soviet Union as the main antagonist of Western freedom removed the stigmas attached to leftist political views, allowing their adherents to carry their banners into mainstream ideological debates and into the human rights arena.

In civil society, "peace" activists who had campaigned for disarmament needed a new cause. Many of them had been strongly under the sway of Soviet manipulation; others were simply in varying degrees sympathetic to critiques of America's actions around the world, and to left-wing politics. More often than not, the dislocated campaigners identified their new causes as struggles for human rights, and so the ranks of a new human rights movement swelled with people whose views were more ideological and less committed to the intellectually rigorous application of principle than those of their Cold War predecessors.

The idea of human rights was perhaps a victim of its own success. It had been carried forth from the repressive Soviet period under a bright halo of moral prestige, much of it won by the heroism of Soviet dissidents. Political "social justice" campaigners and former antiwar activists migrated into the human rights tent erected by the UDHR, which had plenty of room for them, since the potential of economic and social rights was far from being fully exploited. The fight to end poverty and bring about "social justice" could be joined without the embarrassing weight of state socialism, and with the added benefit that this fight was attached to a struggle for freedom. It was as if the ghost of communism had risen from its grave and stolen the banner of those who had buried it.

Meanwhile there was money on the table for human rights projects and for nongovernmental organizations if they could manage to label what they were doing as "human rights." Offers of funding came from private foundations like the MacArthur Foundation, the Ford Foundation and George Soros's Open Society Institute; generous national governments like those of the Scandinavian countries and the Netherlands; and intergovernmental organizations like the Council of Europe and the European Union. Human rights work presented an image of transcendent ethical righteousness, accompanied by generous funding and the promise of enforcing one's demands by international law. Many former Soviet apparatchiks cashed in, being clever at manipulating bureaucracies and adept at ideological sleight of hand and historical revisionism. Campaigners for group rights from around the world found opportunities under one or another category of human rights.

When the UN held its Vienna human rights conference, the institution was under unprecedented pressure to solve new problems, yet it was paralyzed in the face of mushrooming violence and chaos, much of it associated with violations of human rights, and overwhelmed by the pace of positive change as well. Free elections had taken place for the first time in Cambodia, Yemen, Burundi and Paraguay. Apartheid had been taken down in South Africa. Guatemala had overcome a military coup to elect a human rights advocate as president.

At the same time, civil wars had broken out in the newly independent states of Tajikistan, where some estimates put the death toll at 100,000, and Georgia. But no conflict put the UN on the hot seat like the one just a few hundred kilometers south of Vienna. In Bosnia-Herzegovina, an ethnic war raged in a modern European country, perplexing people around the world, not least because the United Nations could not stop it or protect civilian victims. Yugoslavia had been a calm, partially bourgeois socialist society whose citizens lived relatively well thanks to foreign credits that pumped cash into the inefficient economy. They enjoyed freedom of movement, including international travel, and forms of free expression and dissent were tolerated. Latent ethnic conflict had been kept that way by the manipulative regime of Yugoslavia's Communist boss, Josip Broz Tito—indeed, held in check indirectly by the Cold War. It burst into active warfare when Communist rule was ended. Bloody images of civilian casualties right on the periphery of civilized Western Europe, and certainly within Europe itself, entered the Euro-Atlantic mental space and tormented a political community driven by sensationalist television news.

The war was intensifying in the months leading up to the World Conference. Gorazde, a community in Eastern Bosnia that had been designated a "UN Safe Area" to protect Muslim civilians, was subject to a brutal attack by Serbian forces under the psychotic psychiatrist Radovan Karadzic. A devastating political cartoon labeled it an "UNsafe Area." At the same time, the impotent UN forces in Bosnia recorded atrocities by Croats and Bosniaks. The conflict had become an irrational, three-way war beyond the capacity of the UN or NATO forces to contain, or even to understand. With their mandate severely limited, UN soldiers could do little to stop violence, and drew derision as hardly more than "food deliverers," an American diplomat told me.

European states and their American ally could not agree on a unified response among themselves, or with the Russian-speaking eastern states, because some had favorites among the adversaries—relationships based on history and on religious affinities. In America, the Clinton administration and its hapless secretary of state, Warren Christopher, were not yet ready to lead. Russia and her Eastern Orthodox former satellites ensured that the UN Security Council would block any solution that bore the legitimacy of the world community, thus revealing a profound weakness in the organization that its proponents would have preferred to ignore. The new Balkan war had fragmented the international community, and the end of the Cold War, far from ending history, had made events flow more rapidly in unfamiliar and unpredictable directions.

The Yugoslav War and the Postmodern Human Rights Doctrine

The war in former Yugoslavia challenged not only the effort to protect civilians from grave human rights violations, but also the very idea of universal human rights. The ethnically motivated violence inspired moral equivalency. It unnerved a number of influential intellectuals, and provided a launching pad for calls to reject a concept of human rights based on Enlightenment rationalism.

Professor Richard Rorty has been a hero to many who reject what they regard as human rights "foundationalism," considering it unacceptably "Eurocentric." In his 1992 essay "Human Rights, Rationality and Sentimentality," Rorty observed:

> Serbian murderers and rapists do not think of themselves as violating human rights. For they are not doing these things to fellow human beings, but to *Muslims*. They are not being inhuman, but rather are discriminating between the true humans and the pseudohumans.... The Serbs take themselves to be acting in the interests of true humanity by purifying the world of pseudohumanity. In this respect their self-image resembles that of moral philosophers who hope to cleanse the world of prejudice and superstition.[2]

Then, in a dig at a major figure of the "human rights foundation," Rorty noted that Thomas Jefferson regarded his black slaves as not fully human. If the author of the famous declaration that "all men are created equal" did not really believe it, the idea of natural rights appeared an arbitrary and meaningless historical construction masking the hypocrisy of its purveyors.

Rorty saw no "big picture" that allowed anyone to make moral judgments about the violence in the Balkans; no universal principles rooted in an understanding of "the nature of man." The question is not "whether human beings really *have* the rights enumerated in the Helsinki Declaration," a question that is "not worth raising" insofar as "nothing relevant to moral choice separates human beings from animals except historically contingent facts of the world, cultural facts." Therefore, we who live in a "human rights culture" should not try invoking transcultural values to demonstrate its superiority to other cultures; instead, our task is to make it more *powerful*.[3] Bringing more peace to the world depends on changing "moral intuitions" by "manipulating feelings," not by appealing to knowledge or reason. Rorty positioned himself firmly against Kant, who had argued that moral good must be based on reason, not feelings or inclination. He dismissed rationality as nothing more than an "attempt" to construct a coherent "web of belief," and he called the paradigm of reason "morally offensive" to those who did not believe it and useless in view of how most people approach their identity. Rorty seemed to blame reason and the concept of human rights for the failure of unreasonable and abusive people to understand and appreciate them.

Granted, it was difficult—especially for European political and opinion leaders—to discern right from wrong in the Balkan war; the fractured societies, ethnic perspectives and multilateral victimization seemed to shatter truth itself. But the "social pragmatism" of the type advocated by Rorty provides "no norms to judge the cruel and unjust," as one critic warned; instead, it "invites either moral paralysis or the raw display of power."[4] Moral paralysis was indeed apparent in the international community, as embodied by the UN, during the World Conference on Human Rights. It could offer no clear moral refutation of ethnic nationalism as contradicting the principle of universal human rights. Philosophical positions like Rorty's were not irrelevant to the politics of the international community; they informed human rights discourse, weakening its ability to provide rational understanding and moral clarity as a basis for decisions and action. Rorty advised that appeals to sentiment and the cultivation of sympathy were more useful than rationality or "moral law." But of course, the Western world was awash in sentiment and sympathy, thanks especially to television. America was led by a man who took pride in being able to "feel others' pain." There was an overload of "concern" about the war. All sides in the war were busy cultivating sympathy and emotion, and indeed, the aggression in Bosnia was made possible largely by the manipulation of media and the mobilization of the feelings of the Serbs, and it was little different as regards ethnic violence by Bosniaks or Croats.

Concern and sympathy saturated foreign ministries and international organizations, leading nowhere. I recall a meeting in Vienna with some officials of the U.S. State Department about American policy in the former Yugoslavia; NGOs were demanding action to stop the killing. The Helsinki Federation, prompted by the Helsinki Committee in Serbia, was probably the most vociferous proponent of military intervention within the human rights community, advocating such action years before it actually took place. The State Department officials squirmed under our critiques, pointing to how *concerned* they were and "how much time" they devoted to the conflict; they seemed almost to be asking for our pity. Yet the Clinton administration did little at that point. Like European governments, it suffered from confusion; it was steeped in the kind of sentiment that Rorty praised, but it lacked conviction and knowledge. Too easily moved by cheap emotional appeals, American and other Western officials were at the same time suspicious and cynical, without a moral compass to provide orientation, without intellectual methods to make distinctions and choices.

A rational foundation for human rights and for moral action had been eroded both by neglect and by the agitprop of postmodernist intellectuals like Rorty, so our leaders thus lacked the moral clarity needed to address a war driven by ethnic hatred. The idea of human rights had been diluted and degraded, while postmodernists declared human rights to be nothing but a preferred Western value. A crude relativism found an open space in the post–Cold War landscape. Claims of natural rights and freedoms seemed passé in the absence of their old enemy, the dark forces of Soviet totalitarianism. Moral contrasts gave way to facile jargon about finding a "third way." Yet the relativist ethos of postmodernism is not finally about live and let live. It is "ultimately a philosophy of will."[5] It is about imposing a particular vision of "justice" on society, and thus it is the antithesis of human rights. Political interests operating behind the intellectual shield of postmodernist philosophy seized the field, and few, if any, defended the foundations and the integrity of human rights. The concept was up for grabs.

The World Conference and the Meaning of Human Rights

The conference in Vienna took place a few weeks before I began as executive director of the Helsinki Federation, and I attended several sessions that were open to representatives of nongovernmental organizations. Outside the Austria Center on Vienna's eastern Danube bank, next to the monstrous UN complex, Croatian, Bosnian and Serbian activists displayed oversized photographs of bodies dismembered, skinned and burned in ethnoracial violence. Under the widely held but false impression that the United Nations had coercive power, they demanded action. They were joined by others who likewise aspired to put their problems on the UN's human rights agenda, showing graphic images of starvation, poverty, racial and ethnic discrimination, brutality against women and minorities, torture and political oppression. It was like a flea market of global horrors. Anguished editorialists and hyperbolic human rights activists were intensifying the pressure to do something, especially about the war in Bosnia. The World Conference became a repository of frustrations and hopes. The scene was set for an ambitious world movement to divert attention from the UN's ongoing failure to cope with a bloody ethnic war, and for an effort to raise up Human Rights as a solution to a vast array of problems. Human rights had become an elastic concept that could mold itself around all of humanity's problems and demands—or in Rorty's terms, their sentiments and sympathies.

The secretary general of the UN, Boutros Boutros-Ghali, had balked at NATO plans to intervene militarily in the war. Relations between the world institution and the United States were at a nadir. In 1992, Boutros-Ghali had penned an ambitious "Agenda for Peace," setting out how the UN should respond to violent conflict, but it was on his and his associate Kofi Annan's watch that the UN, a year later, would ignore warnings from its own field officers and take no action in response to the threat of genocide in Rwanda. Boutros-Ghali was the only UN secretary general to be denied a second term when U.S. officials, spooked by critics in Congress, vetoed it.

He opened the World Conference with a speech that essentially offered up the idea of human rights to any and all who might attach it to their cause. He espoused the view that its meaning changes as political and social values change with the unfolding of history. Distinctions and oppositions are to be finessed or dissolved. The secretary general's peroration encouraged the conference, and the human rights community, to redefine human rights. "The world is undergoing a metamorphosis," Boutros-Ghali intoned. He declared that "certainties are collapsing...the lines are becoming blurred." While indulging the indulgent and even apocalyptic platitudes of the hour, he mysteriously added that "we need recourse to fundamental reference points."[6]

Boutros-Ghali suggested that the conference would establish links between development, economic and social rights, and civil and political rights. Each cultural epoch, he said, has its own way of implementing human rights, which are "the ultimate norm of all politics." The secretary general showed his progressive evolutionist orientation, yet he blithely asserted that human rights are "both absolute and historically determined." They are "a product of history" and "should evolve simultaneously with history," yet should always remain "universal."[7] Boutros-Ghali embraced the uncomfortable contradiction between natural and positive law at the heart of the Universal Declaration and the UN human rights system, making it into a twisted, unstable principle. He attempted to neutralize the problem with the UN's human rights construct—not just by a facile dismissal, but by holding up the contradiction as a symbol of virtue. He spoke as if he were heroically liberating the concept of human rights from the restrictions imposed by Enlightenment rationalism.

The secretary general went on to say, "Only democracy...can truly guarantee human rights."[8] The political transitions of the 1990s would, of course, prove him wrong about the relationship between democracy and human rights. In the following years, the number of nominal democracies increased dramatically, so that by 1997 the American journalist Fareed Zakaria could report that 118 of a total of 193 countries were democratic or becoming so, but only half of the "democratizing" countries of the world respected civil liberties, indicating the rise of "illiberal democracy."[9]

The vision of human rights embraced at the World Conference was protean and expansive, moving with the development of populist politics and with majoritarian rule in the post-Soviet era. It would mold itself to political definitions and to expediency. While affirming that human rights needed protection from democratic decisions, Boutros-Ghali said that human rights would be defined by politics—a position apparently meant to satisfy all.

For the first time, a United Nations event and its far-reaching results were driven to a significant degree by civil society advocacy. The World Conference had been in preparation since 1989, and civil society groups from five regions met well in advance of the conference to prepare declarations—a process that mobilized a wide range of activist groups, many of them political pressure groups, many organized to support state or party agendas. Around three thousand NGO delegates participated, and the list of participating organizations suggests that only a fraction were there to promote human rights as such. Many represented lobbies for interest groups and minorities. Many of these groups came to Vienna to promote economic and social rights, or the rights of women and specific minority groups. A large proportion were not really independent organizations, but were friendly to regimes or ruling parties and were attending on the government's ticket, so they could be relied upon to toe a political line. Strictly speaking, they were not NGOs, but rather GONGOs: government-organized nongovernmental organizations. The NGO contingents were all kept out of the hall where the official deliberations went on, instead meeting in the lower level of the Austria Center, as if in the bowels of a slave ship.

I took part in the most dramatic and emblematic event of the conference. In the NGO hall, during one of our final plenary sessions, we were to be addressed by Jimmy Carter, the former U.S. president. Carter had sacrificed the reputation of his presidency in bungled efforts to promote human rights at the center of his foreign policy. As he began to speak, a repetitive sound resembling a cloud of locusts rose up and drowned him out. It was a mindless, throbbing, collective buzz. Radical leftists had sparked the protest, angered that a former American leader had been given a prominent role. Looking around, I could see hardly anyone who was not making the sound. The "human rights" NGO representatives, disregarding civility and freedom of speech, had formed themselves into a mob. I approached a young man and asked him why he was preventing Carter from speaking. He looked at me for a few seconds and then admitted that he did not know. Evidently, the imperative to join the mob had been reason enough.

Pierre Sané, the eloquent Senegalese director of Amnesty International, tried to calm the crowd. He feared that the chaos at the NGO meeting would discredit the efforts of civil society; referring to the diplomats meeting in the upper floors, he warned, "They are laughing upstairs." (Perhaps it is worth noting that Sané would face ideological turbulence during his tenure at Amnesty International, when the organization's precise human rights mandate fell before the demands of members seeking to broaden it into the realm of "economic justice." He told me, years later, that Amnesty International "had a mandate, but the mandate kept changing.")

Perhaps some of the diplomats in the main chamber snickered at the embarrassing incivility of civil society that night, but they were also listening and bending to the will of the human rights mob. The outcome of the World Conference was to liquefy the idea of human rights and pour it into vessels shaped by popular political opinion. Western diplomats in Vienna did virtually nothing to prevent the destruction that happened there. Instead of defending the concept of human rights, they encouraged and participated in a process of dissolving it. In the run-up to the conference, Western states had focused on the challenge of "cultural relativism," anticipating that various

UN member states would, as usual, insist that their own particular cultural values allowed them to interpret human rights in ways that were at variance with universal standards.

In his speech to the conference, the U.S. secretary of state, Warren Christopher, proclaimed that "we cannot let cultural relativism become the last refuge of repression." Yet representatives of the United States and other liberal democracies evidently did little in preparation for the conference, while state and civil society organizers from South America, Africa, the Middle East and Asia had been refining their positions and demands. One critic noted that the United States was "outmaneuvered and outvoted" in Vienna: "The U.S. and its allies made no proposals, and made no coordinated statement of principles and objectives."[10]

The Vienna Declaration

Let us move directly to the *concrete outcomes* of the World Conference, which are recorded in the "Vienna Declaration and Programme of Action,"[11] a document to which UN officials and human rights activists often refer today.

Reaffirming Authentic Human Rights. The Vienna Declaration included a number of reaffirmations of civil and political rights that were and still are regarded as important victories. The universality of human rights was reaffirmed, despite intense conflicts before the meeting, when a number of states tried to weaken the official UN doctrine on universality by giving states more space to implement human rights on the basis of cultural relativism. While emphasizing the "right to development," the concluding document says that development and democracy are "interdependent and mutually reinforcing," a statement seen to bind autocratic Third World states to a commitment to democracy if they sought development aid. But democracy does not guarantee human rights.

The "Indivisibility" of Human Rights. The most consequential result of the Vienna conference was the endorsement and promotion of the idea that human rights are "indivisible." Representatives of the 171 states attending the conference proclaimed the concept of the "indivisibility, interdependence and inter-relatedness" of all human rights, and the equality of all rights, thereby elevating the idea to the level of a ruling mantra of the international human rights system. The next section of this chapter focuses on this concept and its consequences.

Emphasis on Economic, Social and Cultural Rights. Economic and social rights were stripped of the soiled garments of Communist and Third World propaganda, dressed in a new coat of political respectability, and propped up alongside freedom rights. Human rights were officially and openly bound together with a broad political agenda. Human rights work would now burn with the fires of political passion, and the UN human rights system turned into a world stage for demanding welfare-state benefits as mandated by international law. A large part of the human rights community became a vast, diffuse social-democratic lobby, with legitimation by the Vienna Declaration.

Poverty and Human Rights. The conference established that human rights were to be realized by economic policies, and that fighting poverty was a human rights activity. A "rights-based approach" would transform the alleviation of poverty from a moral duty into a legal obligation. The idea of voluntary charity was to be denounced in favor of international law to compel the redistribution of wealth, and indeed to force the implementation of a particular economic and political model. "Extreme poverty and social exclusion constitute a violation of human dignity," said the Vienna Declaration (par. 25), calling for "urgent steps" to be taken to understand the causes of poverty, "including those related to the problem of development, in order to promote the human rights of the poorest, and to put an end to extreme poverty and social exclusion."

Former President Carter opined at the conference that "a starving family will have no interest in the freedom of speech." This could only be taken to mean that economic rights had priority.

Women's Rights and Group Rights. At Vienna, the women's rights movement came to exert a large influence on the UN's entire approach to human rights, driving a redefinition of universality and perhaps even a redefinition of the human person. Subsequently, in the work of international organizations, a person would be seen largely as defined by subcategories of humanity—by sex, age, class, ethnicity, etc. Women's rights activists had mobilized to a hitherto unknown intensity in the lead-up to the conference. A worldwide petition drive, organized mainly by a U.S.-based NGO,[12] collected over half a million signatures from more than 120 countries. The petition presented at the World Conference demanded that discussions of all specific human rights issues include consideration of how women would be affected.[13] Women's rights activists dominated civil society activities at the conference, organizing over sixty workshops and seminars.

Feminism put its stamp on human rights, but this effort also reflected a broader concern to change human rights, international law, and society itself. The aim, for the most ambitious members of the movement, was to renegotiate the universal human rights framework in light of women's experiences in particular cultures and class backgrounds. Women's rights activists attacked what was left of the international community's belief in the priority of civil and political rights, expressing a revolutionary impulse to recast human rights. Far from being gender-neutral, they claimed, all human rights instruments assume men to be the bearers of basic rights.[14] The implication was clear: a human rights treaty should focus on a specific group, not humanity as such; the idea of universality was a fraud, and now obsolete. The major treaties defining human rights had not been drafted with victims in mind, so new treaties were needed to rectify historical injustices.

The conference rightly focused on a number of groups whose members' human rights were vulnerable, including "national or ethnic, religious and linguistic minorities," indigenous peoples, migrant workers, children, and the disabled, in addition to women. But it promoted the notion that vulnerable individuals should be protected *as members of groups*—that groups would be the focus of human rights. The conference set in motion a process that challenged the transcendent vision of universal human rights, in favor of a divisive emphasis on group rights and identity politics. The idea of protecting individual rights came to be associated with a possessive individualism, while human rights fell under the smothering blanket of a soft collectivism.

"Non-State Actors." Women's rights activists branded the perpetrators of domestic violence, which is or should be a crime, as human rights violators. The primary responsibility of states to honor human rights was thus clouded over by the trendy, bogus concept of "non-state actors," i.e. civilians, being held culpable for human rights violations. The distinction between crimes and human rights violations faded. It is true that domestic violence, a common crime, becomes a violation of human rights when it is not prosecuted and thus the state is not offering equal protection under the law. But some in the human rights community wanted the perpetrators of crimes themselves to be considered guilty of violating human rights. Lawyers influenced by feminism and critical legal theory have looted human rights terminology to bring the weight of international law down on wife-beaters, twisting legal human rights terms like "torture," which has (or had) a precise, limited meaning under

international law, to claim that spousal abuse is torture. In the past fifteen years, the human rights community has been preoccupied with "trafficking in human beings," a criminal matter that has landed in human rights, which makes no sense when some human rights activists insist on a human right to work as a prostitute.

Tolerance and Xenophobia. Another way the World Conference contributed to bending the concept of human rights was by suggesting that various attitudes and sentiments are human rights violations, and tasking human rights institutions with changing them. Indeed, the World Conference put human rights more sharply into conflict with the freedom of speech and conscience. The final document declared that "xenophobia and related intolerance is a priority task for the international community." No one can deny that xenophobia and intolerance are unhealthy and potentially dangerous, or that they are often associated with crimes and violations of human rights. But while human rights had generally meant protecting the freedom of speech and other core freedoms, the Vienna conference encouraged efforts to suppress various forms of thought and expression in the name of human rights. Many totalitarian governments had long sought to do this by supporting legislation against "hate speech" and "incitement to hatred," concepts that are vague and easily abused.

In the years since the World Conference, the intergovernmental machinery of international human rights as well as national governments and civil society have all poured resources into "combating xenophobia and intolerance." Recently, the eradication of "Islamophobia" has become a central objective (see Chapter 6 below). It is one thing for civil society campaigns to try to change the attitudes of citizens, but when state organs do so, the process can drift into propaganda and threaten freedom of thought and speech.

It is difficult for many people to understand that human rights do not compel individuals to uphold particular moral beliefs, such as the value of charity or tolerance. Governments are obligated by human rights principles and covenants to refrain from and even prohibit discrimination. Indeed, the core human rights principles of freedom of religion and speech were clarified as European societies came to terms with religious pluralism. But human rights should not be used to police and prosecute attitudes when they do not pose direct threats to others. Human rights should even protect attitudes that may be abhorrent, making a clear distinction between attitudes and behaviors. Since the early 1990s and the World Conference, the human rights trend has been toward an overreach into mentalities, attitudes and beliefs. The concept of human rights has morphed into a set of moral and political prejudices rather than a mechanism to shield individuals from repression.

In September 2016, the UN's Office of the High Commissioner for Human Rights asked in a rhetorical tweet if free-market economics posed an "urgent threat."[15] Within a few days, the high commissioner, Zeid Ra'ad Al Hussein, gave an impassioned speech in The Hague singling out "populist" parties and individual political leaders including Marine Le Pen, the head of the National Front in France; Geert Wilders, the Dutch MP; Nigel Farage, the British "Brexit" advocate; and Donald Trump, then a U.S. presidential candidate.[16] A short time later, addressing the 33rd Session of the UN Human Rights Council in the context of a statement defending international organizations, he warned that "[a] number of elections will be held in well established democracies, with dangerous xenophobes and bigots running for office."[17] Not a single media commentator or civil society representative, as far as I could determine, pointed out the inappropriateness of these expressions—how they violate the principle of political neutrality so essential to the credibility of human rights activism.

The "Indivisibility" Movement

The political core of the Vienna Declaration was to endorse the concept of the "indivisibility of human rights." The fifth article states:

> All human rights are universal, indivisible and interdependent and inter-related. The international community must treat human rights globally in a fair and equal manner, on the same footing, and with the same emphasis. While the significance of national and regional particularities and various historical, cultural and religious backgrounds must be borne in mind, it is the duty of States, regardless of their political, economic and cultural systems, to promote and protect all human rights and fundamental freedoms.[18]

The indivisibility of all human rights is today typically considered a basic principle of human rights, along with universalism, freedom and equality.[19] All things in existence are ultimately indivisible and interdependent. What then is actually meant by the "indivisibility of human rights"? The idea was implicit in the Universal Declaration, where economic and social rights were bound together with civil and political rights to reflect diverse understandings of human rights. Asbjørn Eide, the scholar of economic and social rights, regards the idea as fundamental to the "very establishment of the United Nations."[20] The concept of human rights at the core of the UN system is one in which the placement of authentic human rights and social rights together in the UDHR implicitly established their indivisibility, and thus the moral and legal unacceptability of seeing real human rights apart from economic and social rights.

As we have seen, the idea of indivisibility had already been deployed by some factions of the international community as a means of extracting economic assistance, and by others as a way to push for economic and social rights. Now it was embraced by the entire UN membership as a primary principle, or more accurately as a slogan or mantra. Neither the United Nations nor any interpreters of the Vienna Declaration or other proclamations about the indivisibility of human rights have fully explained what it means or how it works.

The most charitable way to interpret "indivisibility" is that it refers to the complementary nature of human rights, the view that all human rights (or human rights in addition to economic and social rights) are best realized when implemented together. Some rights clearly support other rights, and there is two-way support between some pairs of rights. But Professor James Nickel has shown that "widespread" or "system-wide" indivisibility is not plausible.[21] The complementarity among authentic civil and political human rights needs little defense. But indivisibility has never been framed by its proponents in that way; it has always referred to the relationship between civil and political rights and economic and social rights—between the two "types" of human rights. In fact, *indivisibility is a purely political idea, a normative, persuasive, ideological idea whose practical aim is to force states and civil society to accept the existence of economic and social rights as human rights.* It is an idea reflecting a range of goals: to resolve political differences, to promote economic and social rights as human rights equal to authentic human rights, to turn criticism of economic and social rights into a heresy, and even to direct human rights away from the protection of individual freedom, toward planned economies and societies where individual freedom is restricted in the name of equality and economic security.

The Politics of Indivisibility

The main practical effect of the words about indivisibility in the Vienna Declaration has been to promote the false notion that the natural right to freedom cannot be enjoyed without specific social policies; that respect for real human rights is contingent upon social services that are not human rights at all. The entire edifice of human rights is made dependent on a particular kind of state, a welfare state. One might think that indivisibility would work in both directions, yet the suggestion that economic and social rights cannot be realized without freedoms is almost never heard in human rights discourse; indeed, the idea is absurd, and demonstrably false given the social protections offered by totalitarian states. Instead, economic and social rights are always given priority as the conditions for enjoying freedom.

Indivisibility is arguably the main instrument by which international human rights has been comprehensively politicized, linking the *universal* right to freedom with a *particular* economic system in UN doctrine. The World Conference made an ironclad dogma of the notion that freedom rights are not viable without a state guarantee of adequate food, housing, education and medical care. Freedom would thus be held hostage to redistributionist welfare spending. Indivisibility means that freedom rights are subject to a form of "proportionality" whereby it is legitimate to ration freedom, especially economic freedom, in order to maintain the welfare state. The elevation of indivisibility into the core governing principle for human rights at the UN has dragged international human rights down into the banal political process of dividing the spoils of society.

The early 1990s saw a worldwide resurgence of left-wing politics under a range of slogans providing cosmetic dissociation from communism and state socialism. Various movements presented themselves as countering "global-ization," "neoliberalism," transnational business enterprises and free trade, and campaigning for redistributive policies, including the seizure of private property and land. Many fashioned themselves as "human rights" campaigns, promoting economic and social rights and asserting that civil and political rights by themselves are a recipe for exploitative, even racist capitalism. But these were (and are) movements essentially advocating coercion in the name of human rights. Indivisibility has become the human rights catchword animating a loosely defined political movement toward global economic collectivism. According to international human rights principles, we cannot have freedom without some form of socialism.

The dominance of the indivisibility principle represents a victory for all who demanded a single legally binding international human rights covenant, not the two that were achieved as a weak victory by free and democratic governments. It was, in fact, a major setback for authentic human rights, returning the world community to ideas that had been discredited forty years before. With the hyped-up emphasis bestowed by the World Conference, indivisibility has deeply eroded the very meaning of human rights. By saying that authentic human rights are the same kind of thing as economic and social rights, it implies that there is no such thing as human rights based on natural law.

UN institutions, in particular the Committee on Economic, Social and Cultural Rights (which oversees the ICESCR), played a vanguard role in twisting human rights into an economic doctrine through the concept of indivisibility. The UN resolution establishing the World Conference indicates that the promotion of economic and social rights was a primary objective of the meeting. At the time, more than sixty members of the United Nations had not ratified the treaty on economic and social rights, and the status of those rights was still open to debate.

In the spring of 1993, leading up to the conference, a contribution by the committee made the case for the "equality of rights" and for an optional protocol to the ICESCR giving the vague treaty legally binding teeth.[22] This document provides a candid condensation of the ideology behind indivisibility and other major decisions of the World Conference. The committee insisted that "respect for both categories of rights must go hand in hand," a principle that had been endorsed "on innumerable occasions by the General Assembly." It was thought "imperative that full and careful consideration be given to the various ways and means by which the principle of indivisibility can be implemented and the situation of economic, social and cultural rights be improved."

It is clear that "indivisibility" was to be the mechanism to promote economic and social rights, and in fact to *prioritize* them. The document attacks the idea that a realization of economic and social rights in the form of stronger state programs will "flow automatically" from respecting civil and political rights and respecting economic freedoms. The authors were frustrated by the "shocking reality" that "violations of civil and political rights continue to be treated as though they were far more serious, and more patently intolerable, than massive and direct denials of economic, social and cultural rights."

The rejection of state socialism and the widening acceptance of liberal democracy had put the proponents of economic and social rights on the defensive. The committee's memorandum, while composed by human rights "experts," was essentially a political pamphlet against "neoliberalism." The authors warned about the consequences of ignoring economic and social rights:

> Political freedom, free markets and pluralism have been embraced with enthusiasm by an ever-increasing number of peoples in recent years, in part because they have been seen as the best prospect of achieving basic economic, social and cultural rights. If that quest proves to be futile the pressures in many societies to revert to authoritarian alternatives will be immense.

It reads almost as a threat—indeed, the same kind of threat that had led Bismarck to provide basic social benefits: Recognize economic and social rights, or face the end of freedom and democracy.

Social safety nets needed to be established and secured by international law, and they "must be formulated in terms of rights rather than charity or generosity." This echoes the nineteenth-century "property is theft" notion of the anarcho-socialist Pierre-Joseph Proudhon—the idea that there is a right to wealth beyond what one has earned, because all wealth is collective property. Proudhon and his followers called it "social wealth" or "social property."[23]

The committee took on the problem of the justiciability of economic and social rights with a tactic that would be replicated many times in succeeding decades. They wrote that making such rights justiciable would require "innovative practices," presumably meaning that the rules of justiciable interpretation would bend the law to accommodate the implementation of such rights. An "optional protocol" providing a legal mechanism whereby individuals could lodge complaints would make the treaty on economic and social rights "more clear"—an odd sequence of thought, suggesting that if laws and the principles behind them are not clear, they will be cleared up by more enforcement. In the committee's view, "one of the basic objectives of the procedure is to enhance understanding of the normative content of the rights and thus shed more light on aspects of the notion of justiciability." An optional protocol would make social rights fully equal to the rights protected by the International Covenant on Civil and Political Rights. In essence, an act of faith, a belief in the legitimacy of bringing about social justice via human rights law, would make it happen. Such a protocol was in fact adopted by the UN General Assembly in 2008, and entered into force in 2013.

In fact, the views put forth by the Committee on Economic, Social and Cultural Rights had long been promoted in the United Nations, mainly by the Soviet bloc, and were taken up strongly at Vienna. The World Conference mobilized and gave vent to the feeling that economic and social rights had been willfully neglected or even suppressed by the rich, capitalist West; that civil and political rights were the rights of the "haves," who had denied and wished to continue denying economic and social rights to the "have nots" in the Global South and in their own societies. At the conference, Western leaders jumped on the bandwagon. They advocated a kind of affirmative action or restitution for the oppressed, for those who had been neglected and victimized. For example, Gareth Evans, the Australian foreign minister (who later gained global influence as head of the International Crisis Group), spoke of the "victory for personal freedom that was won with the end of the Cold War," but like a number of others he implied that this victory *compelled concessions*. Referring to the "sad neglect" of economic and social rights over the previous twenty-five years, he said, "The World Conference should, as one of its primary objectives, put forward specific measures to promote the implementation of economic, social and cultural rights." This might avoid the risk of "driving a greater wedge between the governments of the North and South."[24] The indivisibility scheme would be a compensatory mechanism for prior neglect, a guilt tax; it would rebalance the notion of human rights after the defeat of communism; and it would buy peace with the Global South—all of which are political objectives.

The leaders meeting in Vienna apparently imposed the notion of the indivisibility and interdependence of human rights on the world without reflecting on its lack of logical or empirical justification, or on its blatantly ideological purpose. The members of the European Community, for example, had previously rejected the argument that civil and political rights are impossible to achieve without a respect for economic and social rights, but they reversed course. The interdependence argument was deeply seductive in the years immediately after the collapse of the Soviet bloc, as it seemed to reconcile polarizing positions and give something to all parties in conflict. It also resonated with the post-Sixties generation's ideological map as a Hegelian synthesis, by positing that two sets of rights associated with opposite sides of a profound political divide are not only compatible but necessary to one another. Indivisibility is a formal principle built upon a mirage.

Indivisibility and Human Rights Discourse

Virtually the entire international and human rights community has bought into the idea of the indivisibility and interdependence of human rights, or at least ignored its negative implications. For example, the late Professor Kevin Boyle, a widely respected authority on human rights, published an analysis of the World Conference in 1995, in which he lathered praise on the delegates for ending decades of "sterile East-West ideological confrontation over human rights to address the most pressing of many global dilemmas: how can a common commitment to a single standard of human rights help transform relations between the developed minority world and the developing majority world?"[25] He saw the conference results as a way of addressing a global economic challenge by massaging the concept of human rights.

Boyle praised the conference for reversing the putative neglect of economic and social rights, and for giving broader legitimacy to the "right to development." He commended the "acceptance by the North that peoples of the South have a right to development and that guarantees of basic economic and social rights are necessary...if political stability and respect for civil and political rights are to be ensured." Presumably this meant that foreign assistance was necessary. The largely undemocratic states of the "South" had extracted commitments to economic aid in return for empty promises to respect civil and political rights. Western states, feeling secure without the threat of Russian missiles looming over them, thought they had purchased a compromise. The "South" supposedly accepted that sustainable development "requires a democratic society, not measured alone in the holding of elections, but in the full participation of the entire population, men and women, in decisions affecting them." But again, indivisibility is virtually never invoked to insist on protecting basic freedoms; on the contrary, it is used as an argument for the responsibility and power of states to provide economic and social rights. What is more, a habit of using "human rights" and "democracy" interchangeably had invaded discussions, skating over the need to protect the freedom of individuals from majority rule.

The most destructive way the idea of indivisibility and interdependence has affected human rights discourse is in relativizing and contextualizing human rights violations. Moses Moskowitz, the legal scholar, wrote that the notion of "interdependence" among human rights "gives aid and comfort to Governments which seek refuge in excuses for policies and actions that are violative of human rights." The doctrine establishes "causal relationships of undetermined validity and places responsibilities on all and none. [It] does not move from evidence through reasoning to conclusion to serve as a practical guide for action." Moskowitz concluded that the international community had a "need to restore intellectual discipline" in the face of "cant" and "compulsory clichés."[26]

Indivisibility and interdependence have distorted the way human rights violations are perceived in civil society. An example comes from Yoani Sanchez, the brave Cuban pro-democracy blogger. Finally allowed to travel abroad in 2013, after many years of being banned from doing so, she met with human rights activists in the Netherlands. She recounted part of her conversation as follows:

> It's my turn to speak. I tell about the acts of repudiation, the arbitrary arrests, the assassination of reputations and a nation on rafts crossing the Florida Straits. I tell them of divided families, intolerance, of a country where power is inherited through blood and our children dream of escape. And then come all the phrases I've heard hundreds, thousands of times.
>
> I've barely said the first words and I already know what is coming: "But you can't complain, you have the best educational system on the continent"…"Yes, it might be, but you can't deny that Cuba has confronted the United States for half a century"…"OK, you don't have freedom, but you have a public health system"…and a long repertoire of stereotypes and false conclusions taken from official propaganda.[27]

Sanchez wrote that she could no longer communicate with her colleagues following these remarks, as the "myth" perpetuated by the Cuban regime had prevailed.

The idea of indivisibility supports the view that violations of human rights can balance or justify each other—that violations of freedom can either be offset by social programs, or rationalized by the difficulties of developing such programs. A Cuban dissident at a UN Human Rights Council briefing I observed in Geneva in 2013 explained what this actually meant for the people of his country, saying, "Our health care system and our education system are not free. We have paid for them with our freedom." That price seems rarely if ever to concern those who promote the indivisibility of human rights. When Fidel Castro died in late 2016, his human rights legacy was widely described as "mixed," in view of "improved access to public services such as health and education."[28] Delegates to the Human Rights Council stood for a minute of silence in honor of a dictator who had deprived his people of their human rights for decades and had severely persecuted those who objected.

Linking authentic human rights to the provision of state services is now a common way of dismissing complaints about the denial of fundamental freedoms. Respondents to such complaints may point to economic injustices in liberal societies, or suggest that if people receive certain benefits from their government, they have no right to complain about not being free. Even the Democratic Peoples Republic of Korea, a Stalinist regime with hundreds of thousands starving in concentration camps, defends itself, and is defended by a few Communist ideologues and rogue states, on the grounds of its supposed respect for economic and social rights (as we will see in Chapter 4).

By such reasoning, no human rights violation can stand scrutiny as an objective fact in itself, but must be viewed against the totality of social facts. But the notion that no human right can be realized without all other human rights becomes more absurd and more malignant as "new human rights" proliferate, enlarging the grounds on which violations of freedom can be trivialized. Any human rights violation can thus be intellectually and morally "deconstructed" with the tool of indivisibility, which most often serves a crude Marxian reductionism.

Vienna and the Bureaucratization of Human Rights

When the World Conference took place, the United Nations was failing miserably to stop violence and promote peace and human rights in former Yugoslavia. But the international community responded at Vienna by enlarging the UN's human rights bureaucracy and giving it vast new responsibilities. The World Conference marked the beginning of a process by which international human rights came to be dominated by a centralized bureaucracy. With the enthusiastic support of civil society, governments pushed questions of human rights away from themselves and onto an international level where unaccountable civil servants reigned; they subcontracted human rights to an institution dominated by states that did not respect those rights.

One of the major "achievements" of the Vienna meeting was a mandate to empower a UN office, the Centre for Human Rights, to "coordinate" and "mainstream" human rights. The conference's Programme of Action recommended that more funding be allocated to beef up the capacity of the Centre for Human Rights, and that governments strengthen their own official human rights institutions. Human rights became a growth industry in earnest, dominated by state-controlled institutions sucking up valuable resources that could be better used by independent organizations. The Office of the High Commissioner for Human Rights now has well over one thousand staff members.

The post of high commissioner was established by the UN General Assembly following the Vienna conference. Even Boutros-Ghali, who himself had ambitious plans for expanding the role of the UN, evinced skepticism at "proposals for new bureaucracies, high-level positions, more procedures and permanent forums."[29] The charge of the high commissioner was basically to *enforce the new human rights regime* that emerged from the World Conference. He or she would

> be guided by the recognition that all human rights—civil, cultural, economic, political and social – are universal, indivisible, interdependent and interrelated and that, while the significance of national and regional particularities and various historical, cultural and religious backgrounds must be borne in mind, it is the duty of States, regardless of their political, economic and cultural systems, to promote and protect all human rights and fundamental freedoms; [and]...Recognize the importance of promoting a balanced and sustainable development for all people and of ensuring realization of the right to development, as established in the Declaration on the Right to Development.[30]

It is this job description, not the concept of a high commissioner per se, that is concerning. The idea of a powerful human rights official had been around since before the establishment of the UN itself. René Cassin, the French Nobel Peace laureate who helped draft the Universal Declaration, envisioned an "attorney general for human rights," who would petition a human rights court on behalf of victims.[31] The post eventually created was far from that concept. The high commissioner's job was not to be simply to monitor and protect rights, and advocate on behalf of victims, but to promote a reshaped concept of human rights, and to keep the lid on debate about the nature of human rights. This mandate was the product of a working group led by José Ayala Lasso, an Ecuadorian diplomat who was himself appointed the first UN high commissioner for human rights.

With these ambitious initiatives, the world community moved resolutely toward defining human rights as a challenge for a global legal and regulatory system, as opposed to a challenge for constitutional and legislative policy at the national level. When the main human rights laws are international treaties, they lose their connection to citizens, who themselves lose the sense of ruling over themselves, obeying laws they themselves authored, which is how some have defined freedom.[32]

Human Rights Hollowed Out from the Inside

Human rights, properly understood, originated in a rational analysis of the requirements for individual freedom and dignity. The World Conference modernized the idea of human rights under the heavy influence of a new progressivism that had been developing since the 1960s, responding to the needs and demands of various interest groups and emerging social and political movements. The conference melted the distinction and contradiction between freedom rights and economic and social rights, and fused them all into an ideology that has little to do with authentic human rights. The irrational mingling of political values with human rights was made into an article of faith.

As the distinction between human rights and the legal rights of positive law faded away, human rights became a rhetorical tool of movements for social change,[33] or a process of "distributive justice." Liberal democracies, on the defensive over charges of pushing their own cultural priorities as universal values, accommodated claims to group rights. It was essentially a step backwards. The British philosopher Roger Scruton clarifies the point by noting that individual rights

> force people to treat you as a free being, with sovereignty over his life, who has an equal claim on your respect. But the new ideas of human rights allow rights to one group that they deny to another: you have rights as a gipsy, a woman, a homosexual, which you can claim only as a member of that group. To think in this way is to resurrect the abuses to which Locke and others were in search of a remedy—the abuses which led to people being arbitrarily discriminated against, on account of their class, race or occupation.[34]

Human rights came to be dominated by the effort to overcome inequalities, and would increasingly be invoked to violate freedoms in order to ensure equality and access to wealth. Rights conceived as claims on resources "inevitably point to the state as the only possible provider."[35]

The Vienna vision of human rights put little emphasis on constraining the power of the state—the problem that had preoccupied the founders of human rights.[36] On the contrary, human rights would be a service of the state that further empowers the state, and would imply the dependency of individuals on states. The World Conference ushered in an era of positive human rights law, obligating the state to "create the conditions" for the enjoyment of human rights. The new human rights are indistinguishable from social policy—a global scheme to achieve particular social and political goals, rather than a principle served by duty.

The World Conference reflected significant changes in the way civil society approached human rights, and in turn it influenced those approaches. All of the major initiatives outlined above were enthusiastically promoted by independent human rights groups. The human rights community revealed itself to be thoroughly committed to broad state action to improve the situation of various groups. It approved of the state reaching into society in an effort to change attitudes, even at the expense of freedom of expression.

Perhaps most important, the World Conference advanced a stultifying intellectual conformism and complacency regarding human rights. The meaning of human rights had been officially proclaimed by state authorities in Vienna, as if by a politburo declaring official ideology, and was obediently accepted by civil society. The slogans adopted by states at the conference became an almost unquestioned dogma. The conference marked the end of most debate about the relationship between what were considered the two sets of human rights, and thus the end of most serious political discourse in human rights terms.[37] It marked the onset of an intellectual narcosis that has retarded the march of freedom by sidelining freedom rights and giving credence to a human rights argument for restricting individual rights. At Vienna, political will overran clear legal principles—the principle that negative liberties, the legal translation of natural rights, are distinct from state-given, politically determined rights; the principle that human rights violations are actions by states, not crimes to be punished by states; the principle that negative liberties are politically neutral, while positive policies are by nature political and thus matters for citizens to decide by legislation.

A disenchanted shadow of the concept of human rights—a principle upon which liberal, democratic civic states were built—took up residence in the halls of the global political establishment.

PART II

The Consequences
for Liberty

CHAPTER 4

Toward Human Rights without Freedom

A human rights conference rarely has much impact on the world, but the intellectually embarrassing results of the World Conference of 1993 are an exception. A dysfunctional understanding of human rights was elaborated and locked in place by politicians. Human rights officially ceased to mean guarantees of individual freedom from abuse by the state, and instead became a justification for more state power and control. Individual freedom has been pushed away from the center of the human rights concept. The moral boundary of human rights was already breached in the Universal Declaration, and at Vienna the international community made peace with its contradictions, claiming ostentatiously to transform them into operative principles but really papering them over with morally obligatory slogans. Within the expanding perimeter of what are now called human rights, individual freedoms have increasingly been balanced against a range of political, economic and "social justice" objectives.

These changes permeate the human rights world and are celebrated by the human rights establishment as a remarkable moral achievement. In 2013, marking twenty years since the World Conference, United Nations human rights officials and human rights activists gathered again in Vienna to commemorate the meeting. I was there to observe, keeping silent and scribbling on my notepad, sitting next to my old friend and colleague Ludmilla Alexeyeva, who mainly focused on a word puzzle.

In the commemoratory events, Navanethem (Navi) Pillay, who was then the UN high commissioner for human rights, hailed the Vienna Declaration as "the most significant overarching human rights document produced in the last quarter century. It crystallized the underlying principles that human rights are universal, indivisible, interdependent and interrelated." Ms. Pillay made reference to the context of the Vienna conference, and the fall of the Berlin Wall. She said that by equating economic and social rights with civil and political rights, the conference had "succeeded in breaching a second wall that had divided states over the previous decades." A triumphal mood prevailed; a great victory had been achieved, of which the "indivisibility of human rights" was the emblem. It was, in effect, a victory of politics over natural rights. Almost like a meeting of Soviet bureaucrats, speaker after speaker obediently praised indivisibility, which had fused human rights to welfare-state politics and brought human rights down to the level of regulatory law.

The twentieth anniversary of the World Conference was an opportunity to identify human rights priorities for the future. In a letter written to UN delegations, in which she claimed to speak on behalf of "peoples of the United Nations," Pillay outlined principles that should animate a "post-2015" human rights agenda. The principles included "substantive equality of both opportunity and result under the rule of law." Equality of opportunity is part of the bedrock of fundamental human rights. But invoking equality of *results* implied that the goal of human rights law was to ensure that every person of the world should live at the same material standard. Ms. Pillay was unselfconsciously invoking the Marxist interpretation of equality. These far-reaching proposals were justified on the grounds that "poverty itself represents a complex of human rights violations," and that the "global climate change crisis is also a human rights crisis" threatening the realization of "universally guaranteed entitlements."

At another "High Level Expert Conference" to commemorate the 1993 Vienna event, UN officials and human rights leaders from civil society paid homage to the "paradigmatic shift" that it had brought about, mainly by establishing the indivisibility of human rights as an undisputed principle. The expansive "post-2015" human rights agenda would include a "fully integrated human rights approach" to development, climate change, and the regulation of transnational corporations. Here is an example of this approach, from an "analytical study" on human rights and climate change published by the Office of the High Commissioner in 2016:

> All human rights are universal, inalienable, interdependent and interrelat-ed. In the context of the right to health, these characteristics are eminently clear. Enjoyment of the right to health is contingent upon the availabil-ity of, inter alia, good quality health services, safe working conditions, adequate housing, food, water and sanitation, a healthy environment, and education, all on the basis of non-discrimination, as well as stakeholder participation in health policy formulation and implementation.[1]

The program of the UN's central human rights bureau is hubristic in its reach into diverse regions of social and economic life. In her report to the Human Rights Council for the 17th Session, beginning on May 30, 2011, Ms. Pillay provided an illustration of the broad range of concerns that are being taken up by the human rights apparatus of the UN. They included: defining indicators to be used in research to measure progress in attaining economic and social rights; "preparing an analytical compilation on good and bad practices to prevent maternal mortality and morbidity"; organizing a con-sultation on land issues; organizing an "expert group meeting" to provide "a comprehensive overview of the social situation, well-being, development and rights of older persons the world over"; publishing a training manual on budget monitoring as pertinent to "the realization of economic, social and cultural rights"; advising the government of Moldova on a draft education code; organizing a workshop in Serbia on the right to adequate housing; tak-ing up the issues of lead poisoning in Kosovo, mental health in East Timor, poverty in Afghanistan, bonded child labor in Nepal, exploitation of natural resources in the Democratic Republic of the Congo; and raising the general issues of human rights and trade, and human rights of persons displaced in emergencies. Indeed, the Office of the High Commissioner drums up business for itself by encouraging campaigners for goals like "urban transformation" to frame their issues in terms of human rights.[2]

After the World Conference, the international human rights system morphed into a sprawling regulatory bureaucracy having very little to do with protecting basic individual freedoms, and often baldly reflecting a leftist political ideology. The "proliferation," "inflation" and "dilution" of human rights has become a serious but largely ignored problem. James Griffin, a philosopher of human rights at Oxford University, acknowledged that the extension of the term has changed the meaning of human rights.[3] It becomes more and more difficult to locate the protection of freedom in the vast and incoherent field of international human rights.

The Proliferation of Economic and Social Human Rights Law

Human rights are called forth to govern an ever-widening range of human activity at the behest of leftist social-justice campaigners, politically biased nongovernmental organizations, regulation-promoting lawyers, activist judges, international civil servants and interest groups. The proliferation of human rights laws has led to a devaluation of human rights. As two colleagues have written, "If human rights were a currency, its value would be in free fall, thanks to a gross inflation in the number of human rights treaties and non-binding international instruments adopted by international organizations over the last several decades." There is a huge number of human rights agreements binding states, particularly European countries, as various interest groups have sought "the trump card of having their cause recognized as a human rights issue." Also contributing to this trend are "international human rights advocates, some national governments, and technocrats in international orga-nizations seeking larger bureaucratic domains."[4] Interest groups and lobbies promote international human rights treaties that would mandate their own services, and benefit them materially.[5] The official human rights community, anxious to rein in transnational corporations, is itself largely an unregulated, government-run growth industry.

Respect for the unifying idea of equal, universal, individual human rights has given way to the view that the rights of specific victimized groups must be recognized explicitly in legislation if they are to be taken seriously. The international community has adopted human rights treaties designed to protect the rights of people who face particular challenges to realizing their fundamental rights and freedoms—challenges like discrimination on the basis of gender, race or ethnicity. A treaty that focuses on protecting the freedom of women or children or the disabled would likely duplicate the International Covenant on Civil and Political Rights (ICCPR), which applies to all people. Human rights campaigns often focus on members of threatened groups as a practical and even necessary tactic that need not undermine the principle of universal, individual human rights. The IHF, for example, organized projects on women's rights and discrimination against Muslims following 9/11. But human rights *treaties* that apply to members of particular groups may be divisive and distracting. Human rights law in the service of "identity politics" and group grievances runs counter to promoting understanding and respect for the universality of human rights. This fragmented and conflictual model of human rights has the effect of diminishing our appreciation for universal, individual human rights based on our common humanity.

A number of the international human rights treaties focusing on collective rights to government services have also called for respecting basic freedoms. For example, the International Convention on the Elimination of All Forms of Racial Discrimination (CERD, 1969), in Article 5, stresses the need to guarantee basic civil rights. The Convention on the Elimination of All Forms of Discrimination against Women (CEDAW, 1979) focuses on antidiscrimination legislation in its "agenda for equality." The Convention on the Rights of the Child (CRC, 1990) seeks to guarantee protection of basic civil rights of children, including, for example, their freedom of expression. The Convention on the Rights of Persons with Disabilities, which went into effect in 2006, addresses fundamental rights like the right to life, equal protection before the law, freedom from torture, and freedom of expression.

But the real problem with the array of treaties and resolutions emerging since the International Bill of Human Rights (the UDHR plus the ICCPR and the ICESCR) is that they represent the proliferation of entitlements that are not authentic human rights. They mandate positive state actions, placing economic burdens on governments, imposing themselves on democratic political processes, and reaching toward a coercive, bureaucratic, regulatory utopia.

Economic and Social Rights in UN Collective Rights Treaties

In proliferating international human rights legislation, we find vague phrasing and definitions that arouse unrealistic expectations about the allocation of resources. Human rights treaties promote, and indeed require, a model of the state whose main function is to impose taxes and fund social programs for different classes of people in need. They entrust new legal powers to state entities, while largely ignoring the role of civil society. They remove both resources and responsibility from individuals and from voluntary civil society organizations. International human rights law has enlarged the power of the state and reified the United Nations.

Elaboration of Rights in the Main Economic and Social Rights Treaty. The full implications of the International Covenant on Economic, Social and Cultural Rights (ICESCR) have been rolling out in a process that will likely never stop, owing to the vagueness of its terms. Government-sponsored access to numerous necessities has been named a human right by the responsible treaty bodies and by resolutions of the Human Rights Commission and Council (which replaced it in 2006), and of the UN General Assembly. A few examples will show the general tendencies.

The Committee on Economic, Social and Cultural Rights declared in 1999 that the right to "adequate food" named in the covenant means that "the State must proactively engage in activities intended to strengthen people's access to and utilization of resources and means to ensure their livelihood, including food security."[6] Furthermore,

> The strategy should give particular attention to the need to prevent discrimination in access to food or resources for food. This should include: guarantees of full and equal access to economic resources, particularly for women, including the right to inheritance and the ownership of land and other property, credit, natural resources and appropriate technology; measures to respect and protect self-employment and work which provides a remuneration ensuring a decent living for wage earners and their families....[7]

The human right to "adequate food" is thought to require that states protect their citizens from junk food. The special rapporteur for this topic advised that "states are obliged to ensure effective measures to regulate the food industry, ensure that nutrition policymaking spaces are free from private sector influence and implement comprehensive policies that combat malnutrition in all its forms."[8]

A "right to water" is based on Articles 11 and 12 of the ICESCR. In 2010, a UN resolution declared a human right to "safe and clean drinking water and sanitation," calling upon states and international organizations "to provide financial resources, capacity-building and technology transfer, through international assistance and cooperation, in particular to developing countries, in order to scale up efforts to provide safe, clean, accessible and afford-able drinking water and sanitation for all."[9] Some countries—including the United States, Canada, Australia, New Zealand and several European nations—reportedly tried to block the resolution in hopes of minimizing their future obligations; an official from the United Kingdom was quoted as saying that developed countries "don't want to pay for the toilets in Africa."[10] The resolution was approved by 122 states, while 41 mainly developed countries abstained.

The Committee on Economic, Social and Cultural Rights has pronounced the existence of a "right to health," which "must be understood as a right to the enjoyment of a variety of facilities, goods, services and conditions necessary for the realization of the highest attainable standard of health."[11] In order to honor this right, any government would incur huge responsibili-ties for living conditions. In 2016, the UN Human Rights Council passed a resolution on "Access to medicines in the context of the right of everyone to the enjoyment of the highest attainable standard of physical and mental health," which was based on the principle of "the primacy of human rights over international trade, investment and intellectual property regimes."[12] The resolution stated that it was "the responsibility of states to ensure access for all, without discrimination, to medicines, in particular essential medicines, that are affordable, safe, efficacious and of quality." As one representative to the UN objected, the demand was "untenable by law, and not within the remit of government's responsibility,"[13] certainly not a government whose citizens had opted for limitations on bureaucratic control in favor of individual and civil society responsibility. At the same session of the Human Rights Council, a resolution was passed on "promoting the rights of everyone to the enjoy-ment of the highest attainable standard of physical and mental health through enhancing capacity-building in public health." This resolution was sponsored by Algeria, Brazil, China, Egypt, Iran, Pakistan and South Africa.

The open language in the ICESCR and the "indivisibility" formula suggest an all-encompassing and mutually reinforcing web of entitlements, whereby anything deemed good can be shown to be a human right. The United Nations Population Fund, the UN's "reproductive health and rights agency," declared in 2012 that contraception is a human right. A document with the title "By choice, not by chance: family planning, human rights and development" said that family planning is "universally recognized as an intrinsic right, affirmed and upheld by other rights" such as the right to equality.[14] According to the

RightsInfo blog, the right to contraception is "vital for both gender equality and women's equality, as well also helping to reduce poverty—all ideas which link strongly to our human rights."[15] In the United States, the issue had become particularly divisive when a Georgetown University law student, Sandra Fluke, insisted that the Jesuit institution had to provide contraception in its student health plan under the terms of the Affordable Care Act.[16]

In 2008, proponents of economic and social rights achieved a longtime goal of making such rights "justiciable" when the optional protocol of the ICESCR came into force, establishing an individual complaint mechanism by which the covenant's treaty body can recommend remedies in particular cases through a semijudicial process. Spain became one of the first to ratify the optional protocol, and in 2015 the Committee on Economic, Social and Cultural Rights decided on an individual complaint for the first time. In the case of *I.D.G. v. Spain*, the committee recommended that the Spanish government provide a remedy for a homeowner who, having missed numerous mortgage payments and apparently being unaware of numerous attempts by the lending bank to inform her of their proceedings, was denied access to justice when eventually served with a notice of the auction of her property. Media reports on the case held that the "economic crisis" and high unemployment were factors in the case, which is considered a "vital reminder" of the obligations of governments toward reaching the UN's "Sustainable Development Goals."[17]

Economic and Social Rights Guarantees in Other Treaties. The International Convention on the Elimination of All Forms of Racial Discrimination (CERD) is essentially a treaty protecting civil rights, but it also requires states parties to intervene positively in a wide range of social institutions in order to end racial prejudice. Article 7 directs that

> States Parties undertake to adopt immediate and effective measures, particularly in the fields of teaching, education, culture and information, with a view to combating prejudices which lead to racial discrimination and to promoting understanding, tolerance and friendship among nations and racial or ethnical groups....

The convention goes much further by permitting its signatories to use "special measures" to achieve its objectives, and ensuring that such measures "shall not be deemed racial discrimination" even if they objectively treat people from different groups unequally.

The Convention on the Elimination of All Forms of Discrimination against Women (CEDAW) is also devoted in part to protecting individual freedom, but it presupposes a state that involves itself with the family and family institutions. It obligates states, in Article 8(c), to "encourage the provision of the necessary supporting social services to enable parents to combine family obligations with work responsibilities and participation in public life, in particular through promoting the establishment and development of a network of child-care facilities." Then it puts governments in the position of orchestrating a cultural revolution, to abolish customary differences in the life patterns of men and women. Article 5 directs that "States Parties shall take all appropriate measures: (a) To modify the social and cultural patterns of conduct of men and women, with a view to achieving the elimination of prejudices and customary and all other practices which are based on the idea of the inferiority or the superiority of either of the sexes or on stereotyped roles for men and women." Article 10 enjoins states to work toward eliminating all stereotypical concepts of male and female roles in society, while Article 12(1) demands that signatories ensure access to family planning.

The Convention on the Rights of the Child, which almost every member of the UN has signed, goes far beyond guaranteeing children's freedom from exploitation and abuse; it confirms a range of welfare rights they are entitled to receive from signatories. While acknowledging (Article 27) that parents or guardians "have the primary responsibility to secure, within their abilities and financial capacities, the conditions of living necessary for the child's development," the treaty directs that "States Parties, in accordance with national conditions and within their means, shall take appropriate measures to assist parents and others responsible for the child to implement this right and shall in case of need provide material assistance and support programmes, particularly with regard to nutrition, clothing and housing." The treaty also mandates (Article 28) that states parties "recognize the right of the child to education" and "take appropriate measures such as the introduction of free education and offering financial assistance in case of need." It specifies that different forms of secondary education (general and vocational) should be offered.

The Convention on the Rights of the Child has aroused intense criticism in some sectors for potentially handing over parental responsibilities and discretion to state authorities. A child's freedom to "receive and impart information and ideas of all kinds" and in "any...media of the child's choice" is guaranteed in Article 13(1). States parties are to ensure (Article 17) that "the child has access to information and material from a diversity of national and international sources." Article 16(1) states that "no child shall be subjected to arbitrary or unlawful interference with his or her privacy," suggesting that parents have no right to search a child's room, or be informed if a child is arrested or has an abortion. Article 19(1) prohibits corporal punishment. The convention clearly puts the state in the role of making decisions about the moral education of children. What is more, it necessitates a powerful and intrusive state apparatus with the capacity to know and act upon information about intimate family matters. It therefore has serious *political* implications.

The Convention on the Rights of Persons with Disabilities prohibits discrimination against the handicapped, but it also commits its signatories to a wide range of positive actions that "open the door for extended government reach into many aspects of life and business," as critics observed.[18] Article 4(2) of the convention mandates that every state party "take measures to the maximum of its available resources and, where needed, within the framework of international cooperation, with a view to achieving progressively the full realization" of economic, social and cultural rights for persons with disabilities.

The treaty can impose vast policy changes on its signatories. In October 2015, for example, the UN Committee on the Rights of Persons with Disabilities issued concluding observations on the European Union's compliance with the legal obligations it incurred by signing and ratifying the convention. The committee recommended that the EU conduct a "comprehensive review of its legislation in order to ensure full harmonization with the treaty's provisions, and actively involve representative organizations of persons with disabilities and independent human rights institutions in the process."[19] The committee also linked the protection of the rights of disabled people with other social objectives, including gender equality, recommending that the EU "mainstream a women and girls with disabilities perspective in its forthcoming gender equality strategy, policies and programmes, and a gender perspective in its disability strategies." The committee recommended that the EU "develop affirmative actions to advance the rights of women and girls with disabilities, establish a mechanism to monitor progress and fund data collection and research on women and girls with disabilities."[20] In essence, this meant discriminating against handicapped men and boys.

In response to the UN committee's report, the European Parliament's Committee on Employment and Social Affairs presented a resolution demanding that the European Commission implement these recommendations.[21]

I fully endorse protection of the civil and political rights of the disabled, and common standards for government services, but the UN Convention on the Rights of Persons with Disabilities leaves too much room for utopian interpretations. It is impossible to implement, and because it intrudes far into political and economic issues, its antidiscrimination elements can too easily be dismissed along with its wide-ranging demands on positive law. Even the antidiscrimination prohibitions are far too broad, extending into the private sphere. As Richard Rahn of the CATO Institute has pointed out,

> Article 4(1)(e) demands that "every person, organization, or private enter-prise" must eliminate discrimination on the basis of disability. Taken literally, which some lawyers are sure to do, every homeowner might be required to install wheelchair ramps or even elevators in their homes, regardless of the cost. This also means that the legal standard for the number of handicapped spaces required for parking at your local stores or houses of worship would be established by the U.N.[22]

The excesses of the convention will, I fear, work against its worthy goals. They will turn the protection of people with disabilities into a political issue, so that the unique problems of the disabled are likely to be exploited in the service of efforts to transform the political and economic fundamentals of society.

Economic and Social Rights in Regional Human Rights Treaties

The American Convention on Human Rights came into force in 1978. As noted earlier, while it contained twenty-three articles protecting civil and political rights, it also reflected the growing body of then-soft international law establishing positive state obligations to ensure the "conditions" for everyone to enjoy "freedom from fear and want," with their "economic, social, and cultural rights." Chapter III calls upon states parties to

> adopt measures, both internally and through international cooperation, especially those of an economic and technical nature, with a view to

achieving progressively, by legislation or other appropriate means, the full realization of the rights implicit in the economic, social, educational, scientific, and cultural standards set forth in the Charter of the Organization of American States....

With the Protocol of San Salvador in 1988, the Organization of American States (OAS) went whole hog for economic and social rights, saying in its preamble that "fundamental economic, social and cultural rights have been recognized in earlier international instruments of both world and regional scope."

Finally, a Social Charter of the Americas came into force in 2012, owing its existence and content to the late socialist Venezuelan dictator Hugo Chavez. The document affirms that "social justice and equity are essential for democracy." It moves regional human rights legislation far toward mandating positive state actions to deal with the "underlying causes" of "poverty, social exclusion, and inequity," and to "create favorable conditions for achieving development with social justice" (Article 3). According to Joel Hirst, a Latin American affairs analyst, the Social Charter "is being pushed not as the extension of the civil and political rights already protected under the OAS. It is instead being advanced as the replacement of or alternative to civil and political liberties: the services delivered by caudillo governments in exchange for the total loyalty of their subjects."[23]

Contemporaneous with the passage of the ambitious Social Charter, leading elected members of the OAS, including President Evo Morales of Bolivia, took steps to limit the independence of the Inter-American Commission on Human Rights, or even abolish the body.[24] The commission has been critical of Venezuela's human rights abuses, and has faced a crippling financial shortfall.

The European Charter of Fundamental Rights waters down the protection of authentic human rights with a large admixture of social and economic entitlements, some of which are trivial. Containing fifty substantive articles, the charter combines and equates fundamental political and civil rights with "solidarity rights" (Chapter IV), including the "right to protection against unjustified dismissal" (Article 30); the "right to social and housing assistance" (34); the "right of access to preventative health care and the right to benefit from medical treatment" (35); the right to a "high level of environmental protection" (37) and "consumer protection" (38); and the right to "good administration" (41).

The charter is emblematic of the historicist and politically expedient approach to defining human rights. The EU's website explains (with bolding):

> The rights of every individual within the EU were established at different times, in different ways and in different forms. For this reason, the EU decided to clarify things and to include them all in **a single document which has been updated in the light of changes in society**, social progress and scientific and technological developments.... The Charter is a very modern codification and includes "third generation" fundamental rights, such as: data protection; guarantees on bioethics; and transparent administration.[25]

This elastic approach suggests that the charter will be amended to include new human rights on an ongoing basis.

The charter incorporates a possibly wider array of rights and freedoms than any other human rights treaty, including "the right of access to a free placement service." As one legal analysis remarks, this provision may be "worthwhile," but it is hardly "on the same level as the prohibition against slavery."[26] It is tempting to make light of such a mandate, but it is a serious degradation of human rights, and worthy of outrage. The dogma of the indivisibility and equality of human rights would suggest that there is no moral difference between a "right to free placement services" and the right to be free from torture, or the right to freedom of speech. Those real human rights are trivialized by their association with bogus human rights.

I raised this problem in a question to Navi Pillay, who was then the UN high commissioner for human rights, and to the EU special representative for human rights at a meeting of activists in Brussels in 2012. I also reminded Ms. Pillay that her own office's report found that the UN human rights treaty body system had doubled in size since 2004, with overlapping reporting requirements and low state compliance.[27] A chill seemed to come over the room. Pillay responded dismissively that she believed in respecting "all human rights."

Human Rights Council Mandates That Have Little to Do with Human Rights

The human rights monitoring system of the UN has developed in a way that confuses the protection of authentic human rights with partisan political and economic agendas, and diverts attention from violations of individual freedom.

Beginning in 1967, the UN Human Rights Commission established "mandates" to focus on states that were seriously abusing human rights; the first such mandate was the Ad Hoc Working Group on South Africa. A special rapporteur would be appointed to monitor the situation and provide reports to the commission, and these reports were often of great value to independent civil society monitoring groups. By taking such an action, the Human Rights Commission reached out directly to try to protect individuals within a state, generally against the wishes of their government, demonstrating that the government in question would not protect the human rights of its own people. A "country mandate" was thus an international humiliation that delegitimized a regime in the eyes of the world and of the country's own citizens, which had potential for leading to political change. It is fair to say that a large part of the resistance to the imposition of country mandates, while generally couched in general principles like noninterference, neutrality, and respect for sovereignty, actually arose from fear of losing legitimacy and being overthrown.

The Human Right Commission also established "thematic" mandates to monitor specific human rights problems that occur in numerous states, and the political impact of thematic mandates is not as straightforward. Thematic mandates concerning civil and political rights focus on problems common to countries of all regions, with diverse political systems. The work of the special rapporteurs of these mandates carries with it some of the same political hazards to states as country mandates: states can be embarrassed, isolated and politically destabilized by their reports and consequent condemnation. But particular states are not the focus of such mandates, and states can and do refuse to grant visas to special rapporteurs and then ignore their reports, which can be denounced as "biased" for relying on secondary sources.

Since the "indivisibility" principle was established as dogma, a large proportion of new mandates from the Human Rights Commission and Council have dealt with economic and social rights, "third-generation" rights, or political issues having little to do with human rights at all.

At present, the Human Rights Council has established forty-one thematic "special procedures." In addition to the mandates noted above, they monitor such diverse matters as "the right to safe drinking water," "human rights obligations related to the environmentally sound management and disposal of hazardous substances and waste," "the right of everyone to the highest attainable standards of physical and mental health," the right to "adequate housing," "human rights and international solidarity," and "the effect of foreign debt on human rights, particularly economic, cultural and social rights." All of these involve serious social and political challenges, and areas of suffering and deprivation that democratic processes need to address. Some of them will also require international cooperation among UN member states. Making these problems into human rights issues leads logically to the political conclusion that states, rather than civil society, can and should solve them through the power of courts.

The proposals of the UN special procedures examining these issues typically recommend strong state intervention, even though interventionist states have tended to be the violators of human rights properly understood. The new UN human rights proposals will lead to more powerful states and international bureaucracies with more coercive powers over the individual. Meanwhile, UN special rapporteurs on human rights such as freedom from torture, freedom of expression and freedom from discrimination toil away with diminishing efficacy, as the Human Rights Council creates more and more mandates to monitor more and more "new human rights."[28]

In the framework of the Freedom Rights Project, Jacob Mchangama and Aoife Claire Holly Hegarty examined the established mandates in 2012, and found that about half concerned either economic and social rights, or hybrid combinations of those with civil and political rights, or with "third-generation" rights. The increase in mandates of these types has been a relatively recent phenomenon, with most having been established since 2000. Compared with both country-specific and thematic mandates pertaining to civil and political rights, these mechanisms have been much less confrontational as regards the sensitivities of particular states. They have rarely resulted in harsh opprobrium, either in the form of censure by the community of nations, or in disgrace that may have internal political consequences.

The Freedom Rights Project also analyzed political support for the creation of all human rights mandates established by the Human Rights Commission and the Human Rights Council in relation to the political systems of members of these bodies. An analysis of voting records in the Human Rights Commission and Council found that while free, democratic states favored establishing country-specific mandates, there is a clear pattern of opposition to such mandates by unfree states.

For example, the mandate on the "Effects of Foreign Debt and Other Related International Financial Obligations on the Full Enjoyment of Human Rights," introduced by Cuba, was opposed by twelve free states and passed with the support of fifteen partly free and ten unfree countries. Speaking on behalf of European Union members of the council, the representative of Slovenia said the issue "goes beyond the competence of the Council." But the representative of Sri Lanka said it reflected a will to look at human rights in a "holistic manner" that would seek to understand the "roots" of human rights violations—suggesting that states violated human rights because of their debt burden, and, it may be inferred, that if creditors would forgive debts, the violations would end. The Sri Lankan representative said the resolution had the virtue of "bridging" the divide between civil and political rights and economic and social rights. When the mandate came up for renewal in 2011, the representative of the United States said, "It is incorrect to treat the issue…as a human rights problem" and that doing so "diverts the focus and finances of this Council away from serious human rights issues." Support dropped in 2011, but the measure was still renewed.

In another debate, the European Union raised serious misgivings about the "Cultural Rights" mandate. The representative of Germany, speaking on behalf of the EU members on the council, said there was "no compelling evidence on the need to add a new thematic mandate," noting that respect for cultural rights depended on honoring civil and political rights. The German diplomat warned that the proposal suggested "invoking cultural diversity to infringe on human rights." Thirteen free states opposed the mandate on "Adverse Effects of the Illicit Movement and Dumping of Toxic and Dangerous Products and Wastes on the Enjoyment of Human Rights," some expressing anxieties that it lacked a clear focus on human rights. But political and ideological pressure to support mandates on economic and social rights has been intense. In 2000, the United States was the only member of the Human Rights Commission to vote against establishing a special rapporteur on the "right to food."

The mandate on "Promotion of a Democratic and Equitable International Order," sponsored by Cuba, was opposed by eleven free countries and passed with the support of thirteen partly free and ten unfree states; it was one of the most polarizing special mechanisms yet proposed. Poland, on behalf of EU members of the council, sought to introduce an amendment that would give the measure more focus on promoting democracy at the state level; the Polish representative stated that in proposing the amendment, it was "trying to find some minimal addition that would at least give [the mandate] the potential to make a meaningful contribution to human rights." Cuba retorted that supporters of the amendment were trying "to impose an Anglo-Saxon order on humanity: and to annihilate [a] desire for a better, fairer, more democratic world." The individual appointed as special rapporteur of this mandate was a known ideologue. Alfred de Zayas, a lawyer and expert on international law, is renowned for his defenses of the human rights records of authoritarian and dictatorial countries, and for his harsh accusations against the United States and against Israel. He has a record of scholarly revisionism concerning World War II, claiming that the Allied powers were guilty of "a form of genocide," as well as a record of anti-Jewish statements.[29]

Philip Alston, a human rights expert, notes that China has been leading a "concerted push" by major developing nations to eliminate country-specific UN human rights resolutions. The result is "a clear trend indicating that it will be very difficult in the years ahead to obtain targeted resolutions in relation to all but the most egregious cases."[30] A move away from the tactic of "naming and shaming" was one of the "reforms" thought to mark the transition from the Human Rights Commission to the Human Rights Council in 2006, along with the creation of the Universal Periodic Review.[31] Country-specific mandates are a quintessential example of naming and shaming, and a strategy that many civil society activists regard as essential to holding a state accountable for its legal commitments and answerable to its citizens. Such mandates are also dangerous to undemocratic governments that are vulnerable to political unrest when human rights criticisms emerge out of international institutions. Self-reflective democratic states may reject criticisms with the claim that they are politically motivated or based on a lack of understanding of internal mechanisms that allow their citizens to change policies and obtain remedies for abuses, but such states have rarely rejected "naming and shaming" per se.

The UN resolution that established the Human Rights Council (60/251), however, signaled a different direction by stressing "impartiality," "non-selectivity," and "constructive international dialogue and cooperation."[32] These words are often code for a policy of appeasing human rights abusers. A number of country mandates were taken off the roster with the transition from commission to council. "Only *three states remained on the 'black list' of states* criticized for their gross and systematic human rights violations and subjected to review by country-specific Special Rapporteurs inherited from the former Commission," specifically, "Israel/Palestine, North Korea and Burma/Myanmar."[33] While several new country mandates have been established by the council, it is clear that a number of states that censor criticisms by their own citizens want also to silence criticism from other members of

the international community. Flooding the human rights system with mechanisms that have little if anything to do with human rights serves that purpose.

Economic and Social Rights as Ideological Weapons

In washing over into the realm of positive law and regulation, human rights
law has opened itself up to manipulation in the service of political agendas
and ideologies. Indeed, human rights discourse is rife with the form of
politicization that promotes leftist statism. Only a particular kind of political
system can implement the ambitious economic and social rights set forth in
the international human rights system, a fact not lost on political activists.
In their article "Economic Reform Is a Human Right" in *The Nation*, Radhika
Balakrishnan and James Heintz asserted that "the full realization of economic
and social rights requires a strong state, international cooperation and robust
social institutions."[34] It follows that those seeking a strong redistributionist
state can do so under the cover of promoting human (economic and social)
rights.

Under human rights treaties, Balakrishnan has noted, "humans have rights
and governments have duties, among those the duty to use the 'maximum
available resources' to realize the basic human rights of its people."[35] This view
brings political debates over the allocation of scare resources into the framework of international human rights law mandating that all available financial
resources be directed to a range of different welfare priorities—an intrinsic
contradiction. In recent years, many states have reduced their welfare benefits
under "austerity" budgets to control the debt that threatens national and
international financial systems. Some activists and politicians have expressed
concern that austerity programs in the EU have included "no recommendations on how to guarantee citizens' economic and social rights."[36] The Council
of Europe's Committee on Social Rights ruled that several austerity measures
were directly at odds with the European Social Charter—a treaty that serves
as Europe's regional version of the ICESCR—and thus illegal.

UN human rights authorities often make blatantly ideological pronouncements and recommendations when they enter public discussions on economic
and social questions, and I have never seen political statements of this kind
that did not take a leftward direction. My research indicates that such pronouncements virtually always make collectivistic, socialistic points on the

basis of economic and social rights. The efforts of governments to deal with recent financial crises prompted numerous illustrations of this pattern. For example,

> Addressing the United Nations General Assembly in New York on 23 October 2012, the Chairperson of the Committee on Economic, Social and Cultural Rights, Ariranga Govindasamy Pillay, noted that although States face tough decisions when dealing with rising public deficits, austerity measures are potentially violations of the legal obligations of States Parties to the International Covenant on Economic, Social and Cultural Rights.... By ratifying the Covenant, States Parties have a legally binding obligation to progressively improve, without retrogression, universal access to goods and services such as healthcare, education, housing and social security and to ensure just and favourable conditions of work, without discrimination, in accordance with established international standards.[37]

The UN official further clarified that these rights must be achieved "by using the maximum of available resources," and shared his economic wisdom by asserting that "austerity measures are also a disincentive to economic growth."

Around the same time, the UN special rapporteur on extreme poverty and human rights, Magdalena Sepúlveda, asserted that states are obligated to employ "the maximum of their available resources to ensure the respect, protection and fulfillment of rights," and to ensure that "adequate resources are raised and used for the realization of the human rights of persons living in poverty." For this reason, "States must protect budgetary resources from being compromised by future bailouts and commit to creating a regulatory framework that ensures such resources are not directed to failing financial firms." The UN independent expert on foreign debt and human rights, Cephas Lumina, likewise called for more "effective regulatory measures" to restrain "the excesses of the financial sector." Mr. Lumina said that "while it is widely accepted that the current Eurozone sovereign debt crisis is largely a consequence of huge banking system bailouts, other financial sector actors, such as credit rating agencies, financial speculators and hedge funds, have played a central role in fuelling the crisis." The independent expert on the promotion of a democratic and equitable international order, Alfred de Zayas, was critical of austerity measures that cut into social programs, saying, "There are perfectly viable alternative solutions to the financial crisis, such as reducing the so-called 'defense' budget and significantly reducing all military expenditures."[38]

In March 2016, Juan Pablo Bohoslavsky, then the UN independent expert on foreign debt and human rights, presented a report to the Human Rights Council in which he asserted that "international human rights law has something to say about economic inequality." According to the Office of the High Commissioner for Human Rights, Bohoslavsky's report is clear on the point that "States have the obligation to prevent inequality undermining the enjoyment of human rights." The report said:

> While human rights law does not necessarily imply a perfectly equal distribution of income and wealth, it does require conditions in which rights can be fully exercised. As a consequence, a certain level of redistribution is expected in order to guarantee individuals an equal enjoyment of the realization of their basic rights.

Bohoslavsky recommended that states, in their responses to financial crises or their efforts to prevent them, should take measures to address inequality, including regulation of financial markets, minimum wages, progressive taxation and social protection floors.[39]

The United Kingdom's economic policies came under harsh criticism by the UN Committee on Economic, Social and Cultural Rights following the committee's review of the UK's compliance with the treaty in June 2016. The committee said that the minimum wage was too low, and that "the increase in the threshold for the payment of inheritance tax and the increase of the value added tax, as well as the gradual reduction of the tax on corporate incomes," resulted in "persistent social inequality."[40] *Mother Jones* magazine noted with evident satisfaction that after a "human rights alliance" called the Just Fair consortium had testified, the committee "issued an unequivocal assessment, condemning austerity policies for their impact on homelessness, unemployment, health care access, and discrimination against women and minorities, among other things."[41] The motto of Just Fair is "Justice and fairness through human rights." Jamie Burton, who leads the group, wrote that austerity programs had contributed to disillusionment and mistrust of "experts," which in turn increased support for leaving the European Union in the "Brexit" referendum of June 2016. Echoing a common ideological reflex of the left, Burton wondered how so many people could have voted against "their own interests."[42] Another NGO, the Govan Law Centre, wrote that the governments of the UK and of Scotland "must always be raising living standards and not violating the human right to an adequate standard of living."[43] The Labour Party shadow minister for work and pensions opined, "It should concern us all that the UN is having to publish a report saying that Government policies are contravening the public's human rights."[44]

Economic and social rights are regularly called forth as weapons in ideological disputes. For example, Honduran human rights organizations and social movements found that the "right-wing" government's "neoliberal" policies violated the economic, cultural, and social rights of indigenous peoples, women, and *campesinos*.[45]

The country visit to Canada in 2012 by Olivier De Schutter, the UN special rapporteur on the right to food,[46] became a partisan political football. It was the first visit to a developed country by the special rapporteur, and some objected that numerous other states deserved attention more. Others lauded the visit, noting, inter alia, that a high percentage of people in Canada's remote northern communities lacked adequate access to nutritious food. There had reportedly been a rise in reliance on food banks, with 850,000 citizens using them each month. Another fact invoked to justify the attention of the UN human rights official was the shocking revelation that high-quality food, including fresh produce, is more expensive than less nutritious packaged and fast food, and especially hard to get in the far north. Would he complain about difficult access to ice cream in an equatorial African country?

De Schutter's visit was ruthlessly exploited by critics of the Conservative government, whose policies they blamed for a "hunger crisis in Canada." Bob Rae, the leader of the Liberal Party, used the visit to bludgeon the government of Stephen Harper, stating that the unprecedented investigation of a developed country by the special rapporteur on the right to food was "nothing short of a failure for the Harper Conservatives."[47] He criticized the government for cutting funds for the national child-care program and for health programs for Canada's aboriginal population, and for the lack of a "national poverty strategy," all of which Rae claimed had led to an erosion of "food security" in Canada. The event prompted numerous calls for a "national food policy" that would ensure respect for the "right to food." These proposals invariably see the answer in more central planning and government-controlled redistribution.

De Schutter, a Belgian law professor, has demonstrated a strong affinity for leftist human rights inflation. In a *Guardian* article, for example, he claimed that "we can overcome the problems of delivering collective action on climate change by treating mining, deforestation, ocean degradation and more as violations of human rights."[48] In a 2010 report to the UN General Assembly, De Schutter stressed "land redistribution" as essential "for the realization of the right to food," and called the free-market system a threat to the livelihoods of "peasants, fishers, pastoralists, and indigenous peoples."[49] By making such claims, and by advocating for a particular kind of government policy to address hunger, he was violating a central moral obligation of international human rights advocacy, which is to be scrupulously nonpartisan and politically neutral.

His position clearly played to one side of a partisan ideological controversy in Canada, and apparently by design. One can only imagine the reactions of Canada's left wing had De Schutter come with ideas like reducing taxes and regulation to stimulate economic growth as a strategy for improving access to food through higher production and greater general wealth. Presumably, conservative politicians would not have been able to resist using such recommendations for their own political advantage, which would be just as wrong as the exploitation of human rights by left-wing ideologues. Indeed, any conceivable recommendation for reducing poverty and hunger in Canada would be essentially a political recommendation, to be considered and decided in a democratic process by the citizens and their representatives.

A more recent country visit by a UN official monitoring economic and social rights also assumed a blatantly partisan form. Philip Alston, serving as special rapporteur on poverty and human rights, inspected the issue in the United States for two weeks in late 2017. He attacked President Donald Trump for supposedly turning the country into the "world champion of extreme inequality," and sharply criticized a particular tax bill under consideration. During his visit, Alston met with Senator Bernie Sanders, a self-declared socialist, who used the occasion to amplify his own criticism of government policies.[50]

In May 2012, United Nations human-rights officials issued a call for a global financial-transaction tax "to offset the costs of the enduring economic, financial, fuel, climate and food crises, and to protect basic human rights." The statement is among the most blatant examples of how far the international human rights community has strayed from human rights principles, blundering into complex and highly partisan political debates on economics.

De Schutter, not surprisingly, took part in the call for a global tax on financial transactions. Referring to widespread job losses, to "socialized private debt burdens," and to a risk of "significant human rights regressions through wide-ranging austerity packages," he described such a tax as "a pragmatic tool for providing the means for governments to protect and fulfill the human rights of their people." Magdalena Sepúlveda, the UN special rapporteur on poverty and human rights, expressed confidence that the revenue stream from a financial-transaction tax "would fill government deficit holes," but stressed that the funds "should be channeled to fighting poverty, reversing growing inequality and compensating those whose lives have been devastated by the enduring global economic crisis."[51]

Some UN treaty bodies have insisted that authentic constitutional rights be interpreted so as to ensure entitlements via positive state legislation. When the UN Committee on Economic, Social and Cultural Rights examined Canada in February 2016, it expressed concern about such issues as the government's level of social spending and the degree to which local governments allegedly neglected to provide various social benefits as per the ICESCR. Committee members invoked Canada's Charter of Rights and Freedoms, which is a guarantee of basic political rights, and insisted that Section 7, which guarantees the "right to life, liberty and security of the person,"[52] be interpreted as ensuring economic and social rights. According to Amnesty International, a member of the committee told Canadian representatives, "It's time for Canada to take a step forward and set out a more ambitious, braver interpretation of the Charter to enable it to fully protect all ESC rights as enshrined in the covenant."[53] Canadian antipoverty NGOs used the committee's pronouncements to assail the government. Harriett McLachlan, president of Canada Without Poverty, intoned,

> It would seem that the government views ESC rights as second class rights, they are not to be held in the same regard as civil and political rights. As a result, people who are living in poverty—who are hungry, have no secure place to live or even clean drinking water—have no means to claim these rights. This is a failure on Canada's part.[54]

Meanwhile, human rights courts have subverted authentic human rights protections by turning them into a justification for expanded state benefits. For example, the European Convention on Human Rights was established to protect fundamental human rights and freedoms, and does not mandate government interventions to solve social problems. But the jurisprudence of the European Court of Human Rights is replete with examples of interpreting the convention in a way that expands government intervention in society. In the 1970s, the document came to be seen as a "living instrument" to be adapted to meet an increasing demand for government services. For example, the court held in *McDonald v. The United Kingdom* (2014) that a British woman's right to private life had been violated when the state did not provide her with assistance in using a chamber pot at night. Local authorities had decided that incontinence pads were sufficient, but the woman argued that this alternative was "a grave infringement on her right to dignity and her right to private life under Article 8" of the convention.[55] The decision represents an intellectually dishonest twisting of negative liberties into positive state obligations. One observer remarked (approvingly) that if unsatisfactory care packages are treated as "a potential breach of the negative obligation not to interfere with the applicant's right to respect for her private life," it follows that "there will no longer be a need for applicants to establish that the State had a positive obligation to provide the applicant with the necessary assistance."[56]

Judicial activism of this kind has seriously undermined the legitimacy of the European Court. Jacob Mchangama has pointed to other rulings that disguise social policy choices as human rights issues. For instance, the court has decided that the right to "peaceful enjoyment of possessions" includes a right to welfare benefits.[57] Andras Sajó, a judge at the court, has warned of the danger of "constitutionalizing welfare rights," which should only be done by state legislators.[58]

Human rights have become the positive laws of a global order of states, rather than principles restraining those states, and are invoked as a means for achieving broad, generally leftist global governance goals. In a speech before a "high-level thematic debate" in the UN General Assembly on July 12, 2016, Secretary General Ban Ki-moon imparted a vision of human rights as inseparable from a political program of global regulation and wealth redistribution. He repeatedly confused human rights with positive legislation to achieve the political goals of societies and the international community, and he even spoke of human rights as *subordinate* to those goals, as means to other ends. According to an official UN report, Ban claimed that human rights, rather than being "abstract ideas," must be a "main tool" for "meeting development targets." He said, "In our deeply connected world, all Member States have a shared best interest in promoting individual and collective human rights as a basis for global peace and prosperity."[59] Ban's main theme was clearly not violations of fundamental human rights and freedoms by tyrannical states, but rather human rights as "the most powerful driver of peace and development," essential to achieving the UN's seventeen "Sustainable Development Goals."

"New Human Rights"

Nothing shows the intellectual corruption of human rights more clearly than the proliferation of "new human rights," which invariably give more power to states. Their proponents dubiously claim that such rights improve the "conditions" for enjoying freedoms, though in fact they hem in the freedom of the individual within a thicker layer of global and national regulation. The imagination of utopian social scientists, jurists and activists has been set alight with visions of new human rights that will make the world more just and protect members of threatened groups.

The European Court of Human Rights has played fast and loose in declaring "new human rights." It has asserted a human right to be protected from noise pollution, again on the basis of Article 8 of the European Convention on Human Rights, concerning respect for private life. Responding to a complaint originating in Hungary, "the Court considered that there rested a positive obligation on the Hungarian authorities to adopt measures to secure respect for the applicant's right to respect for his private life and home."[60]

UN resolutions proclaim new human rights, which then enter official discourse and gain legitimacy. When the General Assembly proclaimed a "human right to clean drinking water and sanitation," American officials objected, stating the view that no such right existed under international human rights law. A review of the relevant legal instruments, they said, "demonstrates that there is no internationally agreed 'right to water.' Neither the Universal Declaration of Human Rights (UDHR) nor the International Covenant on Economic, Social, and Cultural Rights (ICESCR) mentions water at all."[61] The "right to water" as declared by the United Nations has led to the banning of independent (nongovernmental) sources of water; courts blocked the privatization of water sources in Greece as part of a bailout program.[62] Giving states a monopoly on water supplies actually restricts and threatens access to water.

In 2012, the UN Human Rights Council began a process to establish a "right to peace."[63] The United States was the only country voting against the motion, while European countries abstained. The motion passed with the support of such states as China, Cuba, Libya, the Russian Federation and Saudi Arabia, states for whom "peace" meant acceptance of the powers that be, by their own citizens and by other states.

In 2014, the independent expert on "Human Rights and International Solidarity," a mandate created in 2005, presented a draft UN resolution to the Human Rights Council to establish a new human right. "The right to international solidarity is a fundamental human right enjoyed by everyone on the basis of equality and nondiscrimination," the independent expert said.[64] The main thrust of the draft resolution is the obligation of wealthy states to provide financial assistance to poorer countries in order to help them honor economic and social rights. Such assistance has always been a key component of the "right to development."

Treaty bodies interpret vague wording in UN human rights covenants expansively in order to create new human rights. All treaty bodies of international human rights covenants issue statements ("concluding declarations") after reviewing compliance by individual states parties to treaties, and they also offer "general comments" clarifying questions of interpretation. Where there are individual complaint mechanisms, they act as quasi-judicial bodies, making recommendations that have no coercive power. Yet these comments and recommendations have become important sources of "soft law." Treaty bodies have been targeted by activists and lobbyists seeking to "locate their cause under the banner of human rights," through a broad interpretation of treaty terms.

One illustrative case is the effort by abortion rights activists, funded by UN agencies, to establish that international human rights laws affirmed a human right to abortion. Two critics of the way treaty bodies routinely ignore their legal mandates described how the activists went about doing this:

> With immense financial resources, lobbyists conceived and ran a conference in Glen Cove, New York, to "dialogue" with representatives of six major human rights treaty bodies, seeking to expand the activity of these treaty bodies in the field of women's health—specifically reproductive and sexual health. Not only was this meeting avowedly the "first occasion on which members of the [then six] human rights treaty bodies met to focus

on…a specific thematic issue," but the theme they discussed was unrelated to the mandates of any of the treaties in question.

This kind of lobbying is comparable to the phenomenon of "regulatory capture," in which regulators fall under the sway of interested parties, and it is "to be expected in the current human rights treaty body system."[65]

In 1999, three years after the Glen Cove meeting, the CEDAW Committee ruled that Article 12 of CEDAW, in effect, established a right to abortion. The argument was that banning any medical service needed only by women was a form of discrimination, in contravention of the treaty.[66] Here is the actual text of Article 12:

1. States Parties shall take all appropriate measures to eliminate discrimination against women in the field of health care in order to ensure, on a basis of equality of men and women, access to health care services, including those related to family planning.
2. Notwithstanding the provisions of paragraph I of this article, States Parties shall ensure to women appropriate services in connection with pregnancy, confinement and the post-natal period, granting free services where necessary, as well as adequate nutrition during pregnancy and lactation.

The committee interpreted this language creatively to conclude that a right to abortion is essential to the "equality of men and women" in access to health care.

It appears that "sexual rights" may be emerging as a human rights growth area, based on language in CEDAW and on international conferences of women's rights groups and population control organizations. A publication of the International Sexuality and HIV Curriculum Working Group speaks of a wide range of sexual rights, including a human right to sexual expression and to seek sexual pleasure, as falling within the framework of international human rights.[67]

The international community appears to have little concern about the ideologically motivated distortion of consensual treaty language, about the dilution of attention to existing human rights, about the duplication of human rights, about the proliferation of the human rights bureaucracy, or about the marginalization of classical freedom rights in the face of expanding economic

and social rights, as academics, UN officials, human rights activists and interest groups identify "gaps" in legislation and then campaign for new treaties.
Decades ago, the legal scholar Moses Moskowitz foresaw that the idea of the
"interdependence" of various kinds of rights would cause human rights to
"lose in depth what they gained in range."[68] Indeed, the idea of human rights
has been rolled out into a thin, weak cliché.

The Cynical Process of Creating New Human Rights

Creating new human rights is a tactic of interest groups that seek to gain the
backing of international human rights law for specific entitlements. It is a
goal of international officials who want expanded human rights structures,
a goal often supported by human rights lawyers who see good in more
international legal rights. Civil society has been a primary driver of the
process, which is described in detail, and in positive terms, by contributors
to *The International Struggle for New Human Rights*, edited by Clifford Rob.[69]
The book provides candid accounts of how the human rights movement
has set aside principles and "adopted" new economic and social rights for
"strategic" (and political) reasons, mainly in order to broaden constituencies
and funding bases, and pander to groups insisting that their grievances are
human rights violations.

A progressive realpolitik holds that human rights are a tool for achieving
political objectives, based on a "realistic appraisal of rights claims and rights
law as politics." Human rights reflect interests and cannot be detached from
interests. Defining human needs, grievances and problems as human rights
issues is presented forthrightly as a matter of strategy: "Reframing these issues
as rights violations is a strategic choice aimed at exerting greater pressure to
solve them."[70] It is essential that "gatekeepers," i.e. influential NGOs, take up
grievances as human rights issues in order for an international consensus to
establish this as a reality. Gatekeepers "may embrace new causes" as a way
to "appease crucial constituencies, maintain funding, and 'stay relevant.'"[71]

Until the mid-1990s, major human rights organizations adhered mainly
to an agenda of defending civil and political rights. Since then, both Amnesty
International and Human Rights Watch have expanded their agendas. A fore-
runner of this trend was the International Commission of Jurists, which in
1986 published the Limburg Principles clarifying and elaborating economic

and social rights. One reason for the shift of emphasis was the ending of the Cold War, which removed the ideological stigma from support for ESCR. The Cold War had left little "cultural and political space" for NGOs to campaign for those rights. According to *The International Struggle for New Human Rights*, the United States "led an almost single-handed campaign to assign a secondary status to economic and social rights," and it was U.S. pressure that resulted in the promulgation of two separate covenants rather than a unified one. The winding down of the Cold War opened up room to elevate ESCR because it "de-linked the struggle for human rights from the geopolitical conflict between East and West." Economic and social rights could then be reframed "as being consistent with a liberal state rather than requiring a form of totalitarian socialism for their implementation."[72]

Ideological opposition to "neoliberalism" is also cited as a major reason for the embrace of ESCR, in the belief that neoliberal policies "created significant new threats to subsistence in many regions." Human rights were made into "one of several main organizing frames for mobilizations against 'neoliberal globalization'" and against what many regarded as "an unjust global economic system."[73]

Resistance to new human rights is seen as a self-interested reaction by those who benefit from classical liberty rights—as if universal individual rights protected only a particular interest group, whose members do not want others to enjoy their own human rights. Warnings about rights inflation are viewed as a way to "rationalize" the rejection of new rights claims, and are thought to pose little more than technical obstacles. "Shifting political currents in larger societies move gatekeepers," it is said. Aggrieved groups "are unlikely to be deterred by abstract assertions that they should forgo *their* rights in the interests of the human rights 'core.'"[74] Worries about rights proliferation are "overblown," it is asserted. "Human rights are political, and their precise scope will always remain disputed." Rights are to be seen as "tools of political conflict."[75] Therefore the defense of economic and social rights "requires taking a more political (and thus less moral) stance."[76]

In this analysis, the expansion of Amnesty International and Human Rights Watch into the arena of economic and social rights is openly portrayed as opportunistic—as a way to attract new, younger, more geographically diverse members, and to secure more funders. "When the antiglobalization movement ignited in the late 1990s in the global south, the message was reinforced that the legitimacy of human rights organizations depended in part on advocating for economic and social rights."[77] At the same time, the "development community" has cleaved to human rights language, using a "rights-based" approach to endow demands for transnational assistance and concessions from private enterprise with the leverage and the prestige of international law.

New Human Rights in the UN Pipeline

In this politicized atmosphere, several new human rights treaties are under active consideration in the UN system.

The Human Rights of the Elderly. United Nations human rights officials, lawyers' groups including the American Bar Association (ABA), nongovernmental organizations and influential governments are promoting a "UN Convention on the Rights of Older Persons." The proposal has been spearheaded by Argentina, Chile and other Latin American and African countries.

The proposed treaty would institutionalize services to the elderly not as government policies but as rights protected by international law. According to its proponents, the rights of older persons are "invisible under international law" because those rights are not "recognized explicitly." They say that universal human rights protections afforded by the main UN conventions on civil and political rights and on economic and social rights have not worked to protect the aging from discrimination, exploitation and deprivation. At a strategy meeting to promote advocacy for a convention, sponsored by the ABA, a top Argentine diplomat said the main rights treaties came into force at a time (in the 1970s) when people only "thought about white males." Universal human rights protected all "in theory," but additional treaties were needed to protect children, women, racial minorities, indigenous peoples, migrants, those with disabilities, and now the aging. A UN human rights official said that the lack of a dedicated human rights protection system for the elderly was an affront to the rule of law. Older persons are victims, and international law is the most effective way to make changes in society; thus the "progressive development of international law" is a worthwhile investment, as "states turn to the U.N. to solve problems more cheaply."[78]

NGO representatives say a new treaty will raise the profile of the issue and force states to assign resources and create institutions to comply with legal obligations, "mainstreaming" the rights of older people and applying a "rights-based" approach to social services. The project of advocacy for a treaty has become a unifying campaign for civil society groups that want a UN treaty dealing with their own area of work. It is also a strategy to generate funding streams and lock them in with binding legal obligations.

The UN General Assembly gave a major boost to the creation of a new treaty by establishing an "open-ended working group" to "identify possible gaps in the existing UN framework by considering the feasibility of further instruments." The working group, open to input from civil society, appears to institutionalize the treaty-making process, making it virtually inevitable. A communication from the working group states: "Existing instruments and mechanisms do not appear to provide sufficient specificity about quality and accessibility of health and long term care for older persons."[79] Addressing the UN Social Forum in 2014, the high commissioner for human rights gave unqualified support for a new treaty, saying, "We have found that articulation of dedicated instruments laying [out] the specific rights of certain groups can be of invaluable assistance in focusing world attention—and action—on key groups at risk." The rights of older persons have been included in the agenda of the Human Rights Council, which has appointed an independent expert to report regularly on the issue.[80]

Some resistance to this initiative has reportedly come from the United States government, the European Union, China and other powerful states, with the argument that the rights of older people are already protected by existing international law. But democratic states fear conflict with "like-minded" allies and political backlash from their large aging populations. And they have no intellectual tools to resist human rights inflation. European human rights officials wanted to oppose the treaty, but did not know how without placing themselves in political jeopardy. A confidential memorandum from the EU's Working Party on Human Rights (COHOM) in July 2013 referred to a growing lobby, especially in Latin America, for a convention on the rights of the elderly, and said:

> The EU and many others are opposed to a new convention, as they say that all rights are already covered in existing treaties and are wary of the creation of a new treaty architecture, reporting, treaty body etc. However, the OHCHR [Office of the High Commissioner for Human Rights] has also come out clearly in favour of a new convention. The EU is still looking at other options... but ultimately the lobby for a new convention might be too strong.[81]

Without guidance from clear principles, there is apparently no way to resist the proliferation of collective human rights treaties.

Human Rights, Transnational Corporations and Other Business Enterprises.[82] Activists and UN officials have declared the human rights impact of transnational and other business enterprises to be a top global priority. The issue has emerged as a human rights problem particularly in the context of consensus in the human rights community that non-state actors can be responsible for human rights violations, one of the contributions of the World Conference in Vienna.

No one can or should deny that severe crimes and deprivations are associated with the activities of some transnational corporations. Many have shameful records of exploitation and environmental degradation, and have clumsily tried to cover them up. Child labor is a scourge that tragically robs children of their childhood, their health and their future. It is a global problem, and one that requires international cooperation to pressure governments to institute economic reforms and impose and enforce sound labor standards. In many cases, national laws protecting children need to be strengthened. Transnational or other corporations that exploit children need to be prosecuted to the full extent of the law, and also punished by consumers.

Unfortunately, some of the states with the world's worst child labor records are promoting the establishment of a new UN business and human rights treaty that is unlikely to have any benefit for victims, but will obscure their own corruption and irresponsibility in a fog of anti-free-enterprise rhetoric. Given the tendency of abusive states to foster meaningless global human rights legislation and institutions, it can be assumed that their support for such a treaty is part of a diversionary strategy.

In June 2011, the UN Human Rights Council adopted Resolution 17/4 to "establish an open-ended intergovernmental working group with the mandate to elaborate an international legally binding instrument on Transnational Corporations and Other Business Enterprises with respect to human rights." The aim of the treaty would be to "clarify the obligations of transnational corporations and other business enterprises with respect to human rights," and to provide remedies in such cases where domestic jurisdiction cannot do so.

The measure was cosponsored by Ecuador, a country where "children, in particular indigenous children and Afro-descendants, are engaged in the worst forms of child labor, including hazardous forms of agriculture and dangerous street work," according to the U.S. Department of Labor.[83] Child labor is prohibited by the Ecuadorian constitution. Apparently it was assumed that a UN treaty with Geneva-based monitors would be more effective in protecting vulnerable children in Ecuador.

Supporters of a new treaty include India and Pakistan, both of which scored "zero" on the Child Labor Index, putting them among the world's worst with regard to "the prevalence, gravity and impunity of child labor under the age of 15... which directly or indirectly limits or damages a child's mental, physical, social or psychological development." Other supporters are Congo and Ethiopia, which rate among the world's twelve worst abusers; China, ranked thirteenth; Indonesia and Vietnam, where children are at "extreme risk"; Russia and Venezuela, judged to be "high risk" countries for children.

Of the twenty members of the Human Rights Council that supported new global "human rights" regulation of transnational businesses, only four respect human rights principles enough to be ranked as free countries by Freedom House, an independent nongovernmental organization. On the other hand, all fourteen of the states opposing the resolution are free, and only one, Romania, has a serious problem with child labor. Other problems that are the focus of treaty advocates, like pollution, toxic dumping, and harm to lands of indigenous peoples, have also been addressed more effectively in democratic states.

John G. Ruggie, who produced the UN "Guiding Principles on Business and Human Rights" and was the UN special representative on the issue, warned that "business and human rights is not so discrete an issue area as to lend itself to a single set of detailed treaty obligations." He said it was "hard to imagine" such a treaty "providing a basis for meaningful legal action." He recommended avoiding "largely symbolic gestures, of little practical use to real people in real places." Indeed, from the perspective of victims, he said, "an all-encompassing business and human rights treaty" would be "a profound deception."[84]

Nonetheless, more than five hundred nongovernmental organizations, promoting a false contradiction between free enterprise and human rights, lobbied for passage of the resolution, claiming that opposition meant being subservient to "corporate actors" and their "public relations strategies." Friends of the Earth Europe accused the European Union of "standing up for corporate interests instead of human rights." The NGO propaganda evidently scared numerous states into abstaining from the Human Rights Council vote, allowing the measure to pass. Human Rights Watch said the proposal was "too narrow," faulting it for not also dealing with national and other businesses "that should also be required to respect human rights." In May 2016, Human Rights Watch urged governments, employers, and trade unions attending an International Labour Conference "to seize the opportunity to begin the process for the adoption of a new, international, legally binding standard that obliges governments to require businesses to conduct human rights due diligence in global supply chains."[85]

As Professor Ruggie noted, an international treaty on business and human rights would not have much effect on the practices of transnational corporations. But it *would* give states that fail to protect their citizens an opportunity to hide their failures behind ideological slogans. And by diluting attention to fundamental rights, it would further diminish the capacity of the international human rights system to hold governments to norms by which citizens can be empowered to solve complex problems like child labor through democratic processes.

I raised these questions in 2014 at a meeting organized by the ABA, described as a "multi-stakeholder conference examining the prospective legal dimensions of a binding international treaty on business and human rights." The participants were mostly human rights lawyers. I also added the kamikaze point that new UN treaties provided jobs for the legal profession. My concerns were met with silence.

European states appear to be taking a passive stance as regards the formation of a treaty. A petition sent by Friends of the Earth and left-wing activist groups to the president of the European Commission complained that the EU and its members states were absent from negotiations.[86]

Proposed UN Convention on the Human Rights of Peasants. Formal consideration is being given to proposals for a global treaty protecting the human rights of peasants. This initiative has been led by La Via Campesina, an alliance of more than 140 peasant organizations from 69 different countries, claiming to represent more than 200 million peasants. Other NGOs have also joined the effort. The campaign for a human rights convention specifically focused on peasants is seen as emblematic of "new rights advocacy," that is, the expansion of human rights claims since the World Conference. La Via Campesina represents a movement to "challenge the hegemonic ideology of neoliberalism in global economics," according to a sympathetic observer.[87] At the International Conference on Peasants' Rights held in Jakarta in June 2008, La Via Campesina adopted its "Declaration of the Rights of Peasants - Women and Men." Their next project was to make it a UN declaration.

The UN human rights system reacted to the call of La Via Campesina in the context of responding to the "global food crisis" of 2008. The following year, the Human Rights Council and the General Assembly both invited La Via Campesina to give its views on the ways in which the food crisis could be remedied. On September 24, 2012, the council adopted a resolution on the "Promotion of the human rights of peasants and other people working in rural areas."[88] Sponsored by Bolivia, Cuba and South Africa, the resolution was adopted with twenty-three votes in favor, fifteen abstentions and nine votes against, including European states and the United States. The resolution led to the creation of yet another open-ended intergovernmental working group with the mandate of negotiating a draft United Nations Declaration on the Rights of Peasants and Other People Working in Rural Areas. Negotiations started in July 2013.

An examination of which members of the Human Rights Council supported the creation of the new treaty is revealing:

- *In favor:* Angola, Bangladesh, Benin, Burkina Faso, Cameroon, Chile, China, Congo, Costa Rica, Cuba, Djibouti, Ecuador, Guatemala, India, Indonesia, Kyrgyzstan, Malaysia, Peru, Philippines, Russian Federation, Thailand, Uganda, Uruguay.
- *Against:* Austria, Belgium, Czech Republic, Hungary, Italy, Poland, Romania, Spain, United States of America.
- *Abstaining:* Botswana, Jordan, Kuwait, Libya, Maldives, Mauritania, Mauritius, Mexico, Nigeria, Norway, Qatar, Republic of Moldova, Saudi Arabia, Senegal, Switzerland.

The creation of new, collective human rights is clearly a *political strategy*—a way of weaponizing and instrumentalizing human rights to accomplish political goals of the left.

Exploiting ESCR to Defend Oppression

Since the founding of the modern international human rights system, repressive dictatorial governments have exploited the concept of economic and social rights as a way of masking their violations of freedom while posing as defenders of human rights, and also as a weapon to attack and undermine the legitimacy of liberal democracies whose governments respect individual freedom.

The main outlines of this tendency were established by the Soviet Union in the early years of the international human rights system. Soviet propagandists were obsessed with the concept of human rights, seeing it clearly as the strongest philosophical threat to their hegemony and their appeal to the Third World. At the same time, economic and social rights were central to the self-presentation of Soviet communism—the garb in which it dressed itself up for global inspection. The human rights embraced by the USSR were painted as more consequential than individual freedom rights. "The unity of state and society, and the reality of mass participation in its structures, made Soviet rights stronger than those that existed in the capitalist West," in this view. "Unlike in the West, rights were founded on true principles of equality, which flowed out of the individual's organic status inside the state-society unity...."[89] Economic and social rights were material gifts of the state, not illusions based on the abstract concept of natural law. Economic and social rights offered concrete necessities, while the individual freedom at the heart of civil and political rights was a recipe for class exploitation, inequality, poverty, moral corruption and disorder.

Soviet ideologues thus turned human rights on their head, making them an instrument for aggrandizing rather than limiting the power of the state. At the Washington Summit of 1987, Mikhail Gorbachev denounced America's rejection of economic and social rights, asking, "What moral right do you have to give us lectures?"[90] When the Soviet Union was coming apart in 1989, he still vigorously defended the economic and social rights it promised, pushing back against claims that the system trampled on human nature.

Soviet theorists constructed a template for rationalizing oppression by invoking respect for economic and social rights—a pattern that has become traditional since the end of the Cold War. The elevation of the "indivisibility" of human rights to an official doctrine of the United Nations has encouraged this theme to spread around the international community. It has become an accepted truism that freedom cannot be enjoyed without "conditions" being provided by the state. Repressive states have increasingly gone on the offensive about human rights, using the concept of economic and social rights to undermine their critics and clothe themselves in moral legitimacy. Elliott Abrams provided this example of dictators "reviving the old Soviet Line":

Just before his visit to Washington [August 2009], Egypt's President Mubarak did an interview with Charlie Rose, who raised the issue of human rights (tepidly, it must be said). Mubarak was ready for him, having apparently opened the old Soviet textbooks Egypt used to have before Sadat broke with Russia. "Look, please," Mubarak replied. "Your concept of human rights is a merely political one. Human rights are not only political. You have social rights. You have the right to education. You have the right to health. You have the right to a job. There are many other rights. And we are doing well on these fronts. But what we are not [is] absolutely perfect, and nobody's perfect.... It is not merely a political concept. It is social, it is health, and it is amalgamated as one."[91]

Defending Repression in the Universal Periodic Review Process

Compliance with international human rights standards of all members of the United Nations is examined every four years under the Universal Periodic Review (UPR), a process set up with the reform of the UN Human Rights Commission in 2006. Three documents form the basis of the UPR: a national report submitted by the state under review, a compilation of UN information by the Office of the High Commissioner for Human Rights (OHCHR), and a summary (also prepared by the OHCHR) of reports submitted by nongovernmental organizations and other stakeholders. The UPR yields what is considered a comprehensive assessment of human rights conditions in each country. Yet the world's most repressive states fare well, notwithstanding the abject misery of their citizens, because the review process weighs fundamental freedoms against social and economic policies. The UPR has become a forum in which abusive governments can trivialize their own crimes while they belittle the civil and political rights enjoyed by citizens of liberal democracies. The vital question of freedom is crowded out in the examinations, which is exactly what totalitarian and authoritarian states had in mind by promoting the concept of indivisibility. The UN human rights system has institutionalized their strategy.[92] A few examples follow.

China paraded out its compliance with standards for economic and social rights in its 2013 UPR examination, deflecting criticism of its denial of fundamental, authentic human rights.[93] China's national report cited, inter alia, 9.3 percent per annum growth in gross domestic product, low unemployment, investments in education and culture, housing policy, and poverty relief.

Although it claims the second highest GDP in the world, China refers to itself as a developing country with "over 100 million people living in poverty," implying that it cannot afford to grant its citizens the freedoms allowed in the West.

In the "interactive dialogue" where UN members could question China on the basis of its own report as well as reports submitted by NGOs, 141 states participated, a huge number. That left only fifty seconds for each intervention. The vast majority of those 141 states praised China, often using the same phrases, suggesting that Chinese authorities gamed the process to drown out criticism.

States repeatedly praised China for assistance to citizens in rural areas, to the disabled and to children; for its cultural events; even for environmental protection. Numerous delegations praised human rights education in China. Turkmenistan praised China's success at including minorities in the National Congress of the Communist Party. The highest praise for China was voiced by Syria, whose delegate looked forward to China's election to the Human Rights Council.

Several states shamelessly applauded and encouraged some of China's most egregious human rights violations. Singapore praised China's strict Internet censorship. Saudi Arabia urged China to continue to prosecute those who "offend others in the name of promoting human rights." None of the Muslim states mentioned China's often-violent suppression of the Uyghur Muslim minority.

Only twenty-five UN members expressed even mild concerns about human rights violations in China, most centering on use of the death penalty, violations of freedom of religion, expression and association, persecution of human rights defenders, and mistreatment of minorities, especially the people of Tibet. The strongest critiques came from Australia, Canada, the Czech Republic, Germany, the United Kingdom and the United States. Pushing a wide-ranging series of recommendations into the scant fifty-second time slot, the USA even got in a mention of Xu Zhiyong and Yang Maodong, two persecuted human rights defenders.

The Chinese delegation said it was regrettable that security actions were called ethnic cleansing, that criminals were considered human rights defenders, and that "political procedures" were called persecution. Reacting to several references to the disappearance of Cao Shunli, an activist who had attempted to participate in the UPR, China defended its right to prosecute civil society activists when they sought to "instigate unlawful gatherings to make trouble." Freedom of assembly was "guaranteed" as long as it did not "undermine the legitimacy of the state" and "social stability." The Chinese delegation said the state needed to protect "national interests" and citizens from "harmful information" on the Internet. Religious organizations needed to be registered in order to protect their members. Abortions to comply with population policy were always carried out with the "consent" of the mother, it was claimed. The Chinese government said it was considering reforms in the "education through labor" program, and that Tibet had seen notable improvements regarding illiteracy, poverty and life expectancy.

In fact, the Chinese government does not accept the idea of universal, individual civil and political human rights at all. Instead, China subscribes to a version of human rights that is "founded on the country's own experience," according to an official statement. In this view, "human rights are the product of social and historical situations." The Chinese state defines human rights as "the rights society gives to its members." It follows, then, that "society," by which Chinese leaders mean the state, can arbitrarily take away those rights or refuse to honor them, depending on the social and historical situation. A "secret warning" was disseminated to party members, apparently authorized by Xi Jinping, China's leader, admonishing in exhausted Stalinist language about the dangers of "universal" human rights, as well as "Western constitutional democracy," "neoliberalism," and "nihilist" criticisms of past Communist Party problems.[94]

These absurd positions can find a comfortable place in the UN human rights system because the international community has watered down the meaning of human rights, and they receive increasing support even in liberal democracies. When a Canadian reporter raised questions in June 2016 about human rights violations in China, the country's foreign minister, Wang Yi, responded testily, "Do you know that China has lifted more than 600 million people out of poverty?"[95] An Ontario cabinet minister, Michael Chan, defended China's approach to human rights, saying it should be viewed from the perspective of "basic livelihood." Chan argued, "The inner meaning of human rights is very broad, but the right to survival and a basic livelihood are important components of human rights."[96] Apparently the approximately 45 million Chinese citizens murdered by the Communist regime between 1958 and 1962 in the name of collective economic and political progress were somehow an exception to China's commitment to the "right to survival."

North Korea, or the Democratic People's Republic of Korea (DPRK), is the world's most repressive state. In 2013, the Human Rights Council appointed a commission of inquiry to look into allegations of grave human rights violations and crimes against humanity there. The commission found that "crimes against humanity have been committed in the Democratic People's Republic of Korea, pursuant to policies established at the highest level of the state." Specifically, it found:

> These crimes against humanity entail extermination, murder, enslavement, torture, imprisonment, rape, forced abortions and other sexual violence, persecution on political, religious, racial and gender grounds, the forcible transfer of populations, the enforced disappearance of persons and the inhumane act of knowingly causing prolonged starvation. The commission further finds that crimes against humanity are ongoing in the Democratic People's Republic of Korea because the policies, institutions and patterns of impunity that lie at their heart remain in place.[97]

Yet when the DPRK underwent its Universal Periodic Review in May 2014, the regime's crimes against humanity were balanced against its claims of respect for economic and social rights. North Korean authorities boasted of the country's social programs:

> A series of human rights-related laws, including in the areas of education, health care, the protection of the rights of the child, women and persons with disabilities, and disaster prevention were adopted or amended during the reporting period.... The Government made efforts to improve economic construction and people's living and to build a socialist civilized country....
>
> Progress had been made in protecting and promoting the rights of children, women, the elderly and persons with disabilities. Special attention was given to health care and education for children without parents....
>
> Measures had been taken for the care of older persons with no one to depend on and a new support system had been established. The delegation stated that alleged discrimination based on social classification of people was unimaginable in the country, where all people were the masters of the State and society, and noted that equality was guaranteed by the Constitution and in practice.[98]

Eighty-five national delegations made interventions in the discussion of North Korea's record on human rights. Of these, *thirty-nine praised the DPRK's performance*, citing its social programs as demonstrating compliance with economic and social rights treaties. Far less attention was paid to its contemptible inhumanity to its own citizens. In decades of contact with victims of torture, I never heard worse accounts than those of former prisoners in the DPRK's concentration camps, a number of whom I interviewed in South Korea in 2013. During several of these interviews I found myself nauseated and on the verge of tears. Yet the cruel regime has managed to offset its crimes with reference to bogus human rights.

What is more, both China and the DPRK have taken active measures to suppress criticism. China has blocked the participation of critical NGOs in the Human Rights Council and imprisoned Chinese citizens attempting to provide independent information.

I can even cite an apparent attempt at intimidation directed against myself. Articles and interviews of mine that were sharply critical of China had been translated into Chinese. Ahead of the China UPR discussed above, I traveled to Geneva to meet with UN delegations concerning China's forcible and illegal repatriation of North Koreans who had fled the regime. Meeting in the Serpentine Lounge in the Palace of Nations with a diplomat, I noticed an Asian woman staring directly at me, clearly watching me, and when I left, she left too. Later I made my way to a hotel across the French border. As I checked in, another Asian woman fell in behind me, and appeared again in the dining room when I did. When I opened my email account the next morning, I found it had been hacked over thirty times—from an IP address inside the hotel. I have no proof, but think it is likely that these events reflect what is called "overt surveillance" intended to discourage my activities. (Some months before, when I urged foreign ministry officials of a major European country to raise the repatriation question at the China UPR, they said they could not send me a follow-up email because their system was being monitored by Chinese intelligence services.)

When *Turkmenistan* had its UPR in December 2008, Dr. Shirin Akhmedova, who led the delegation, "declared unwavering implementation of the international obligations undertaken by the State." She said that Turkmenistan "is carrying out broad and important reforms in education, health, social security, in the legal sphere and in improving the well-being of people, including those living in remote areas of the country." She said "the rights and freedoms of the citizens of Turkmenistan have been broadened," stressing that "Turkmenistan is a socially oriented state."

Despite having signed the Helsinki Accords committing itself to human rights and the rule of law, Turkmenistan is a dictatorship permitting its citizens no civil or political rights. During the discussions at the UPR, only thirty-five delegations took the floor. Some UN members tried to hold the Turkmen delegation accountable for abuses of human rights. Ten delegations openly criticized Turkmenistan for abuses of human rights defenders, a politicized judiciary, corruption, meager protection of women's and children's rights, trafficking in human beings, and many other problems. Other delegations made anodyne bureaucratic interventions about technical compliance issues. But the majority of delegations that made interventions praised Turkmenistan, focusing especially on "reforms." Not a single delegation mentioned that under the country's rulers, hospitals have been closed, epidemics like tuberculosis have been ignored, and medical standards have been debased in an effort to pretend there are no health problems, although information about these problems was made available to UN members.[99]

When *Iran's* human rights record was examined in 2014, there were statements from 104 delegations. Of those, 61 praised Iran's human rights practices, the vast majority citing economic and social rights. For example, according to the UN documentation,

> Turkmenistan commended the improvement in children's nutrition and the expansion of health services in rural areas....Bangladesh noted that the country would likely meet most of the Millennium Development Goals....Belarus noted the development of national institutions to protect the rights of the most vulnerable....Brazil noted the recent progress, particularly regarding economic and social rights.[100]

Human rights groups consider *Belarus* to be Europe's last dictatorship. At Belarus's UPR in 2015, its delegation bragged about economic and social rights:

> In the past five years, Belarus had climbed 15 places in the Human Development Index; almost all of the Millennium Development Goals had been achieved, five of them ahead of schedule. Other positive indicators had been achieved in the fields of education, gender equality, improving the quality of drinking water and immunization of children.[101]

Cuba is particularly aggressive in defending repression by invoking economic and social rights, noting during the DPRK review cited above that "the State under review was endeavouring to consolidate a socialist society in the face of aggressive imperialist policies directed against its country." According to Human Rights Watch, "When faced with criticism of its civil and political rights record, Cuba often defends its human rights practices by pointing to improvements in economic and social rights...."[102]

But some observers fully accept that calculus for measuring the realization of human rights. Garry Leech, writing in the journal *Critical Legal Thinking* in 2013, accused Human Rights Watch of "bias" for criticizing violations of civil and political rights in Venezuela. Leech pointed to that country's "remarkable successes ensuring that all citizens receive adequate food and housing as well as free healthcare and education; all of which constitute guarantees of economic, social and cultural rights."[103] As of this writing, people of Venezuela cannot find bread to purchase, or toilet paper, mainly due to price controls imposed by the dictatorial government that make all but the most minimal profit margins illegal, while protesting citizens are being shot in the street. The irony and the tragedy of defending the denial of liberty by adducing "economic rights" policies that also result in material deprivation needs no further explication.

A Postliberal Human Rights without Freedom

States that reject criticism of their restrictions on civil and political rights, justifying those actions by pointing to economic and social rights, have been coalescing into an informal caucus at the United Nations.[104] They are becoming more aggressive, strategic and mutually supportive in seeking institutional changes to blunt such criticism in UN forums, and in promoting a "new normal" in international human rights that is compatible with authoritarian regimes. With the election of Cuba, China, Russia and Saudi Arabia to the UN Human Rights Council in November 2013, the trend intensified.

In the Human Rights Council, these authoritarian states—as well as Azerbaijan, Iran, Pakistan, Venezuela and others—defend their policies in part by alleging human rights abuses in states that question them. What is more, the newly energized "antiliberal UN caucus" denounces the practice of citing specific violations of human rights in international forums. They claim that "naming and shaming," one of the central methods of human rights advocacy, should have ended with the UN reform of 2006, and that citing violations of human rights constitutes gross interference in the internal affairs of sovereign states and shows political bias.

Speeches from the "antiliberal caucus" bear the obvious marks of sharing information and ideas, including a common database of problems in liberal democracies such as unemployment, discrimination against Roma and Muslims, and expulsions of immigrants in Europe; as well as poverty, racism and gun violence in the United States, and the government's drone killings, NSA spying, rendition programs, and "anti-Muslim" travel ban. Some of these do represent serious failures that have compromised the West's position as a defender of universal human rights.

At the same time, the West's commitment to supporting human rights and civil society campaigners abroad has been weakened by fear of economic repercussions from confronting China, which stoutly defends itself and other members of the caucus. In previous decades, violations of human rights incurred risks of Western retribution, but the tables have turned and now Western states are often unwilling to run the risks that come with defending human rights, after subjecting the issue to a cost-benefit analysis.

Bullying of human rights NGOs in the UN context has increased dramatically, as have attempts to shut down critical NGO speeches. Some states in the antiliberal caucus submit reports falsely claiming to be written by independent groups, in an effort to subvert UN human rights evaluations. The antiliberal caucus has invested heavily in building fake NGOs, fake human rights bureaucracies and fake parliamentary opposition to create an illusion of respect for human rights.

But it would be a mistake to interpret the pushback against human rights as merely a defensive reaction or political theater. A coherent, alternative human rights ideology is taking shape, fostered by the growing global emphasis on economic and social rights. While championing those rights, members of the antiliberal caucus argue that criticisms about the violation of civil and political rights are disruptive of peace and the international order and are fig leaves for aggressive efforts to force regime change. In their speeches, they appeal to "international cooperation," "even-handedness" and "dialogue," painting themselves as the "party of peace." As memories of the Gulag fade, Western economies falter and the global community adopts an expanded human rights agenda, promises of "stability" and social benefits in return for restricted civil and political rights find wider acceptance. The antiliberal caucus speaks to a new human rights community that increasingly views its area of concern in utilitarian and economic terms, as a matter of ensuring security rather than freedom; in terms utterly inconsistent with the foundations of human rights in natural rights.

The United States and members of the European Union do point out violations of civil and political rights, but they apply a utilitarian calculus. This "pragmatic" posture is incompatible with the obligation to defend human rights for their own sake, as a matter of principle. Liberal democracies do not counter the emerging authoritarian human rights ideology with a strong and clear defense of freedom. As a result, human rights has lost much of its moral charisma, and the UN General Assembly concerns itself largely with discussions about development.

The antiliberal caucus is fighting a war of ideas, but liberal democracies are not fighting back. They seem to have lost the capacity or the will to defend the core concept of human rights that is a legacy of the Enlightenment. If they wish to halt the decay of the international human rights system, they must do more than robotically cite violations. They must better articulate a vision of human rights that cannot be traded off for the paternalistic favors of authoritarian governments. We will return to this theme in Chapter 6.

CHAPTER 5

The Loss of America's Human Rights Exceptionalism

Human rights defenders recoil at the assertion of "exceptionalism" by any state. In the international human rights community, exceptionalism generally signals an excuse to violate human rights. It suggests that each state defines human rights for itself, in accordance with its own "values" and sovereignty, and its rulers can thus defend themselves from demands for freedom based on universal and natural rights. Asian states, among many others, have claimed their own distinct interpretation of human rights in harmony with their cultures and values. In some countries, female genital mutilation is defended on the grounds that it is rooted in a particular culture. This kind of exceptionalism is an expression of a cultural relativism that rejects the existence of any universal human rights that impose a uniform obligation everywhere, trumping culture and politics. It is a rejection of universality.

The idea of American exceptionalism has its own negative baggage. In one sense, it is a truism: the founding and constitution of the United States, and the formation of a society of immigrants coming together as citizens of a democratic, multinational and multiethnic civil state, are without question unique in the world. "The position of the Americans is quite exceptional," concluded Alexis de Tocqueville in 1835.[1] Yet the idea of American exceptionalism has gotten a bad name by being linked with an aggressive national chauvinism.

159

It is "the underlying justification for US imperialism and lawlessness around the world," in one typical statement of this view. "It relies on a claim that the US is beyond international law and has been *chosen by God* to tell everyone in the world what to do."[2]

But America's true exceptionalism lies in its natural rights universalism. American exceptionalism was, and is, its political and legal system based on natural law and individual rights, a government set up to limit its own power in deference to the natural rights of the individual. It was in this sense that Ayn Rand called the United States "the first *moral* society in history." She wrote, "The most profoundly revolutionary achievement of the United States of America was *the subordination of society to moral law*."[3]

The foundation of America's respect for political freedom was a vision of natural rights—inherent, permanent, inalienable. Natural rights were the basis for the American colonists' demand for independence, and the principles upon which the U.S. Constitution was formed. A concern for natural rights was a common theme in American colonial thought and debate, and a lens through which politics and law were interpreted and judged. Now, every July 4th, political and community leaders ritually repeat words about the source of our rights being God, or the Creator, and politicians still refer to natural rights. The idea is compatible with rational and even scientific forms of religion like deism, and thus compatible with the largely secular culture of contemporary America, but the public understanding of natural rights has faded, and with it the connection between natural rights and human rights. Consequently, American human rights exceptionalism is being lost. Instead of exporting its true exceptionalism, America is helping to spread an incoherent and unstable idea of human rights that has effectively become universal, even while embodying a contradiction with the ideal of universality.

Natural Rights in America

The idea of inherent and inalienable natural rights is what gave impetus to the founding of the United States: what drove protests and actions against British rule in the American colonies, and what led to the fateful decision to declare independence and fight for freedom in the Revolutionary War, a major turning point in world history. The very purpose of the new constitutional republic would be to protect natural rights. The Revolutionary War was not fought for economic interests; the American colonies enjoyed a high standard of living, and ordinary people were thriving in comparison with their counterparts in other parts of the world. The revolt initially brought harsh suffering for the Americans, including the Founders. One-third of the fifty-six signers of the Declaration of Independence lost their fortunes, and nine died for their convictions. The Revolutionary War, second only to the Civil War in terms of proportional casualties, was fought to secure natural rights in the form of individual civil rights and political freedoms.

Philip Hamburger, a legal scholar at Columbia University, has painstakingly demonstrated that natural law and natural rights were familiar ideas to public-minded colonial Americans.[4] The idea of inherent natural rights commonly appears in political tracts, sermons, letters, speeches, declarations and colonial constitutions from the years of political ferment leading up to the establishment of a new state. A significant number of colonial leaders had received a classical education and were impressed by the writings of Aristotle, Cicero and others who had contributed to the classical natural law tradition. But the Enlightenment had put a fresh face on classical natural law. A research project on sources referenced by the Framers of the Constitution, examining over fifteen thousand documents, found the three most quoted authors to be Montesquieu, Blackstone and John Locke.[5] Of most importance was Locke's republican, Enlightenment rationalism: the view that government is essentially artificial, existing only to protect natural rights, and that by violating those rights it undermines its own raison d'être. The most frequently quoted text in prerevolutionary political tracts was the Bible.

The revolutionary generation regularly referred to a distinction between natural and conventional law, and to the principle that the laws of governments must be subordinate to a transcendent moral standard based on human nature. At first their arguments were aimed at proving that the American colonists deserved to have their natural rights honored as British subjects. For example, James Otis (who apparently coined the phrase "no taxation without representation") argued in *Rights of the British Colonies Asserted and Proved* (1763) that British taxation contradicted the limits that natural law placed on legislation.

> Every British subject born on the continent of America, or in any other of the British dominions, is by the law of God and nature, by the common law, and by act of parliament, (exclusive of all charters from the Crown)

entitled to all the natural, essential, inherent and inseparable rights of our fellow subjects in Great Britain.[6]

In 1765, the Pennsylvania Assembly resolved that "the inhabitants of this Province are entitled to the Liberties, Rights and Privileges of His Majesty's Subjects in Great-Britain or elsewhere," and that "the Constitution of Government of this Province is founded on the natural Rights of Mankind, and the noble Principles of English Liberty."[7] In the Massachusetts Resolves, Samuel Adams asserted that the peoples of the colony were "unalienably entitled to those essential rights in common with all men; and that no law of society can consistent with the law of God and Nature divest them of those rights."[8]

Thomas Paine, the most forceful advocate of a separation from England, put philosophical ideas into simple, down-to-earth prose. *Common Sense* (1776) was the most popular pamphlet published in America, with 150,000 copies distributed in a few months, and eventually half a million copies were sold. (In proportional terms, it was America's greatest bestseller ever.)[9] Later, in *Rights of Man* (1791), Paine wrote, "Natural rights are those which appertain to man in right of his existence. Of this kind are all the intellectual rights, or rights of the mind, and also all those rights of acting as an individual for his own comfort and happiness, which are not injurious to the natural rights of others."[10] Richard Bland, a Virginia lawyer whose ideas influenced Thomas Jefferson, said that natural rights "remain with every man," so that "he cannot be deprived of [them] by any civil Authority."[11]

As the colonies were pushed toward a radical break with the monarchy, they faced not only the prospect of violent military conflict in their midst, but also a new and uncharted life, with their cultural roots severed, their national identity thrown into limbo, and their political institutions entering a radical transformation. A habitual respect for political authority, which inhered in the Christian political theology of the day, had been weakened by life on the periphery of the empire, relatively detached from contact with the central symbols and sentiments of the British monarchy. Claims for the divine right of kings had effectively been rebutted by the turmoil of the previous century, when kings were dethroned by parliamentarians. A belief in the natural rights of individuals was hard to square with a belief in the inherent power of the royalty, and it inspired criticism and open ridicule of both the king and Parliament. It diminished the colonists' sense of loyalty as subjects, and in some measure their sense of fellowship with British society. The idea and vision of natural rights was the source of their resolve, providing a logic that brought together intellectual, political and religious beliefs. Their confidence in the rationality of natural law, and in the power of reason to guard against anarchy in the exercise of freedom, allowed them to think of themselves as free men and dream of forming a free yet orderly society.

Natural law was the necessary context for understanding natural rights. Just as natural law set limits on positive law, it also put limits on natural liberty through the mechanism of reason. Natural law tempered the exercise of natural rights; it constrained men from violating the rights of others, and thus it preserved order and the liberty of all. According to Professor Philip Hamburger, "Americans derived social obligations from enlightened self-interest...and could talk about natural law both as a law of human nature and as the foundation of moral rules."[12] They cultivated a civil society with civil manners, valuing respect and polite discourse.[13] America had "a blank sheet to write upon," as Paine put it, and its people assumed responsibility for self-determination, with the iron logic of natural law and natural rights as their guide.

The shift to arguing on the basis of natural law and natural rights instead of historic British rights and privileges became complete with the Declaration of Independence, which states:

> We hold these truths to be self-evident: That all men are created equal; that they are endowed by their Creator with certain unalienable rights; that among these are life, liberty, and the pursuit of happiness; that, to secure these rights, governments are instituted among men, deriving their just powers from the consent of the governed; that whenever any form of government becomes destructive of these ends, it is the right of the people to alter or to abolish it, and to institute new government, laying its foundation on such principles, and organizing its powers in such form, as to them shall seem most likely to effect their safety and happiness.

The document remains exceptional in the central place assigned to natural rights and to the natural law we find via reason. "No public document gives more prominence to the idea of natural law," writes James Stoner, "nor relies more crucially upon natural law as a premise, than the American Declaration of Independence."[14] It amounts to an oath before God not to violate natural rights, and an affirmation that violations of natural rights are violations of a sacred order, a sin against both man and God.

The Declaration of Independence was, and is, a call for freedom throughout the world; it was not just about Americans, but about human beings, about mankind. Based on the "laws of nature and Nature's God," it was a clear assertion of a common human nature and of the universality of human rights. It expressed a way of thinking about human beings as such, not as members of any subdivision of humanity. It presented a challenge to aristocracies, to any "unnatural" rule over others, to any form of discrimination in political systems. It was an affirmation, in political terms, of the brotherhood of man that lies at the moral core of Western civilization in the book of Genesis.

Human nature had an objective quality that could be understood by reason. The state needed to be a creation of reason, a contract that would work for individuals of diverse outlooks and capacities living together in mutual respect. The moral charisma of the Founders, which still has force today, seems to reside in their sympathy and respect for individuals paradoxically joined with a rational aloofness; in their concurrent love and detachment. The modern government they established was a product of their capacity for objectivity and for acting on principle. It was not about them; it was not about their reference groups, or particulars of their society, or their time and place. It reflected enduring principles, foremost among them the principles of natural law and rights. The rights articulated in the Declaration of Independence were not simply "posited," but were "rights that would arise for all human beings by nature, and they would remain the same in all places where that nature remained the same."[15] With its invocation of natural law as a measure of national policy, and its appeal to "the opinions of mankind," the declaration was indeed a step toward global international law, toward international human rights based on natural law.[16]

The Americans thus established a new form of government whose purpose was to protect individual human (natural) rights. The government would be a minimalist structure to establish peace and order, intruding as little as possible in the lives of free people and their local governments. Its statutes and laws mainly limited its own powers. In his *Lectures on Law* (1791), James Wilson wrote that government "should be formed to secure and to enlarge the exercise of the natural rights of its members; and every government, which has not this in view, as its principal object, is not a government of the legitimate kind."[17] The Framers sought to promulgate positive law constrained by natural rights. It is the model upon which negative liberties are now protected under national and international law.

The Bill of Rights to the Constitution is, in a sense, an indirect portrait of human nature, reflecting Locke's empirical approach. It lists essential, inherent freedoms, as well as civil rights that can exist only under civil government.[18] These rights are "guaranteed in constitutions because they were essential to restraining government," writes Hamburger.[19] The First Amendment describes the core of American freedom, giving paramount importance to freedom of religion as the first human right. Religion, according to James Madison, the chief author of the Bill of Rights, had to be "immune" from civil authorities, because citizens were first "subjects of the Great Governor of the Universe," before they entered civil society.[20] Natural law existed in an otherworldly realm. No earthly government could have authority over one's relationship with God, or over one's intellectual freedom to define and live by one's perception of ultimate authority and morality. The Framers' understanding of religious freedom was built largely on the legal definition of religion in the Virginia Declaration of Rights, as "the duty which we owe to our Creator," a duty that could be discharged only "by reason and conviction, not by force or violence."

The government's duty to honor religious freedom is inseparable from the duty to respect natural law and natural rights. The freedom of religion stipulates the supremacy of natural law over the laws of government, and thus establishes the intellectual framework for the freedoms that follow. Ján Figel', the European Union's special envoy on freedom of religion and belief, called it a "basic precondition for real freedom."[21] Religious freedom gives substance to all other rights. It works as a guarantee of people's right to attain "immediate contact with the ultimate principles implicit in their beliefs and standards."[22] The freedom of religion found an echo in Principle VII of the Helsinki Final Act, which confirmed "the right of the individual to know and act upon his rights and duties."

Freedom of speech and of the press, freedom of assembly (understood now as "freedom of association"), and freedom to "petition the government for a redress of grievances" were considered natural liberties that protected people against tyranny—including the tyranny of majority rule under a democracy—and also established an environment of intellectual and political freedom in which the exercise of natural liberties would be tempered by reason. In the first years after ratification of the Constitution, legislators began to humanize the laws in conformity with principles of natural rights. For example, penal codes were liberalized, prisons were reformed to focus more on rehabilitation, and the use of capital punishment was limited.[23]

The United States Constitution does not guarantee any "distributional rights."[24] No provision of the document offers any protection of economic rights. There is no record of debate by early Americans about the possibility of inserting material entitlements into the Bill of Rights; the idea that freedom depends on the state ensuring economic equality is nowhere to be found. Economic benefits are clearly not inherent, natural rights belonging to individuals in the absence of any government. They have nothing to do with restraining the government from infringing on natural liberties. The revolutionary generation gave plenty of thought to the matter of assisting society's poor and needy members, placing great value on a benevolence grounded in nature and reason.[25] But the grounding of human rights in natural rights kept the issue of government services completely separate from constitutionally guaranteed natural or human rights. Economic and social concerns would be addressed by civil society and positive law, but had no place in the framework of rights that were meant to constrain the positive law.

From Ambivalence to Rejection

The turbulent first decades of the nineteenth century reveal fewer references to natural law and natural rights by American leaders than are seen in the writings and speeches of the revolutionary leaders. In the new, free country, men's natural rights, excepting those of slaves, were enshrined in the Constitution and in law, and insofar as people did not feel a denial of natural rights, the attachment to the *idea* began to fade. The citizens of the new country were exercising their freedom in the tasks of commerce and nation building, and thus gave less attention to philosophy. Political leaders were dealing with more concrete issues and disputes.

The high value placed upon civility by the revolutionary generation gave way to coarser manners in public life, a lapsing of the self-restraint that the Founders regarded as central to the rational exercise of natural rights. Powerful personalities like Andrew Jackson stepped into the political arena, giving birth to the Democratic Party and a system of political patronage and spoils. Jackson's administration seems to represent the beginning of a postrevolutionary American political creed. According to the historian J. M. Opal,

Jackson and other borderlands elites developed a working theory about how nations and citizens should protect themselves. They did so in conscious reference to both Constitutional and international law, eventually creating a new way of talking and thinking about the American people as "sovereign" within a cruel state of nature.[26]

The Jackson administration had no philosophical objection to a war of annihilation on Native American peoples. Violence was often glorified in the Jacksonian ethos, which saw individuals, and the American people, as having freedom in a state of nature, yet seemingly unconstrained by a natural law of reason-based morals. At the same time, Tocqueville observed a strong attachment in the United States to individual rights against majority rule.

The newly free nation was full of diffuse political and moral energies. Religious enthusiasm—the sense of immediate contact with the divine—took hold in massive Protestant revivals, which pulled the idea of natural law more firmly into the orbit of God's law. In 1828, George Combe published *The Constitution of Man in Relation to the Natural Laws*, which became one of the most influential books of the era. Combe argued that man is subject to natural laws like the rest of nature: "The Laws of Nature have been instituted by an omnipotent, all-just, and all-wise God, and that the observance of these laws is a religious duty."[27]

Natural Rights and the Question of Slavery. The existence of slavery in major portions of the United States posed a contradiction to the natural rights creed, a contradiction that troubled the minds of Jefferson and other fathers of American freedom, and continued to fester in political life through the first half of the nineteenth century. The national controversy over slavery in the run-up to the Civil War brought renewed attention to the idea of natural rights and its necessity to realizing the potential and the destiny of individual rights in the United States. The abolitionist Lysander Spooner denounced slavery as unconstitutional because it was a violation of natural rights.[28] He did so despite his anarchist position against the authority of the Constitution itself.

At the same time, a pronounced ambivalence about natural rights could be seen in the defense of slavery as a particular custom more important than the principle of universal human rights. Criticisms of natural rights in this context revealed doubts about the moral foundations of constitutional rights. They were the beginning of a shameful history that has undermined the political philosophy of the United States, opening the door to infringements on liberty by refuting or contextualizing natural rights. Senator John Calhoun, who had served as vice president under both Andrew Jackson and his prede-cessor John Quincy Adams, wrote in 1848 that the idea of the natural rights of individuals in a state of nature was inconsistent with the true "social and political" natural condition of mankind. No one is ever born free and equal; all "are born subject, not only to parental authority, but to the laws and insti-tutions of the country where born." Man is a "social being." The purpose of government is to "protect and preserve society," not individual freedom. The Constitution was to protect minority rights, including those of slaveholders.[29] Others defended slavery as consistent with natural property rights, believing that slaves were not fully human.

Perhaps Calhoun, in proposing cultural relativism and denying an objec-tive human nature and the idea of individual rights based in nature, was America's first postmodernist. The brewing Civil War was on one level a conflict between a fading but still powerful attachment to natural rights, and an emerging tendency to reduce the human moral spirit to a product of historical and social vicissitudes. Abraham Lincoln, as a young and aspiring politician in 1838, had lamented in his "Lyceum" speech that Americans' com-mitment to "establishing and maintaining civil and religious liberty" was on the wane. Individual rights and freedoms were taken for granted by a new generation, and this led to a disregard for the Constitution and for law itself, as evidenced by rampant crime. Two decades later, Lincoln honored Thomas Jefferson for having had the foresight "to introduce into a merely revolution-ary document, an abstract truth, applicable to all men and all times, and so to embalm it there, that to-day, and in all coming days, it shall be a rebuke and a stumbling-block to the very harbingers of re-appearing tyranny and oppression."[30]

In light of the "abstract truth, applicable to all men and all times," slavery was a violation of natural law. Speaking in Peoria, Illinois, in 1854, Lincoln said that no person could be considered "merchandise," because every per-son possessed "some natural right to himself." In his debates with Stephen A. Douglas in 1858, Lincoln confronted the morally relativistic view that slavery and antislavery could exist side by side. Slavery needed to be opposed because it was wrong, he insisted. It was discordant with natural law, which rests on reason. In demonstrating that slavery was irrational and logically indefensible, Lincoln also proved its immorality and its inconsistency with America's founding principles. And by so doing, "Lincoln affirmed, clarified, and vindicated the unique amalgam of classical natural law and modern natural law that defined American republicanism."[31]

An Accelerating Erosion. References to natural rights by political figures became more and more infrequent in postbellum America, signifying an abysmal custodianship of the nation's political values and ideals. The population was left vulnerable to corrosive doubts and outright attacks on its liberal constitutionalism emanating from local philosophers and legal theorists, and from imported European nihilism.[32] The sacrosanct foundations of human rights were ignored by political leaders and challenged outright by intellectuals in civil society, leaving a vacuum in the moral and legal space once inhabited by natural rights. It would be filled with philosophies and social sciences that diminished respect for the moral autonomy of individuals, while placing greater expectations upon the state to regulate society and solve its problems, even at the expense of constitutionally protected human rights. These currents of thought encouraged new generations of politicians to seek powers for the government that were inconsistent with constitutional limitations. The questioning of natural rights and natural law concepts amounted to an implicit questioning of the rights protected by the Constitution: were they inherent natural rights prior to governments, as the Founders insisted, or were they indistinct from rights conferred by the state, and thus subject to historical and political change?

Jurists and academics moved from natural law to positivism, seeking a science of law. Thomas Cooley, a widely influential legal scholar, maintained in *Constitutional Limitations* (1868) that natural rights are legally protected only if they have been established in the form of positive law.[33] He warned against referring to natural rights in court arguments. Legal positivism as such would not become a formal school of legal theory until the next century, but it grew as a way of thinking about the law, and about the basis for human rights, in the decades following the Civil War. Philosophers and jurists, some influenced by the utilitarianism of Jeremy Bentham (who had famously derided natural law as "nonsense on stilts"), concerned themselves not with the law's underlying moral principles, but with its consequences. At the same time, confidence in America's individual rights creed was waning. The Christian idealist and influential Harvard professor Josiah Royce attracted followers with his call for the sublimation of individual ambitions to the demands or needs of the community of the whole of humanity, and his denunciation of capitalism as morally vacuous.[34]

Intellectuals and politicians began to adopt a philosophy of "pragmatism," a style of inquiry that originated with Charles Sanders Peirce in 1878. According to William James, its primary exponent, "Mr. Peirce, after pointing out that our beliefs are really rules for action, said that, to develop a thought's meaning, we need only determine what conduct it is fitted to produce: that conduct is for us its only significance."[35] Action should be the measure of truth. Pragmatism, as Thomas P. Whelan described it in 1928, "rejected objective evidence as the criterion of truth and substituted therefor, the utility, the fitness, the expediency of a thing."[36] What is important about the virtue of a law is its results, not any judgment about right or wrong, or conformity with an ideal of justice. Law, in essence, consists of "social engineering."[37] Pragmatism, applied to a question like protecting natural or human rights, would draw attention to "social claims and wants and desires...to the exclusion of rights, duties and obligations."[38]

Pragmatism was thus a seductive challenge to the austere natural rights tradition in America, a counterpoint to what Lincoln had called Jefferson's "cool" attachment to "abstract truth." The government based on protecting natural or human rights did not concern itself with specific tangible results beyond freedom itself; what people do with their liberties would reflect their own goals and moral virtues, or lack thereof. Pragmatism, on the other hand, seemed to promise governance that would provide citizens with what they want—a government that would deliver happiness itself, not merely the conditions for the *pursuit* of happiness.

Pragmatism (then and now) provided the logic for an activist government to build upon the ashes of natural rights. It challenged a central principle of the natural law tradition upon which authentic human rights rest: the universality of law, a principle articulated by Cicero (*Republic*, Bk. III). Pragmatism held that ideas, proposals, and laws were not intrinsically good or bad; the good of a thing was contingent upon its results.[39] The implications for human rights would be profound. According to the amoral logic of pragmatism, if the results of freedom—for example, the freedom of expression—are undesirable, then this freedom may legitimately be restricted. If the exercise of individual moral agency leads to undesirable consequences, then the state may limit the space for moral choice. One can see the pernicious effect of pragmatism in the discourse of the contemporary international human rights community: nondiscrimination policies are good because they produce good results; the freedom of religion is good because it promotes stability. But this approach obviously sows the seeds of human rights violations by offering a readymade justification. We can thank pragmatism for burdening human rights with the utilitarianism that subordinates the principle of liberty to other goals.

Progressives Dismiss Natural Rights as Outdated. After pragmatism, the next major influence on the concept of human rights was the progressive movement. Chapter 1 noted the deep influences of progressivism on the Universal Declaration of Human Rights and on the content of international human rights generally. To reiterate, progressives held natural rights to be a regressive ideology; they argued that real freedom could be made possible only by actions of the state to provide the conditions for enjoying freedom. Progressive American intellectuals and political leaders dismissed or overtly attacked the idea of natural rights—the foundation of the country's unparalleled freedoms and its republican form of government—as irrelevant to the challenges of a modern, urban, industrial society.

In academic circles, politics and government were coming to be regarded as a science, and there was growing opinion that political principles needed to be adapted to changing conditions, assisted by social-scientific analysis. Charles Merriam, a leading professor of political science at the University of Chicago, promoted what he called a "new method" of understanding politics in his influential textbook *A History of American Political Theories* (1903), a method that rejected the individualistic philosophy of the early nineteenth century.[40] He held that natural rights ("these alleged rights," he called them) "have no political force whatever, unless recognized and enforced by the state." According to Merriam, "the idea that men possess inherent and inalienable rights of a political or quasi-political character which are independent of the state, has been generally given up. It is held that these natural rights can have no other than an ethical value, and have no proper place in politics."[41] He would go on to become the leading political scientist in the country and a key adviser to President Franklin Delano Roosevelt.

In 1888, John Dewey published *The Ethics of Society*, in which he argued for an "organic" conception of society and the relationship between individuals and societies. "Government is an organ of society, and is as comprehensive as society," he wrote.[42] Equating government with society was recognized as totalitarian by the human rights community in which I worked, yet the concept remains something of a shibboleth among progressives. In *The Public and Its Problems* (1927), Dewey, who admired the philosophy of pragmatism, would challenge the habit of reference to fixed moral principles in legal and political reasoning as an obstacle to "orderly and directed" political and social change.[43] Like Josiah Royce, he found fault with a system focusing primarily on individual rights. Dewey saw individualism as immoral, "a kind of ideology or even dogma, disguising certain motives as universal truths," or a "rationalization for certain special interests."[44] His "deconstruction" to reveal underlying motives and orientations, in the spirit of Hegel and Marx, put the sincerity of Locke into question.[45]

In Dewey's philosophy, communities needed to shame individuals into being mindful of "social consequences" in making decisions. Modern society had to impose more responsibilities while it allowed greater freedom. The state needed to be the guarantor of social and economic standards, which were the conditions for "effective" freedom. Freedom depended on positive government action, not restraint. Freedom was therefore not something inherent to human nature that could be conceived apart from specific societies and governments. On the contrary, an individual person could not be seen detached from society, and society was essentially coterminous with government. In this respect, progressivism indeed represented a soft totalitarianism. The keys to freedom lay in government, and in one's responsible roles in the community.[46] The modern age was a "collective age" requiring a "new" form of individualism. The political culture of America needed to assume new "corporate" qualities, to counteract domination by corporations and the influence of mass-market advertising. Progressivism was itself regressive—a retreat from the moral challenge and responsibilities, and the promise, of individual freedom.

A number of these themes, which emerged in the course of Dewey's long career as a public intellectual, were taken into the politics and policies of America's progressive presidencies, including those of Theodore Roosevelt, Woodrow Wilson, Franklin Delano Roosevelt, and to an extent, Harry S. Truman. They are also associated with the policies of Lyndon Johnson and with the critical legal theory that shaped the thinking of Barack Obama.

Theodore Roosevelt was the "Rough Rider" whose tough talk and actions still inspire Americans, but he road roughly over human rights. He denounced any natural right to property, and judged the concept of natural rights to be "scientifically wrong and morally obsolete."[47] It was duties that were important, not rights. To be concerned about rights was selfish, reflecting unconcern for the common good. In a speech titled "Duty and Self Control" in Madison, Wisconsin, in 1911, Roosevelt said that "the people cannot be greater unless the people think of duty more than of right, just as the individual man who rises has to think first of duty and then of his rights. They must think of rights as developed in duty rather than of only their individual rights." Teddy

Roosevelt promoted a "new nationalism" in which the state would robustly promote economic equality and would respect private property "only so long as the gaining represents benefit to the community."[48] He engaged in conflict with courts when they defended property rights against majorities on the basis of natural rights.[49]

Progressive political ideas took hold strongly in the popular imagination. Oliver Wendell Holmes, a leading legal scholar of the period, ridiculed the idea of any objectively existing natural law, saying that law was nothing more than a reflection of the majority will—a position that identified him as the "American Nietzsche."[50] There was no inherent right to property; it was strictly a creation of the law.

A leading progressive, Frank Goodnow, wrote in *The American Conception of Liberty and Government* (1916),

> The rights which [an individual] possesses are, it is believed, conferred upon him, not by his Creator, but rather by the society to which he belongs. What they are is to be determined by the legislative authority in view of the needs of that society. Social expediency, rather than natural right, is thus to determine the sphere of individual freedom of action.[51]

Goodnow regarded the protection of individual rights through constitutionally limited government as an antiquated notion and an obstacle to reform.[52] His pointed views were really no different from those of the Chinese Communist government as regards the nature of human rights, and may be seen as an ideal type of the progressive approach to rights. Progressives advocated for a planned economy, and a society in which educational programs steered the young toward professions where they were needed for the good of the community, with the aim of efficiency. Progressivism promised a "golden mean" between laissez-faire individualism and Marxist socialism, in a "unifying moral order."[53]

Progressives also favored expansive administrative law to deal adaptively with social problems. A far-reaching civil service, detached from democratic processes, would have wide discretion. Professional experts would objectively assess problems and craft solutions. The state was envisioned as an organism with a life of its own—a take-off from Hegel's doctrine of historical progress. The juridical structure of the liberal state built around a system of checks and balances, as envisioned by America's Founders, was considered passé.

Woodrow Wilson, in his book *The State* (1898), wrote that "Government does now whatever experience permits or the times demand."[54] In his judgment, "abstract rights" were useless and the idea of "inalienable rights of the individual" was "nonsense."[55] Wilson famously advised reading the Declaration of Independence without its preface, which frames the demand for honoring freedom in terms of natural rights.[56] Speaking on "the meaning of liberty" at Independence Hall in 1914, Wilson claimed that the declaration was a "piece of practical business" more than a statement of principles about the rights of man. It was a "bill of particulars" relevant to 1776. "If we would keep it alive," he said, "we must fill it with a bill of particulars of the year 1914." Wilson's government empowered the executive branch while harshly cracking down on civil liberties. His disrespect for minorities has led some activists to seek to disassociate themselves from his legacy, despite its resonance with contemporary progressivism.

More than any other American leader, Franklin Delano Roosevelt transformed the principle of natural rights into a concept of "human rights" requiring positive state actions putatively needed to make enjoyment of freedom possible. But as a shrewd politician, he largely sidestepped knotty problems of political and legal philosophy, leaving only a thin trail of philosophical discourse. He achieved his results mainly by actions, as a political pragmatist.

In his Commonwealth Club address in 1932, Roosevelt set out a view of rights as being defined and bestowed by those in power:

> Rulers were accorded power, and the people consented to that power on consideration that they be accorded certain rights. The *task of statesmanship has always been the redefinition of these rights in terms of a changing and growing social order.* New conditions impose new requirements upon Government and those who conduct government. [Emphasis added.]

Consistent with the progressive tradition, Roosevelt held that natural rights were "inadequate to assure us equality in the pursuit of happiness" given the problems of modern society and the growth of the industrial state.[57] The state needed to create conditions for liberty; Americans thus shared a common responsibility to ensure that all would have an adequate standard of living—a standard to which they had a right.

But Roosevelt devoted little energy to philosophical argumentation against natural rights. "Roosevelt was not engaging with natural rights theories," wrote Cass Sunstein, a legal expert who served in the Obama administration and an avid admirer of FDR's Second Bill of Rights, or Economic Bill of Rights. Rather, he was "contending that government should respect, and try to foster, the rights to decent opportunity and to minimal security."[58] Instead of attacking the founding principles of the United States, Roosevelt and his staff flooded the public square with talk of a new kind of rights, to goods and services, as if there were no contradiction between such benefits and freedom rights. As we have seen, this was essentially the tactic by which economic and social rights were embedded into the Universal Declaration of Human Rights.

Roosevelt was a master of the politics of virtue. By asserting that Americans had economic *rights*, despite their profound incongruity with natural rights, he placed the onus on others to say that such rights were not on the same moral level as freedom rights—and they would do so at their own political hazard. He seized what appeared to be the high moral ground of human rights, bypassing philosophical obstacles as he pulled human rights fully into political territory. Natural rights were dissolved into the cloudy notion of human rights—an unstable composite of natural rights and welfare-state politics—while few realized or cared what was happening. Natural rights were left behind as Americans debated welfare policies largely without reference to underlying principles.

The United States government essentially placed Roosevelt's Economic Bill of Rights, a proposal that was politically unviable in the country itself, on the table when the UN Human Rights Commission set out to consider what was a human right.[59] By doing so (and through the New Deal), America might assume its "rightful place in the world," as both Franklin and Theodore Roosevelt had hoped. To gain more respect, they believed, the United Stated needed to divest itself of its narrow definition of rights—the natural rights doctrine that had made it exceptional in the world. Ending America's natural or human rights exceptionalism and bringing the country into conformity with European-style social democracy is still a goal of progressivism.

The implications of America's depreciation and virtual abandonment of natural rights are thus far-reaching, as Calvin Coolidge foresaw clearly. In defending the Declaration of Independence in 1926, President Coolidge said:

> If all men are created equal, that is final. If they are endowed with inalienable rights, that is final. If governments derive their just powers from the

consent of the governed, that is final. No advance, no progress can be made beyond these propositions.... The things of the spirit come first. Unless we cling to that, all our material prosperity, overwhelming though it may appear, will turn to a barren scepter in our grasp. If we are to maintain the great heritage which has been bequeathed to us, we must be like minded as the fathers who created it.[60]

Coolidge held that the movement to progress beyond natural rights was in fact regressive—an insight of great relevance to political debate in the United States today. If Americans no longer understood their constitutional liberties to be grounded in natural rights, but only in the government's laws, those freedoms would be vulnerable to encroachment. With no solid foundation for respect, they could be sacrificed in the call to sublimate liberty in service to the community, to set rights aside in the interest of duty to society.

Natural rights provided a bulwark against authoritarianism—nationalist, socialist, or some hybrid. But Coolidge was virtually alone in the overt defense of natural rights. What the United States brought to the table of international human rights was a deep ambivalence about natural rights, the basis for the very idea of human rights. Yet American statesmen were also ambivalent about the economic and social rights that their government had helped legitimize.

Ambivalence about Economic and Social Rights

In 2007, at a seminar on democracy promotion in Central Asia organized by the Centre for OSCE Research (CORE) in Hamburg, a participant from a Russian research institute accused the United States of promoting the over-throw of Central Asian governments in the name of promoting democracy and human rights, while itself not respecting economic and social rights. Kyle Scott, who was the deputy chief of the U.S. Mission to the Organization for Security and Co-operation in Europe (OSCE), gave a pithy response concerning economic and social rights: "We don't believe in 'em." He went on to say that the United States considered economic and social rights to be "goals," not human rights.

This reflexive statement, of course, belies a much more complicated and contradictory picture. According to the website of the U.S. Department of State, "The values captured in the Universal Declaration of Human Rights and other global and regional commitments are consistent with the values upon which the United States was founded centuries ago." The statement is manifestly false and amounts to disowning the legacy of the nation's founding documents. The U.S. Constitution does not classify any material government entitlements as rights, but it does protect the natural right to individual freedom. Perhaps the Framers would have approved of the state entitlements that have been granted by legislation over the past century, but with their natural rights orientation it is unlikely that they would have endorsed an expansion of the notion of rights beyond those they appended to the Constitution. Believing that only freedoms should be protected as rights does not mean that one is opposed to welfare policies. It means that one understands the categorical difference between natural rights that place an inviolable, protective canopy over individuals and their choices, and positive legislation aimed at solving the problems of society. Rights are supposed to constrain such legislation, and if they are confused with positive law, the concept of rights loses meaning and force. Indeed, the erasure of the distinction may signal an agenda to discredit and destroy the idea of natural rights.

The human rights expert Philip Alston has often been a sharp critic of American domestic policies, yet he observed that "the United States has been the single most important force in shaping the international human rights regime," whether people like it or not.[61] With only a few important exceptions, American administrations since the end of World War II have consistently ignored or muddled the distinction between human rights and social policies, or perhaps have not been fully aware of the profound implications of that distinction. American administrations have supported the concept of economic and social rights, at the expense of the integrity of the international human rights system, not to mention their own. They have commonly denied that such rights possess the qualities of real human rights, but they have failed to explain the idea of authentic human rights to the international community, the idea that has been their particular birthright. They have acquiesced in the devolution of the concept of human rights, allowing it to stand for an amalgam of natural rights and welfare benefits. They have misused the idea of human rights for strategic, political purposes, so as not to appear indifferent to poverty around the world and to build relations with collectivist governments. Yet Americans are still widely found guilty for not supporting economic and social rights, despite the wide-ranging entitlements provided in U.S. law. American administrations have tried to have it both ways on those so-called rights, but they have neither achieved intellectual integrity nor reaped political and public relations rewards.

The economic and social rights in the Universal Declaration of Human Rights, in the International Covenant on Economic, Social and Cultural Rights (ICESCR), and in the other human rights treaties were put there with American support and encouragement beginning in 1948.[62] American policies on international economic and social human rights reflect the tacit dismissal and tactical avoidance of natural rights by both Franklin and Eleanor Roosevelt. Often seen as a posture of expedient political accommodation, the U.S. approach in fact manifested a general sympathy with the socialist tendency to classify state benefits as human rights, as well as a political strategy to bring the forces of communism into the new world system. It may well have had an underlying domestic motive: to accomplish via the international human rights system what was politically unviable in the United States Congress.

Leading figures in the drafting of the UDHR, for example Charles Malik, saw the economic and social rights articles in the document as being based on Roosevelt's Second Bill of Rights.[63] Economic and social rights were rooted in the "Rooseveltian ideology," which held that individual liberties were insufficient for equality, and that government intervention was required to create the conditions for the realization of freedom.[64]

Eleanor Roosevelt said the U.S. government gave "wholehearted support" to those articles. The UDHR put the state into the human rights picture, making state actions necessary for the realization of human rights, and including state "rights and responsibilities."[65] It defined the kind of state needed to protect human rights. Mrs. Roosevelt said that the United States did not consider the articles on economic and social rights to "imply an obligation on governments to assure the enjoyment of these rights by direct governmental action."[66] But that was how all the states and civilian actors saw economic and social rights, and that is also how her own husband's presidential administration viewed such rights. Anything that is a "right" identifies bearers of that right and a corresponding duty on the part of specific duty-bearers. To suggest that economic and social rights can have meaning and existence without government obligations strains credulity.

Mrs. Roosevelt's remark seems to have been made to acknowledge and preserve an ambivalence about economic and social rights. American officials have typically called economic and social rights "human rights," while treating them as rights in name only. For example, Walter M. Kotschnig, who was a leading foreign service officer representing the United States in international formations, said that "economic, social and cultural rights while spoken of as 'rights' were, however, to be treated as objectives towards which *States* adhering to the Covenant would *within their resources* undertake to strive."[67] But rights and objectives are not the same kind of thing. If economic and social rights, enshrined in the UDHR and in legally binding international treaties, can be dismissed as only suggestions of desirable and unenforceable goals, then they are not in effect human rights at all. And if they *are*, then civil and political rights can likewise be diminished to mere goals—as indeed they have been.

The early 1950s were a time of strong domestic opposition not only to the idea of economic and social rights, but to self-executing international human rights law in general. Senator John Bricker of Ohio, a fierce opponent of centralized government, authored the "Bricker amendment" of 1953, which would have extracted a pledge from the Eisenhower administration against signing any human rights treaties. The measure failed in the U.S. Senate by one vote. The Eisenhower administration veered away from support for the International Covenant on Civil and Political Rights (ICCPR), but "expressed no special animus toward the covenant that dealt with ESCR."[68]

Today the American Bar Association actively promotes human rights inflation in the form of new but obviously duplicative human rights treaties, such as the one to protect the rights of the elderly. But in the 1950s, the head of the ABA viewed human rights as essentially part of a Communist plot against the American system. "Economic and social rights" were a recipe for central planning and the end of free enterprise, with the goal of global socialism.[69] William Fleming wrote in the *ABA Journal* that the inclusion of economic and social rights in the Universal Declaration manifested the "heavy imprint of Eastern philosophy." He regarded Part III of the declaration, listing economic and social rights, as "nothing else but the perfect embodiment of the unadulterated welfare state and unmitigated socialism." Indeed, he foresaw the danger that the growth of economic and social rights would lead to "the establishment of global economic planning by the United Nations."[70]

For most of the Cold War, economic and social rights were defensively and deviously promoted by the Soviet Union, and American officials attached caveats to their legitimacy in that connection. Human rights issues were seen through the lens of geopolitical and ideological disputes, so economic and social rights were generally opposed not on the basis of their inconsistency with universal natural rights, but rather because they were being promoted by a totalitarian state and used as ideological weapons. Yet in the 1960s, officials in the Johnson administration assisted in the drafting of the ICESCR, voted for its adoption by the UN General Assembly, and also urged the inclusion of economic and social rights in the Convention on the Elimination of All Forms of Racial Discrimination.[71]

America's wobbly position on economic and social rights has been a bipartisan affair: In negotiations leading up to the signing of the Helsinki Accords in 1975, diplomats in Republican administrations supported the inclusion of economic and social rights among those the participating states pledged to uphold. The accords committed the participating states to "promote and encourage the effective exercise of civil, political, economic, social, cultural and other rights and freedoms all of which derive from the inherent dignity of the human person and are essential for his free and full development."

In 1977, President Jimmy Carter signed the International Covenant on Economic, Social and Cultural Rights. Yet administration officials gave only halfhearted support to its ratification, promoting it as something less than a legally binding treaty and not actually about human rights—thus leaving the impression of having made only a symbolic gesture, or of promising noncompliance, in order to assuage anxieties in the U.S. Congress. One of Carter's own speechwriters balked at use of the term "economic and social rights," complaining that if the definition of human rights "ever gets so broad that it also includes Milk for Hottentots, its usefulness will be lost." He recognized that "the temptation is strong to define one's pet project as a human right so that the president will appear to be endorsing it, but let's keep human rights to mean human rights, and find another label for economic and social progress."[72]

The question of ratification failed to engage a very wide range of actors or commentators. One witness opposing the treaty, from the Federalist Society, said that economic and social rights were "largely the historical product of Marxist ideology espoused by the Soviet bloc, coupled with the non-Communist world's postwar infatuation with various forms of democratic socialism." While the goals of the ICESCR might be worthy, it was mostly "a document of collectivist inspiration, alien in spirit and philosophy to the principles of a free economy."[73] But opponents generally stressed the danger of higher taxes rather than incompatibility with constitutional principles. In a submission to Congress, the conservative activist Phyllis Schlafly wrote that Article 2 of the ICESCR "could mean that the United States is making a legally binding commitment to legislate unlimited taxes on ourselves in order to support every other country in the world."[74] Most of the testimony, however, favored ratification.

Nevertheless, the ratification process has gone essentially nowhere since the Carter administration.[75] In 1992, the former president claimed that opponents of ratification "believe governments have no obligation to safeguard the rights of their citizens to jobs, education, housing, and an adequate standard of living."[76] Carter in effect smeared anyone upholding the natural rights principles of the Constitution as being indifferent to social problems, suggesting that one cannot be in favor of welfare benefits without regarding them as human rights.

Natural Rights–Based U.S. Human Rights Approaches. Until the 1980s, reservations about economic and social rights among American foreign policy analysts and government representatives were almost completely of a political or technical nature. In the 1950s, some conservatives saw economic and social rights as communism coming in by the back door, while others were primarily concerned that such rights were not justiciable. Few spoke of their inconsistency with the natural rights philosophy that underpins the protection of human rights in the United States.

This changed with the election of Ronald Reagan. President Reagan signaled a new direction in nominating Ernest Lefever to be the assistant secretary of state for human rights and humanitarian affairs. Lefever had founded the Ethics and Public Policy Center, an institution that announced its devotion to defending, inter alia, "the inherent dignity of the human person, individual freedom and responsibility." When Lefever was rejected by the Senate Foreign Relations Committee, Reagan nominated Elliott Abrams for the post.

The Reagan administration's human rights policies have been widely criticized by partisan and human rights organizations; they are judged as being inconsistent and too protective of authoritarian regimes, and belittled as anticommunism in camouflage.[77] The policy was indeed inconsistent, but the same can be said of every U.S. administration's human rights policies since World War II. Civil society is obligated to be consistent and objective in human rights assessments, but governments, being responsible for policies and actions, inevitably weigh other concerns—including traditional alliances, security and economic advantage—against immediate human rights concerns.

The extraordinary feature of President Reagan's policy was its references to natural rights, and in consequence its firm philosophical rejection of economic and social human rights. Reagan linked the defense of natural rights to America's tense military and ideological competition with the Soviet Union. In a confidential 1981 memorandum made public by the *New York Times*, two leading Reagan officials, in recommending Abrams for the human rights portfolio, said that human rights must be the core of American foreign policy.[78] The policy needed to express the principle of freedom as America's Founders had understood it, and back it up with force, in contrast to President Carter's moralistic rhetoric accompanied by appeasement that put Americans' freedom, and that of other peoples, at risk. The way to mobilize the American people to support a hard line against the Soviet Union's aggression was to show that such a policy was, at heart, a defense of America's founding principle of individual freedom. Apathy and weakness resulted from moral relativism and moral equivalence, which encouraged the perception that there was no fundamental difference between communism and the liberal democracy of the West.

Then the authors of the memo touched on the idea of human rights itself, suggesting that "we should move away from 'human rights' as a term, and begin to speak of 'individual rights,' 'political rights' and 'civil liberties.'"[79] The meaning of human rights, as globally institutionalized, was no longer consistent with the concept of natural rights embodied in the Bill of Rights, essentially deriving from the philosophy of John Locke. Reagan's policies, the memo stressed, should reflect the idea of human rights espoused by the Founders, not the one developed in the United Nations. Alexander Hague, the secretary of state, confirmed that "concerns about liberty" would be at the foundation of U.S. foreign policy, not an "add on."[80]

Reagan's has been the only American administration to deal directly with the definition and meaning of human rights in a comprehensive way, referring not only to international law but also to the concept's underlying moral philosophy. It has been the only administration to encourage (sometimes force) those dealing with international human rights issues to respect the principles of classical liberalism. The 1983 State Department report on human rights around the world made reference to economic and social rights, but also included a text by Elliott Abrams that stated in clear terms how the administration viewed human rights. Abrams' introduction said: "The intention of the originators of human rights...seems to have been to select from the vast range of things that men need or want, certain crucial things that they are entitled to by their very nature—human rights—which, when fulfilled, will create the preconditions for the satisfaction of other needs." It referred to a "lack of consensus on these rights." Leaders tended to prefer duties over rights, to "broaden the concept of human rights to include the duty to authority." Economic and social rights were used as a "justification of repression." But societies that respected human rights were more likely to develop economically. The eradication of poverty can provide "a crucial foundation for democratic political institutions." Abrams wrote that "the rights no government can violate should not be watered down to the status of rights that governments should do their best to secure."[81]

A Reagan State Department official, Paula Dobriansky, clarified in 1988 that the administration considered it a "myth" that economic and social rights were actual human rights, and said that there had been "efforts to obfuscate traditional civil and political rights with 'economic and social rights.'"[82] In response, and apparently attempting sarcasm, the prominent linguist and political commentator Noam Chomsky wrote that Dobriansky "denounced the efforts to obfuscate human rights discourse by introducing these spurious rights—which are entrenched in the [Universal Declaration of Human Rights]."[83]

The Reagan administration thus broke free from the American postwar tradition of patronizing economic and social rights in international forums and attempting to swallow the UN's expansive human rights package while remaining true to American principles. In 1986, the U.S. representative to the Conference on Security and Cooperation in Europe (CSCE) said the United States would not focus on the obligation of the participating states to respect economic and social rights, "because we do not believe they concern matters of basic human rights. Rather these 'quality of life' issues concern human goals and aspirations."[84] But even under the Reagan administration there was ambivalence on the subject. At a CSCE meeting in January 1989, the United States agreed to an "effective exercise" of economic, social and cultural rights, and pledged to consider ratification of the economic and social rights treaty.[85]

President Reagan demonstrated the reality of individual human rights by highlighting the personal situation of victims of human rights violations. He repeatedly hosted dissident human rights campaigners, such as Ludmilla Alexeyeva, demonstrating solidarity with individuals and making human rights a vivid, existential issue, and he involved himself in individual human rights cases. In a meeting with the Soviet leader Leonid Brezhnev in the early years of the administration, for example, Reagan pressed him to grant exit visas for persecuted Jehovah's Witnesses.[86]

A Return to Ambivalence. Following Reagan's two presidential terms, the United States slid back into its habitual and contradictory posture concerning economic and social rights, and its neglect of the foundations of human rights. Unlike its predecessor, the administration of George H. W. Bush did not vociferously contest the existence of economic and social rights; the collapse of Communist regimes by itself demonstrated the corruption of the Soviet approach to human rights. The administration of Bill Clinton gave verbal support to economic and social rights being actual human rights. But according to Amnesty International, while Clinton "did not deny the nature of these rights," the administration "did not find it politically expedient to engage in a battle with Congress over the Covenant."[87] In a go-along to get-along mode at the World Conference, the United States was nevertheless not a prominent force in promoting the official expansion of human rights, or in establishing the "indivisibility of human rights" as the principle giving final legitimation to economic and social rights. By the same token, as far as the record indicates, neither did the United States do anything at all to question or curb the excesses of the Vienna World Conference on Human Rights. Again the United States acquiesced to these developments, blending into the global community in its blind embrace of a new human rights concept in which there was no boundary between human rights and social policy, and where UN officials insisted that there were no essential differences between vague entitlements like "high quality food" and the right to religious freedom. Natural rights had vanished, or been expelled, from the international human rights scene, and the United States, the only country founded upon natural rights, was silent.

In 1998, Ambassador George Moose, who served as the U.S. permanent representative to the UN in Geneva, went far beyond acquiescence, stating that

> the United States supports the whole principle of economic, social, and cultural rights. It's an integral part of the Universal Declaration of Human Rights. We supported the provisions on economic and social and cultural rights of the Vienna Declaration, as well as the provisions in that declaration regarding the right to development. We believe strongly that economic and social and cultural development is a fundamental part of creating international peace and stability.[88]

Under the leadership of George W. Bush, the government adopted no policy statements on the problem of economic and social rights. His foreign policy was influenced to some degree by a number of intellectuals opposed to historicism and relativism. Numerous investigative journalists and authors have tried to reveal the workings of a "Straussian" cabal—followers of the natural rights philosopher Leo Strauss—within the government.[89] But approaches to human rights have not been cited as evidence of such influence.

The Bush administration, obviously, aroused harsh criticism from human rights organizations, and in fact a number of basic human rights were compromised in the campaign against terrorists (or "war against terrorism"). The International Helsinki Federation for Human Rights, under my direction, stated in a 2006 briefing paper that after September 11, 2001, the United States had "sought to circumvent its international obligations with respect to torture and ill-treatment in the interrogation and treatment of terrorist suspects, thereby establishing a problematic precedent for other, less democratic states."[90] We reiterated those concerns in numerous other statements, and also opposed the use of military courts for terror suspects on rule-of-law grounds.

But my concern here is to try to shed light on how various American administrations *understood* human rights. Bush spoke vividly and often about promoting freedom, characterizing the terrorist attacks of 2001 as attacks not only on Americans, but on freedom itself. He used moral language: terrorists were "evil," or "evildoers," and evil needed to be clearly identified and fought. Like Reagan, Bush associated himself with human rights dissidents from oppressive societies, and with victims.

Yet the Bush administration had no "clear and comprehensive policy" on human rights.[91] Its approach to economic and social rights was consistent with the ambivalence of other post–World War II administrations, with the exception of Reagan's. In basic outline: Economic and social rights were not rights in the same way as civil and political rights, but were "aspirational" and unenforceable. Civil and political rights were priorities, and implementing those rights was the way to achieve economic and social rights. For example, Marc Leland, the U.S. delegate to the UN Human Rights Commission, noted that "There is no doubt that societies that respect civil and political rights, practice democracy, and respect the rule of law can do a better job of allowing individuals to fully realize their economic, social, and cultural rights."[92] Prosperity would allow the realization of economic and social rights, and the key to prosperity was political and economic freedom. The global infatuation with economic and social rights was thus, in a sense, exploited to promote a "Freedom Agenda." But identifying freedom as the key to realizing economic and social rights is to attach a goal to the obligation to respect human rights, and it expresses a form of utilitarianism.

In 2004, the Bush administration sought to insert a "generic preambular paragraph" in UN Human Rights Commission resolutions dealing with economic and social rights. It would have clarified that sovereign states had different approaches to "realizing the achievement of economic, social and cultural rights and objectives," and that such programs needed to be consistent with particular legal and administrative systems.[93]

Bush appointees thus did not challenge the idea of economic and social rights, raising only technical caveats. What is more, they defended U.S. welfare policies as fulfilling what were considered obligations with respect to economic and social rights. In 2003, a statement before the Human Rights Commission gave assurances that the United States was "committed to providing the conditions for individuals to achieve economic, social and cultural well-being, both at home and abroad."

Philip Alston found that the U.S. government had given "selective," "superficial" and "rhetorical" support to economic and social rights. He recommended that a new administration "revert to a policy that was more or less accepted by a succession of American administrations from Truman through Carter." The conflicted and ambiguous approach to economic and social rights has aroused confusion and criticism, for it suggests a faltering commitment to the interpretation of human rights that is at the core of the American political system. Against this background, some viewed the Bush administration's "Freedom Agenda" as a renewal of human rights exceptionalism. For example, Charles Kesler effused that President Bush did "more to revive the language of natural rights democracy—the 18th century vernacular of American politics—than any Republican President since Abraham Lincoln."[94] Given the overall retreat from natural rights, this is not a strong claim. The uncompromising defense of freedom and the desire to promote and support it are to be admired, yet the Bush administration's approach to human rights displayed a conventional ambivalence about rights that are not rights, if not a neglect of the moral framework of America's own, exceptional human rights principles.

A Human Rights Policy Detached from Natural Rights

The American approach to human rights moved sharply toward the global center under the resurgent progressivism that characterized the administration of Barack Obama. This trend would surely have continued had Hillary

Clinton won the presidency, and the trajectory seems unclear under the Trump administration.

Natural rights has become a marginal idea, living on the periphery of American political consciousness, with little space to flourish and few resources to sustain it. Whenever it pushes through the wall of conformism that shields mainstream human rights approaches, it is quickly beaten down, and its triumphalist critics face little if any intellectual liability. It is generally greeted with sneers, or dressed in scare-quotes. When Clarence Thomas underwent scrutiny as a nominee to the Supreme Court, his orientation to natural law aroused alarm and was considered to put his qualification for the Court in question. Here is what Professor Laurence Tribe of Harvard Law School wrote on the issue in the *New York Times*:

> Clarence Thomas, judging from his speeches and scholarly writings, seems...to believe judges should enforce the Founders' natural law philosophy—the inalienable rights "given man by his Creator"—which he maintains is revealed most completely in the Declaration of Independence. He is the first Supreme Court nominee in 50 years to maintain that natural law should be readily consulted in constitutional interpretation.... Before the Senate decides whether to confirm Judge Thomas, they should explore the implications of his views about natural law as the lodestar of constitutional interpretation.[95]

In the human rights community itself, one can find virtually no references to natural rights. It is virtually an unknown term among human rights activists; it is not ever raised in the defense of basic freedoms, not used as a measuring stick to evaluate developments in international human rights jurisprudence or institutional strategies. In about twenty-five years of human rights activism, the only mention I have heard of natural rights has been by a few Christian advocates of religious freedom, and by myself (in recent years). The human rights community has been virtually occupied by the left and is losing its essential political neutrality. And although natural rights is in fact a politically neutral concept, it has been wrongly characterized as an ideology of the right. Hadley Arkes, analyzing the "drift from natural rights," observed that while natural rights is now considered an ideology, something arbitrary and political, the nonexistence of natural law is thought to be an absolute truth.[96] Arkes called the denial of the ability to know moral truths a form of modern orthodoxy.

Serious debate about the status of natural rights would be welcome, because it would mean that the idea of natural rights was still alive. Even a logical refutation and clear rejection of natural rights would be welcome, because it would mean that a thinking person had examined the idea and perhaps been intellectually enlarged in doing so. The idea of natural rights will leave its impression, and will sow doubt concerning the sterile, ossified positivism that grips human rights today.

Debate about America's natural rights exceptionalism has virtually died out, much as debate about the legitimacy of economic and social rights faded away after the UN human rights establishment officially declared the question closed in 1993. The views of Americans have merged into the contradictory and intellectually unstable global mean, and the predominant stance toward natural rights, among the few aware of the concept, is agnosticism. According to Judge Diarmuid O'Scannlain,

> Too few of us take seriously the notion of natural rights, that is, of objective rights held by all humans as a matter of moral principle. This is why, when people today refer to the freedoms of speech and of religion, they will speak of "the rights we have through the First Amendment," as if their existence depended on the positive law.[97]

O'Scannlain pointed out that natural law is currently dismissed "from both sides": "To the left, it is an invention of mystics and religious conservatives. To the right, it is a dangerous invitation for judges to impose their own sense of justice on the country."[98] This bipartisan skepticism is proof that natural rights are not ideological. Likewise, authentic international human rights are regularly attacked by both leftists and rightists, but in fact they are politically neutral in protecting the freedom of the individual. Authentic human rights do not support ideologies, but create the conditions under which political actors can operate on a level playing field.

The progressive political establishment that governed the United States from 2009 to 2017, like the mainline human rights community, followed the tactic deployed by Franklin Roosevelt concerning the idea of natural rights, the core of the political philosophy that informed the Constitution. It was explicitly dismissed only in private, while in public it is simply bypassed. Rights are considered to have no objective existence; they are expressions of our society and culture, and they change with the times. In this view, the rights honored in the Bill of Rights have no reality apart from being executed in the positive laws of legislatures and the government. Without government, rights do not exist. This was the position used to defend the institution of slavery. But Jefferson and the American Founders saw it differently; they thought of the government as "securing" rights that are natural to all humans.[99]

Progressive politicians and human rights scholars like Philip Alston—ignoring the fact that the United States was the first country in history to accept the universality of human rights, and that it had the world's first human rights policy—claim that the natural rights exceptionalism of the United States has somehow "distorted" the concept of human rights. This perspective seems to have animated U.S. human rights policy under the Obama administration. As secretary of state, Hillary Clinton announced a clear break from the natural rights tradition centered on freedom, and a less ambivalent posture on economic and social rights. In August 2009, Secretary Clinton said it was "important to look at human rights more broadly than it has been defined. Human rights are also the right to a good job and shelter over your head and a chance to send your kids to school and get health care when your wife is pregnant. It's a much broader agenda. Too often it has gotten narrowed to our detriment." She referred to needs in the areas of food, health care and education, and she said the administration's "21st-century human rights agenda" would be to support democracy and foster development.[100]

Speaking to delegates at the Organization of American States, Clinton deflected a question about political prisoners in Cuba by mentioning concerns about the economic and social rights of Latin Americans. She said the United States would work with all countries to promote welfare: "We believe that lifting people out of poverty in our hemisphere, narrowing the intolerable income gap that exists between the rich and the poor in our hemisphere, working for greater social inclusion, improved education and health care—these are our goals."[101] No decent person would deny the worth of such goals, but Clinton substituted them for human rights and implied they had priority.

Secretary Clinton infuriated those concerned about repression in China when, just prior to her first trip to China in 2009, she told journalists that regarding issues for discussion, human rights "can't interfere with the global economic crisis, the global climate change crisis and the security crisis."[102] There is virtually no free press, freedom of speech, free elections, freedom of association, nor any real political and civil rights in China. According to Chinese human rights activists—operating from abroad, needless to say—

Clinton's statement was "ostentatiously" highlighted on the front pages of China's state-controlled newspapers throughout the country, as a demonstration that China's repressive policies, and their justification as necessary for economic growth, wouldn't be challenged by powerful America.[103] Indeed, the statement was a boon not only to the Chinese Communist Party, but to the rulers of all illiberal states who want economic development without challenges to their own authority, and who rely on an inflated definition of human rights to deflect criticism of their repressive measures.

America's pushback against its natural rights foundations could also be seen in the context of relations with Cuba. Together with Jan Ter Laak, who was a Dutch Catholic human rights campaigner, and Maria Luisa Bascur, a colleague of mine from the International Helsinki Federation for Human Rights (IHF), I interviewed numerous persecuted human rights dissidents there in 2006, including Oswaldo Payá, who was killed in 2012 when his car was run off the road in what appears to have been an assassination. I have had close contact with people of many oppressive societies, but a fact-finding mission in Cuba stands out in my memory. It was without doubt the most spiritually depressed society I have ever seen. The decay of buildings in Havana reminds me of descriptions of how a society would look decades after an EMP attack. Indeed, communism killed the energy in Cuba.

During President Obama's historic visit to Cuba in 2016, Raul Castro attacked America's human rights record. Castro claimed that while Cuba was in compliance with international human rights standards, the United States violated human rights with respect to welfare policies. Obama replied, "President Castro, I think, has pointed out that in his view making sure that everybody is getting a decent education or health care, has basic security in old age, that those things are human rights as well. I personally would not disagree with him."[104] Obama missed an opportunity, indeed an obligation, to explain and defend the exceptional American idea of human rights as distinct from economic entitlements. Instead, Obama said he "personally" held an interpretation of human rights at variance with the philosophy of the U.S. Constitution.

His words were bad news for those who defend human rights as natural rights to basic freedoms, and who look to America for support and as an example of the success of freedom. What is more, Cuba has arguably done more than any other nation to subvert respect for authentic human rights in the United Nations. With his response, Obama indirectly but clearly voiced tolerance for Cuba's deeply destructive role in the shaping of international human rights. Cuba has consistently defended the world's worst human rights abusers, like North Korea, from criticism in international forums, claiming that such criticism is "political" and "biased." In fact, Cuba is the most vocal member of the United Nations in trying to weaken the UN's instruments for investigating grave human rights violations and for putting pressure on governments to reform; it favors anodyne "thematic" issues instead. Cuba has been a leader in proposing bogus human rights mandates in the UN Human Rights Council, such as the "independent expert" on the "Promotion of a Democratic and Equitable International Order," which is nothing but a platform for ideological attacks on free societies and free enterprise.[105]

In his speech in Cuba, Obama also suggested a moral equivalence between the American Revolution and Fidel Castro's Communist takeover, events that were motivated by profoundly different principles.[106] Obama's betrayal of the idea of natural rights, and America's own natural rights tradition, was also a betrayal of Cuban human rights campaigners, and of people around the world living under dictators who exploit the conflation of human rights and welfare rights in order to defend oppression. In fact, twenty months after Obama decided to normalize relations with Cuba and ease restrictions on trade and travel, independent monitors found that civil liberties on the island deteriorated still further.[107] What is more, in the process of normalizing relations with Cuba, the Obama administration failed to uphold a distinction between sanctions relief for ordinary citizens and for regime officials. According to the activist Mauricio Claver-Carone, the result is that "neighborhood repressors," members of the "puppet legislature," secret police and intelligence officials can "enjoy unlimited remittances, gift parcels, U-turn banking transactions, communication devices and even employ U.S.-based internet-related services."[108]

The Obama administration's human rights legacy will be a marginalizing of natural rights in order to accommodate the "sensitivities of the world community."[109] It was a policy of bowing to cultural relativism and accepting restrictions on basic freedoms, like the freedom of expression; a policy in which America would be only another state in the world, following along a path toward global communitarianism rather than leading the world toward liberty. International human rights law and regulations, centering largely on economic and social rights, would be "downloaded" into U.S. law in the course of a "transnational legal process," and would supersede the natural rights framework of the Constitution and the clear freedoms protected by the Bill of Rights.[110]

Human rights were not a priority for the Obama administration, but it is clear that President Obama and his administration were in accord with the view, now shared by most human rights institutions of the international community, that political rights cannot be realized if citizens are not properly cared for in a material sense; that effective citizenship is impossible without economic and social rights. Moreover, basic freedoms are negotiable, since freedom is meant to deliver other goods, such as tolerance and security.

Brett Schaefer, an advocate of UN reform, observed that the "lion's share" of Obama's UN General Assembly speech in 2012 "was dedicated to condemning intolerance, beginning with a lengthy condemnation of a YouTube video, and continuing with repeated platitudes about a more inclusive world." The speech gave "unwarranted credence to restrictions on freedom of speech by explicitly acknowledging different nations have differing definitions of such rights." Schaefer noted that "President Obama spent less time defending free speech than he did outlining a vague vision for a world with tolerance and diversity as its key ideals."[111] In fact, the language was similar to what could be heard in Socialist Scholars Conferences in the 1980s, such as the ones that Obama attended. The socialist agenda has re-emerged in the language of human rights.[112]

America's Human Rights Self-Presentation to the UN under Obama. The U.S. Department of State has demonstrated a retreat from America's natural rights exceptionalism in its submissions to the UN Universal Periodic Review (UPR) process. Documents submitted have classified the United States' welfare policies as human rights protections, highlighting "social benefits provided by law," "federal housing assistance programs" and the Affordable Care Act as examples of commitment to human rights.[113]

The 2010 UPR submission indicated that the United States was ready to conform to global trends regarding the definition of human rights. Consistent with reigning UN human rights dogma, the document treated the question of equality not in terms of opportunity but of result, or "substantive equality," placing the government in the role of ensuring that "conditions" for enjoying human rights are met. The submission strongly implied that the U.S. government was on a path toward enlarging its interventions in the economy and social institutions in order to strengthen protections of economic and social rights. The document focused largely on collective rights: of individuals with disabilities, women, minorities, LGBT people, Muslims, Arabs, South Asians,

Native Americans. The means to protect members of these groups are generally discussed as targeted interventions by positive law, rather than more respect for the individual liberties of all.

In language at times both preening and obsequious, the submission acknowledges that constitutional freedoms have allowed America to legislate social justice:

> Throughout our history, our citizens have used the freedoms provided in the Constitution as a foundation upon which to advocate for changes that would create a more just society. The Constitution provided the means for its own amelioration and revision: its glaring original flaw of tolerating slavery, as well as denying the vote to women, have both been corrected through constitutional reform, judicial review and our democratic processes. Human rights—including the freedoms of speech, association, and religion—have empowered our people to be the engine of our progress.[114]

Progressive politicians and citizens have, through law, remedied the insufficient constitutional rights framework. Citing Franklin Roosevelt's "Four Freedoms," the submission said:

> On subjects such as "freedom from want," the United States has focused on democratic solutions and civil society initiatives while the U.S. courts have defined our federal constitutional obligations narrowly and primarily by focusing on procedural rights to due process and equal protection of the law. But as a matter of public policy, our citizens have taken action through their elected representatives to help create a society in which prosperity is shared, including social benefits provided by law, so that all citizens can live what Roosevelt called "a healthy peacetime life."[115]

It is made clear that constitutional rights are not enough:

> [T]his year saw the passage of major legislation that will greatly expand the number of Americans who have health insurance. In every case, the creation of these programs has reflected a popular sense that the society in which we want to live is one in which each person has the opportunity to live a full and fulfilling life. That begins, but does not end, with the exercise of their human rights.[116]

The submission contained passages that are transparently partisan advertisements for the administration's political program of economic and social rights, addressing issues that have little to do with constitutional human rights. For example, it reported that "President Obama signed major financial reform legislation in 2010 that includes a new consumer protection bureau, among other provisions," in the context of a tendentious discussion of the causes and response to the recession in 2008. "The recession in the United States," the report stated, "was fueled largely by a housing crisis, which coincided with some discriminatory lending practices." Those practices, the report strongly implies, resulted in a market where "fewer than half of African-American and Hispanic families own homes while three quarters of white families do." As proof of the administration's eagerness to solve the problem, the report cites its "major financial reform legislation."[117]

As evidence of conforming to human rights standards, the submission cited a law that "reduces sentencing disparities between powder cocaine and crack cocaine offenses, capping a long effort—one discussed at our UPR consultations—that arose out of the fact that those convicted of crack cocaine offenses are more likely to be members of a racial minority." The submission also cited as a human rights problem in the United States that "Asian-American men suffer from stomach cancer 114 percent more often than non-Hispanic white men."[118]

According to Roger Pilon, a legal philosopher and former Reagan administration official, "the report reads like a politically correct campaign brochure, touting everything from stimulus spending to Obamacare as promoting human rights, which renders the idea boundless and therefore meaningless." The government's submission "implicitly sanctioned the conflation of real and supposed rights."[119]

Proactive government interventions to address social problems move the United States toward conformity with the international community's politicized approach to human rights. When numerous UN members questioned the U.S. delegation about failure to ratify the ICESCR, the response was that the United States was progressively honoring those rights via social policy:

> Regarding questions related to economic, social and cultural rights, what Franklin Roosevelt described as "freedom from want," the United States has focused on democratic solutions and civil society initiatives while

courts have defined constitutional obligations primarily by focusing on procedural rights to due process and equal protection of the law. As a matter of broader public policy, the United States is committed to help create a society in which prosperity is shared, including social benefits provided by law.[120]

Furthermore, "The United States is committed to working to pursue laws and policies that will build an economy and society that lifts up all Americans.... In 2010, President Obama signed into law the Affordable Care Act, which is projected to expand health insurance to 32 million Americans who would otherwise lack coverage."[121] But Amnesty International observed that health care was "still not recognized as a universal human right."[122]

The submission correctly affirmed that the United States had provided a social safety net for its citizens, and had done so through democratic processes. Where it went wrong was in suggesting that this has been America's way of implementing economic and social *rights*, guided by an international standard. The State Department seemed to imply that the difference between the international system of economic and social rights and the American constitutional system was only a technical detail.

The State Department was strongly pushed by American and international civil society groups to endorse the concept of economic and social rights, and to claim that American social policy legislation is consistent with those rights. Among these groups, the U.S. Human Rights Network (USHRN) shows up prominently in the UPR documentation of "stakeholder" concerns, and its report noted that "around 30% of the population lacks an adequate income to meet basic needs."[123] The USHRN is not a nonpartisan human rights organization, but a political lobby. Its putative mandate is "human rights advocacy and organizing" to "prioritize the struggles of the poor and most marginalized groups in society." The group's founding executive director, Ajamu Baraka, is a political organizer on the radical left who ran for vice president of the United States on the Green Party ticket. There is clearly no line between politics and human rights in his outlook. In serious human rights organizations like the Helsinki Committee in Poland, members are excluded if they participate in political activities.

America's Retreat from Defending Human Rights Abroad. The effort to detach human rights from natural rights, leaving them with no firm moral basis, has sucked the life out of U.S. human rights policies. It has been a recipe for ambiguity and apathy. Here I am referring mainly to the way President Obama approached human rights violations, not the bureaucracy.

The U.S. Department of State is largely an institution on autopilot, immune from changes in ideology at the top of the executive branch. It is a big, old ship, sailing on established routes. Human rights promotion and defense is a matter of bureaucratic procedure. Regardless of who has been elected president, and even who has been appointed secretary of state, human rights around the world are monitored, and ambassadors and representatives in international forums call out many offenders. Human rights defenders are listened to, and appeals are made for prisoners of conscience. In my experience, based on State Department traditions, no other country shows more respect for human rights advocates.

At the same time, the Obama administration's human rights policy, like its foreign policy in general, was to a large extent centrally managed by the presidential staff. And although the State Department bureaucracy pushed forward with actions in defense of human rights, it became clear that human rights was not an administration priority, and that the government was often prepared to look the other way as it sought to improve relations with rights-violating states. Negligence toward genuine human rights and a politicized view of human rights at the top levels of the government seeped down into the bureaucracy, and into how the international community perceives the United States.

In the early years of the first Obama administration, a spate of newspaper articles raised alarm about the government's neglect of human rights. It seemed to come as a shock to many that the new government was indifferent to human rights, and that the president hardly ever used the phrase. The concerns aroused a form of cognitive dissonance in the human rights community, which had fought the torture and surveillance policies of the Bush administration and enthusiastically supported Obama's election.

The articles were of diverse authorship from an ideological perspective. For example, Joshua Kurlantzick of the Council on Foreign Relations (CFR), citing compromises on human rights, demanded that President Obama "be more aggressive on human rights."[124] Elliott Abrams characterized the human rights policy articulated by Secretary Clinton as a "Soviet bromide" and charged that the Obama administration "does not care" about human rights.[125] In the *New York Daily News*, Rabbi Abraham Cooper and Harold Brackman asked,

"Obama, what about human rights?"[126] The *Jerusalem Post* editorialist Caroline Glick wrote that Obama was "wavering" on support for human rights in China, Iran, Myanmar, Saudi Arabia, Cuba, North Korea, Iraq, Afghanistan, Syria, Russia, Sudan, Darfur and Sri Lanka. Pressure had been relaxed on all of these abusive states. Glick claimed that

> the Obama administration has systematically taken human rights and democracy promotion off America's agenda. In their place, it has advocated "improving America's image," multilateralism and a moral relativism that either sees no distinction between dictators and their victims or deems the distinctions immaterial to the advancement of US interests.[127]

Human rights groups saw the Obama administration equivocating on human rights. Jennifer Windsor, the director of Freedom House, said:

> There has not been sufficient attention paid within this administration on how to counter the major challenges to human rights that we face today. We see authoritarian regimes like China, Iran and Egypt and others getting granted opportunities for dialogue and engagement, but it's not clear from the outside how human rights concerns will be addressed in that engagement.[128]

Another leading American human rights advocate, Kenneth Roth, executive director of Human Rights Watch, wrote about "Obama's hesitant embrace of human rights."[129]

A *Washington Post* article said the United States faced "doubts about leadership on human rights."[130] A columnist for the *Post*, Jackson Diehl, wrote that "Obama's national security strategy is light on the human rights agenda."[131] In the *Wall Street Journal*, Bret Stephens asked, "Does Obama believe in human rights?" He said it appeared that human rights "interfered" with President Obama's campaign against climate change.[132] The critiques continued to dribble out. In 2012, Jimmy Carter called the administration's domestic and international human rights record "cruel and unusual," claiming that "the United States is abandoning its role as the global champion of human rights." Carter cited, inter alia, violations of international human rights standards protecting the right to freedom of expression and the right to be presumed innocent until proven guilty in antiterrorism legislation, and an "arbitrary rule that any man killed by drones is declared an enemy terrorist."[133]

The Obama administration's timidity and temporizing on human rights impressed itself upon me during my work with the International Campaign for Human Rights in Iran, a group I helped establish in 2008. (It is now named the International Center for Human Rights in Iran.) The Iranian presidential election on June 12, 2009, with its clearly fabricated results, set off massive peaceful demonstrations, which were generally not partisan and not calling for "regime change," but simply Iranians united in demanding legality and respect for human rights. The government brutally repressed the demonstrators, killing hundreds on the streets and imprisoning thousands, many of whom were tortured. President Obama was extremely slow to denounce the repression and show solidarity with the Iranian people. According to Jay Solomon, an investigative reporter, Obama's main objective was to open a dialogue with Iran's leading clerics.[134] Some dissidents in Iran also warned against gestures that would make them look like puppets of the United States, and Obama's reluctance may have been justified on that account, but it appears that better relations with the Iranian regime trumped human rights.

Later, our organization made a top priority of securing American support for the establishment of a United Nations special mandate to monitor human rights in Iran, but the U.S. government would not initially support the initiative. State Department officials could not explain the reason, and were clearly frustrated over it; they were obviously being blocked by the White House, and all they could do was blame the divided European Union for not taking the initiative, while European officials in turn blamed a lack of American support. The principle of defending human rights was being subordinated to something else. Eventually a decision was made to support the proposal, which easily became a reality with the United States behind it.

Anne R. Pierce, a political scientist and foreign affairs analyst, tracked the Obama administration's foreign policy in real time and showed in detail how, in a wide range of cases, the government failed to defend individual freedom.[135] Neither President Obama nor Secretary Clinton referred much to human rights, and by Pierce's account they never mentioned individual rights.[136] Obama's use of the word "freedom" was dramatically lower than that of his predecessors, and when he did employ the word it was not in reference to the spread of freedom around the world.[137]

Pierce found that the Obama administration consistently downplayed threats to individual rights in addressing foreign policy challenges. She cites, for example, Obama's "dilatory" lack of pressure on Hosni Mubarak, the former Egyptian ruler, followed by his supplicating outreach to Mohamed Morsi, the Muslim Brotherhood leader—all part of a larger pattern of ingratiating himself to the Muslim world. Obama's intelligence chief called the Muslim Brotherhood a "moderate" and "secular" organization that "eschewed violence" and had no international agenda. Obama courted Turkey's Recep Erdogan, claiming a "bond of trust" with a leader who was trashing the country's secular political norms and who used a coup attempt to decimate the political opposition and civil society. The United States did little to deter aggression in Ukraine; its response was "minimalist" as millions of Ukrainian citizens, including the people of Crimea, were swept into the Russian orbit, where their political freedoms are severely restricted.

According to Pierce, America had "looked the other way" and been "detached and apathetic" while North Korea tightened its grip on its captive, brutalized population and built its nuclear arsenal. Obama's engagement policy played down the regime's totalitarian ideology and human rights atrocities. As noted earlier, the Obama administration also glossed over human rights in its dealings with China, while Secretary Clinton stressed "economic statecraft," de-emphasizing the role of ideas.

To what should we attribute America's sharp shift away from defending human rights? It is clear that President Obama wished to differentiate himself from the policies of George W. Bush, and to improve relations with governments and populations that had become more hostile to the United States because of Bush's policies, as many believe.

From the standpoint of partisan politics, Democratic Party activists are now significantly less likely than Republicans to identify human rights as "very important."[138] There can be no question that the demotion of human rights was part of a "pragmatic" strategy to reduce global conflict. President Obama was clearly wary of the "Freedom Agenda" of the previous administration, which critics painted as an effort to "impose democracy" on other countries, and he regarded global harmony and peace as more important.[139] But Obama was promoting a harmony of *states*, not of their people. He sought solidarity with regimes instead of reaching into repressive states to establish solidarity with their oppressed citizens. He dealt with rulers, not dissidents.

Pierce attributed Obama's unconcern for human rights to his philosophy of cultural relativism, his "moral ambiguity" and neutrality, and a political perspective of "one world socialism." The administration followed a pragmatic policy of seeking unity and peace with other nations in order to achieve broad economic and environmental goals.

The United States was established upon universal principles, on a fixed point of reference, creating a sharp distinction between darkness and light in human rights. But Obama's foreign policy reflected a sense that this Manichean view of human rights was a destructive force in the world, a source of moral imperialism and conflict. His was not a policy driven by attachment to any sense of an objective, transcendent moral order; it was a thoroughly postmodern one, in which the realization of human potential depends on abandoning transcendentals, as Richard Weaver described in *Ideas Have Consequences*. For Obama, human rights had no sacred or transcendent basis; they were temporal and political.

Obama had firmly rejected America's natural rights exceptionalism, the creed that animated America's compulsion to "project its ideas of individual and human rights," as Pierce put it. Lacking a "passion for freedom," he was indifferent to the plight of individuals and willfully neglectful of authentic human rights, while boosting the idea of economic and social rights. Thus he gave force to the progressivism of Franklin D. Roosevelt that was largely responsible for infecting the international human rights system with politics and for eroding the concept of human rights.

CHAPTER 6

A Convergence
against Liberty

America has an imperfect human rights record, like all countries, but America has shown the modern world how natural rights can be the principle of a government of free people, how respect for natural rights can constrain state power and mold it into a guardian of individual rights and civil society. Yet American leaders, either neglecting or disrespecting their country's founding philosophy, stood by while ideology poisoned the international human rights system at its roots, deforming its future development. In this final chapter, I show how a politicized concept of human rights has not only undermined the protection of genuine human or natural rights, but has legitimized and even encouraged the active violation of natural rights. Today's reigning version of human rights is a threat to liberty.

The inclusion of economic and social rights in the Universal Declaration of Human Rights opened human rights up to redefinition. More and more issues have come to be considered human rights issues, and while they are all claimed to be equal and indivisible, these various "human rights" are not all harmonious. In the competition among them, natural rights are being squeezed into a tighter space and are given no priority over, say, economic development goals. UN human rights officials, national leaders and civil society activists have promoted the notion of "intersectionality," a term coined by Kimberlé Crenshaw in 1989. It has come to designate an analytic fad in which many sources of oppression—including race, class, gender, disability, etc.—are claimed to reinforce each other systemically. From this perspective, freedom may be conditioned on a variety of factors in the interest of combating patterns of oppression. Virtually any spontaneous or creative action can be blamed for someone's "oppression," and thus legitimately be repressed.

These tendencies were all promoted by the international community at Vienna in 1993: the emphasis on economic and social rights, on indivisibility, on collective rights; the identification of "non-state" human rights violators; and especially the designation of "tolerance" as a human rights goal. All of these have contributed to turning human rights into a principle of conformism and even a warrant for coercion. Since the end of the Cold War, with the UN's contradictory messaging, human rights has been neutered—drained of its emancipatory moral power, to become an ideology of the status quo, wearing the garb of "stability," "development," "integration" and the like.

Liberal democracies have moved toward the human rights position taken by authoritarian states, backing away from the principle of individual freedom, as they balance natural rights against other human rights claims. The Universal Declaration, in artificially melding the politics of the left with the universalist logic of natural rights, infected Western liberalism with a legal compulsion to conform to a welfare-state model that in essence is a watery neo-Marxism. It covered the globe with a blanket of *political* uniformity, instead of the universality of basic human rights that come from human nature. The principles of the declaration were reinforced at Vienna in 1993 and subsequently pounded into the human rights community with thought-terminating clichés[1] designed to paper over the dissonance between those principles and the logic of freedom in classical human rights.

The international human rights system's entrenchment of Marxian principles has empowered and given legitimacy to authoritarian forms of rule. Chapter 4 above illustrated how such regimes adduce economic and social rights to shield themselves from criticism over violations of basic freedoms. They also actively violate natural rights in the name of ideologies that incorporate parts of the international community's expansive definition of human rights.

Together, these tendencies are converging in a global pincer against individual freedom, powered by a distorted concept of human rights.

The Dynamic of Illiberal Human Rights

The doctrine of the "indivisibility of human rights" has exerted a one-way influence, as we have seen. It has compelled liberal democracies, which respect the "rule based" international system, to comply with a particular politics and implement policies aimed at equalizing citizens. But it has had no corresponding effect in opening up unfree societies. During the Cold War, economic and social rights provided a place for totalitarianism at the moral table of human rights. Today the table is much larger, with room for a wider array of human rights distortions, and more nuanced forms of totalitarianism than what Soviet diplomats trotted out.

Examples are legion. In November 2016, China was re-elected by the UN General Assembly as a member of the Human Rights Council, despite the regime's intensified crackdown on human rights activists and other dissidents. An official source said the endorsement by the General Assembly reflected "the nation's outstanding achievement in human rights protection" and that "both the [Communist] Party and the Chinese government have been committed to economic and social development, people's well-being, social justice and protection of human rights by applying universal principles of human rights." The announcement further stated that "China treats development as a part of human rights and prioritizes right to life and right to development [*sic*], which are not only the basic needs of the developing world, but also their contributions to theories and systems of international human rights." More words followed about China's international cooperation on behalf of the "2030 Agenda for Sustainable Development."[2]

Obviously there are strong currents within China's complex culture that emphasize the individual's obligations to groups, but that is no license to restrict individual freedom. China's justification for tightening political control and negating individual rights is that it comports with traditional Chinese culture. It is an assertion of Chinese exceptionalism. Over the decades, China has often stressed that the "right to development is a part of basic human rights."[3] The "right to development" can generally be taken to entail an obligation on the part of wealthy states to provide development assistance, but it also includes China's right to develop a modern military,[4] and to interpret human rights in its own way. An Asian human rights defender wrote that this "economic model" of human rights often leads to "unfreedoms" and economic and social inequality, where freedoms of people, particularly that of the marginalized groups and the poor are increasingly compromised. There is resurgence in discrimination and the repression of the voices of dissent and democracy in several parts of the region. China, the biggest economy in the world, in many ways indicates the rise of "unfreedoms" in the most evident manner, despite economic development.[5]

China has improved its living standards and welfare rights, while more forcefully and brutally repressing basic freedom, especially the freedom of religion—thus demonstrating that "indivisibility" is a myth. The UN's new secretary general gave encouragement to these trends when he visited China in November 2016. There, Antonio Guterres stated that what was needed, "in a world torn by war, [was] a United Nations able to enhance diplomacy for peace." Also needed, "in a world where so many rights are not respected, [was] to make sure that there is an effective combination in human rights, of the civil and political rights and the economic and social rights in a balanced way."[6] He was mirroring China's routine explanation for denying basic freedoms to her citizens.

This kind of equivocation on basic freedom affects billions of people. Yet more potent threats to liberty in the new global human rights dynamic can be seen in two aggressive statist ideologies: Eurasianism along with its populist offshoots, and political Islam. Both are expansionist and both wield enormous influence in the world today.

"Eurasianism": An Antimodern Challenge to Liberal Human Rights

As a political idea, Eurasianism has commonly stood for a longstanding Russian dream of blending "Eastern" and "Western" cultures and political values.[7] In a sense, Eurasianism is a mirror of the UDHR. It has come into sharper focus with the rule of Vladimir Putin and renewed confrontation between Russia and the Euro-Atlantic political community following Russia's conflict with Georgia in 2008, the annexation of Crimea in 2014 and Russian military involvement in Eastern Ukraine. The term is associated with an ambitious vision in which Russia and other former Soviet states will be ideologically united with European societies by a common determination to govern according to their own national traditions, excluding fundamental principles that are enshrined in the international human rights system, and eschewing the political values of "neoliberal" Atlanticism. A number of opposition political parties in Europe have adopted main elements of the political vision of Eurasia.[8]

Eurasianism thus stands for an "exceptionalism" in human rights, claimed for societies considered to be part of the Russian cultural space, though its outlines are embraced by other societies as well. It is carried largely by leaders of the Russian Federation and allied states, using familiar arguments of cultural relativism to justify a rejection of universal human rights standards. While the human rights component of the Eurasian political idea is generally expressed in a defensive posture against criticisms of human rights practices, it is increasingly also a *positive* doctrine of human rights and freedom. Eurasianism is "antimodern," giving primacy to national traditions and cultural identity and to a conservative Orthodox Christianity, as against a universal obligation to protect individual freedom and civil society on the basis of a common human nature and natural rights.

Eurasianism is known by a number of names: It has been called, among other things, "19th-century Russian imperialism," "neo-czarism," "nationalism," "national socialism," "neo-totalitarianism," "neo-Sovietism," "fascism" and "neofascism." Its human rights doctrine is overtly hostile to individual and natural rights, while emphasizing economic and social rights. Eurasianism was what raised its head at the Moscow meeting in 1993 about the "Red-Brown" movement, to which I referred in the Introduction.

The Eurasian View of Human Rights. At the heart of the Eurasian human rights doctrine is a harsh critique of international human rights, viewed as a product of postmodernism. Few if any references to international legal human rights obligations may be found in explanations of the Eurasian approach to human rights, as if they are of no import whatsoever. Yet the Eurasian view is consistent with several principles that the international community endorsed at the 1993 World Conference.

A primary source for the Eurasian approach to human rights is the Russian Orthodox Church, which in 2008 published its "Basic Teaching on Human Dignity, Freedom and Rights."[9] The document was developed with the assistance of the Russian political philosopher Alexander Dugin. In his book *The Fourth Political Theory*, Dugin proclaims the virtue of a seamless unity between the state and the individual, as opposed to a society in which independent institutions struggle to ensure the freedom of individuals from state control.

Freedom, for Dugin, means freedom from disharmony between one's own ethos and that of society; from the dichotomy of "subject and object." His book reads like a turgid, utopian college term paper from the 1970s. Yet Dugin has emerged as the primary intellectual architect of Eurasianism and a significant influence on President Vladimir Putin and the Russian political and religious elite. And his admirers include a number of rising political leaders and other citizens in Europe and the United States.[10]

According to the Basic Teaching, it is legitimate for the state to limit the freedom of expression, since "public statements and declarations should not further the propagation of sin or generate strife and disorder in society," an argument that mixes a political rationale with religious and moral reasons for restricting speech. The document says, "It is especially dangerous to insult religious and national feelings, to distort information about the life of particular religious communities, nations, social groups and personalities," and that blasphemy "shall not be justified by the rights of the artist, writer, or journalist."

The Basic Teaching praises citizen participation in government as long as it is supportive of the government. It cautions that "the use of political and civil rights should not lead to divisions and enmity." The document refers to an "Orthodox tradition of conciliarity," which "implies the preservation of social unity on the basis of intransient moral values. The Church calls upon people to restrain their egoistic desires for the sake of the common good." Following on this theme of unity, in a section on "Collective Rights," the document says, "The rights of an individual should not be destructive for the unique way of life and traditions of the family and for various religious, national and social communities." It further states:

> Unity and inter-connection between civil and political, economic and social, individual and collective human rights can promote a harmonious order of societal life both on the national and international level. The social value and effectiveness of the entire human rights system depend on the extent to which it helps to create conditions for personal growth in the God-given dignity and relates to the responsibility of a person for his actions before God and his neighbors.

The Basic Teaching thus incorporates the "indivisibility of human rights," suggesting and indeed encouraging a larger state role in promoting human rights, conceived as dependent on conditions that require an activist state.

In an extension of collective rights, the Basic Teaching says that a "civilization" has a right to its own values, and "civilizations should not impose their lifestyle patterns on other civilizations." Dugin has stated that he is "deeply convinced that the conception of human rights varies from one culture to another, from one society to another, inasmuch as the very concept of the person varies."[11] From this perspective, since the Russian culture is different from others, Russia naturally has its own concept of human rights.

At a news conference on April 17, 2014, Putin himself reportedly framed the point in essentially biological terms, saying, "The powerful genetic code of the Russian nation, that makes us Russians, is different from other nations and especially compared to the so-called Western genetic code." Putin ominously continued by asserting that a feature of the "Russian genetic code" is the ability "to die for the common cause publicly, in front of the eyes of the community."[12]

The statements obviously suggest a form of traditional Russian ethnic or cultural nationalism. Filling an ideological void that had existed since the end of communism, numerous Russian intellectuals and political leaders have embraced the notion of Russia as an ethnic nation, in which "the purpose of individual work was to aggrandize Russian culture," a view held by Alexander Herzen (1812–1870), one of the fathers of Russian nationalism.[13] Putin's stated goal of creating a "single cultural space" has broad implications for minority rights in a country with 180 different ethnic groups. As one observer put it, Putin's ambition would "undercut nationality as such for Russians by promoting a more expansive definition of Russianness."[14]

The political philosophy of Ivan Ilyin has evidently informed this agenda. Ilyin, who died in 1954, was a proponent of monarchy and of promoting Russian nationalism even beyond Russia itself. In *National-Socialism: The New Spirit* (1933), he advocated for fascism. The theme that unifies his diverse writings is the primacy of state interests over those of individuals. "Ilyin believed that individuality was evil. For him, the 'variety of human beings' demonstrated the failure of God to complete the labor of creation and was therefore essentially satanic," writes Timothy Snyder. For Ilyin, "the purpose of politics is to overcome individuality, and establish a 'living totality' of the nation."[15]

From Political to Cultural Control. An interview with Dugin in November 2016 clarified that he "equates liberalism with moral license and spiritual poverty. 'Liberalism is totalitarianism,' he says, 'an invasive weed that Orthodox Russia, forever poised between East and West, must resist.'"[16] The emergence of a distinctly illiberal, Eurasian approach to human rights in the Russian

Federation is evident in changing patterns of human rights violations. Especially since 2000, the Russian Federation has become a "managed democracy," meaning that obstacles have been constructed to prevent any deep political change, quell conflict and encourage political loyalty. Public opinion on political questions is strongly influenced by a dominant state-controlled media, while only a small number of independent media have escaped closure. Citizens' groups and journalists who have made independent investigations with critical results have been met with harsh treatment, including assassinations. New legislation has severely restricted the ability of nongovernmental organizations to receive and use funds from foreign donors, including organizations that seek to monitor the government's human rights practices. (This is called the "foreign agents law," a term with extremely negative connotations of dangerous espionage by hostile powers.) The major independent Russian human rights groups have been shut down or severely disabled. Although the court system had made significant steps toward professionalism and independence after the end of the USSR, it has regressed and is far from being independent of the executive branch, particularly in politically sensitive cases of conflict between individuals and the state.

Those kinds of violations of political rights are familiar. But in the past ten years especially, human rights violations in the Russian Federation have evolved in the direction of restricting freedoms not only with the aim of securing political hegemony, but also to forge cultural, religious and spiritual harmony and unity. "Spiritual security," a concept frequently invoked by the Orthodox Patriarch, has become an important component of national security, and one that legitimizes restrictions on fundamental freedoms.[17] In 2017, the Russian Federation banned the Jehovah's Witnesses, which is arguably the most flagrant assault on religious freedom to occur in the Euro-Atlantic region since the end of the Soviet Union. The denomination has faced increasing persecution in Russia for decades. The ban, which was confirmed by the Russian Supreme Court, now makes it a crime for about 170,000 Russian citizens to practice their faith.[18]

Censorship has developed from being mostly a mechanism for stifling oppositional political voices, into a way of shielding citizens from a range of ideas, images and texts thought to conflict with dominant cultural and religious values. The Internet has come under new restrictions, with an increasing number of sites blacklisted by the Federal Service for Supervision in Telecommunications, Information Technology and Mass Communications

(Roskomnadzor). While the number of mass media outlets not under strong government control had been very small for a number of years, those remaining have come under increased pressure, sometimes leading to closure. There has been further consolidation of mass media in the hands of the state itself or owners loyal to the government, and limits on foreign ownership. Legislation has made it a crime to allow publication of "false anti-Russian information."[19] The Russian government regards news media not as an institution of civil society, but as "instruments for reaching a goal inside the country, and abroad," according to an independent journalist.[20]

Bans on a range of products are intended to remove influences seen as incompatible with Russian religious and moral values. Russian politicians have recommended banning advertisements for condoms, pregnancy tests, and birth control medications; banning importation of medical equipment and telephones produced abroad; and prohibiting artistic and literary works that "romanticize the criminal world."[21] A bill has been passed to protect children from information that "denies or distorts patriotism," defined as "the love of the fatherland, devotion to it, striving to serve its interests through one's action."[22] The Russian government has made special efforts to suppress public displays of lesbian, gay, bisexual and transgender orientation, as well as any support for the rights of LGBT citizens. Homosexuality and the blurring of gender differences appear to be a central concern, indeed an obsession, of Eurasianism as articulated by Dugin, who has devoted considerable analysis to what he considers an unnatural and corrupt "postmodern" tendency by Western societies to break down clear divisions between the sexes, resulting in the phenomenon of the "transhuman" person.[23] Russian legislation has outlawed "homosexual propaganda," thus infringing on a number of fundamental civil and political rights. Armenia, Belarus, Kazakhstan and Kyrgyzstan are among other states adopting or considering the adoption of similar legislation.[24] In December 2014, the Russian government named being transgender, bigender, asexual and cross-dressing as personality disorders that disallow a person from holding a driver's license.[25]

Freedom in the Context of an Ideology of State Power

Today's Russia-led Eurasianism is an antitheses to classical liberalism based on natural rights, and holds that respect for individual human rights claims is a mark of a weak and unhealthy society. In Eurasianism, the cosmopolitan idealism and scientific detachment of the Soviet dissidents have been turned upside down, and labeled a sociocultural pathology. Freedom, according to this model, exists not when individuals challenge the status quo and the rules of the state on the basis of abstract principles, but rather when they find their essence within the organic whole of a society fully encompassed by the state. Eurasianism's main challenge to the "uncontroversial core of human rights" lies in its ideology of state power, and the allure of its vision of the state as the embodiment and guardian of culture and tradition. States are viewed not as artificial arrangements through which individuals protect their security and guarantee their liberties through a social contract, as claimed in the liberal political tradition, but as organic entities outside of which individual life has no purpose or meaning. The political system "gives us our shape," says Dugin.[26] Echoing the Nazi-friendly philosophy of Martin Heidegger, Eurasianism holds that identity is "installed in us by the state."[27]

Liberalism, with its basis in social contract theory, its pluralism and its concept of an independent civil society, is viewed as an "absolute evil," the "repudiation of God, tradition, community, ethnicity, empire and kingdoms."[28] Liberalism creates enmity between the state and the person. It detaches the person from the state as his or her natural spiritual home, resulting in "transhumanisation" and an "uncertain identity." A state must not be "neutral" on moral questions; this would be to neglect the sustaining values of historical communities. Dugin asserts that the Russian conception of human rights does not include "the right to sin," and that the state has an obligation to protect itself from sinful influences.[29]

Human rights in the sense of natural rights is thus an alienating idea, an attempt to nullify values and hierarchies that are essential to the fulfillment of the individual in the context of society and the state. Human rights, with its necessary subjection of state practices to objective scrutiny and civil control, depends on a separation of the person from society, which in the Eurasian view means a separation of the person from himself. Desecrating the bond between the person and the state results in identity-threatening ambiguity, a form of spiritual bondage.

Eurasianism's ideology of power claims to confer freedom on citizens; the state is the source of freedom, not a threat to freedom. By this logic, state censorship nurtures freedom. In Communist-ruled Hungary, the dissident Miklós Haraszti wrote in *The Velvet Prison*, "Censorship professes to be freedom because it acts, like morality, as a common spirit of both rulers and the ruled."[30] Today, authorities in Russia and elsewhere, including Belarus and nearly all the Central Asian republics, have de jure or de facto rejected the concept of natural, individual rights as an alien imposition by the West. At the same time, they are promoting an alternative notion of freedom and of human rights, compatible with and supportive of authoritarianism. It is founded on the ideal that Haraszti called a "common spirit," and upon the duties of the individual to the state as the source of freedom.

Beginning in 1996, delegations from the International Helsinki Federation for Human Rights (IHF) visited Belarus numerous times in attempts to support the persecuted human rights community there and appeal to the authorities. The country had lost little of its Soviet atmosphere. Under the iron grip of Alexander Lukashenko, former Communist state farm director, it was moving toward a new Soviet-type society posing as a democracy. Civil society was to harmonize with the state; no real political opposition would be allowed, none being deemed necessary. It would be a semisocialist society, run by state authorities and private-sector elites without dissent, and one with humane policies toward disadvantaged citizens. But the harsh violations of basic liberties, especially the manipulation of democratic elections and the crackdowns on independent NGOs and media, aroused condemnation in the international community. Dissident politicians disappeared, and human rights defenders were jailed and beaten, including some of our colleagues. A Belarusian diplomat came to a briefing in the IHF offices in Vienna with an archaic Soviet-era tape recorder in his shoe. One time, leaving from the Minsk airport, I was followed by some sort of government agent, even into the men's room when I transferred in Frankfurt.

Alongside such actions smacking of Stalinism, Belarusian authorities began programs of "human rights education" in secondary schools that impressed international observers. The main idea in these curricula is that human rights are inseparable from duties and obligations to the government. Human rights do not exist in a reality outside of positive law and shielded from it; in fact, the "human rights" teachings fed to Belarusian schoolchildren are largely elements of administrative and criminal law. According to a Belarusian colleague and expert on human rights in the country, the meaning of civil and political rights is "respect for the rights of others," meaning limitations imposed by the state. The Belarusian government was proud to exhibit its "National Human Rights Education Plan," and a government-controlled organization asked the Organization for Security and Cooperation in Europe for assistance to "bring human rights education experience from

Tajikistan, Kazakhstan and Russia,"[31] suggesting an intra-Eurasian human rights education network.

In 1997 and 1998, my colleagues and I met several times with a Belarusian intellectual, Alexander Potupa, a scholar and frustrated former consultant to Lukashenko. He was obsessed with the idea of Belarus becoming a model for a new kind of post-Soviet state. The head of the Belarusian Helsinki Committee, Tatsyana Protska, said similar things. They felt something was happening in their country with wider implications, and they were frustrated by the inability of others to grasp it. What they were speaking about was clearly Eurasianism. During the 26th Session of the UN Human Rights Council in June 2014, Ambassador Mikhail Khvostov of Belarus, when confronted with a report alleging serious violations of basic freedoms and the rule of law, said that his government had been successful at "organizing the political life of society," that the legal system is "secondary to politics," and that "without politics there is no purpose and without purpose there is no state." The state, Khvostov submitted, "is the guarantor of our system of values and way of life."[32] From the floor of the Human Rights Council, the ambassador had essentially shut out the entire concept of universal human rights, and his bold, pseudo-philosophical assertions, highly unusual in a diplomatic context, went unchallenged by diplomats from liberal democracies, who passed up an important opportunity to explain human rights. I wondered how Belarusian human rights activists, and victims, felt to hear that such words and ideas were received in silence.

Western policy elites tend to ignore Eurasianism, but they do so at their peril. According to Adam Michnik, it is more than a "coarse and primitive nationalism."[33] It partakes of a human rights doctrine that, with its emphasis on economic and social rights, can be seen as consistent with the Universal Declaration of Human Rights, and thus it aspires to global legitimacy. Indeed, in the revisionist rhetoric of contemporary Russian officials, the global, postwar human rights ethos owed much to core values driving the Russian Revolution.[34]

Marxist authoritarian states invoke human rights in their defense, and as the framework in which liberties are denied. At the UN in 2016, Venezuela, where dozens of opposition leaders were political prisoners, called itself a "country guarantor of human rights" that accepted the "new conception of human rights as indivisible and comprehensive." In 2012, Venezuela had been elected to the Human Rights Council, receiving more votes than the United

States, Germany or Ireland. Members of the international community thus endorsed Venezuela's Marxist logic that the violation of liberties was necessary and legitimate in order to create a socialist state where economic and social rights would supposedly be realized.

While such retrograde, explicitly Marxist approaches to human rights are largely in retreat, the tendency to undermine basic freedoms in accordance with the Eurasian human rights vision is becoming more pronounced. Pro-Russian leaders are finding success in eastern Europe, some under the label of "socialist," but others mixing nationalism and socialism in the "Red-Brown" sense associated with fascism, and similar political movements are gaining strength in western European states as well. According to the Political Capital Research and Consulting Institute, based in Budapest, "Most major European far-right parties typically fall in the 'committed' category, openly professing their sympathy for Russia."[35] The group further concluded:

> There have been many signs of Kremlin's increasing efforts to influence both decision-makers and the general public in the EU and member states. One of the political tools to exert such influence is through co-opting certain far-right (and far-left) parties and organizations within the European Union.[36]

Virtually nothing is said about human rights by the leaders of these movements or in their party manifestoes. When the topic comes up, a concern about human rights is routinely associated with "globalism," the erasing of national borders, political correctness, the threat of Muslim immigration, and ideological multiculturalism that scorns national traditions and Christian values. There are references to protecting freedoms, but only in the context of preserving national sovereignty against EU and UN regulations and multinationalism, and against the constraints on free speech imposed by hate-speech legislation. Complaints are raised about attacks on the exercise of free speech when it involves anxieties about immigration and encroachments on the rights of native Europeans in favor of minorities and immigrants, but freedom of speech is not asserted as a *principle*. Human rights activism is associated with cultural corruption and political weakness. The idea of defending the natural rights of the individual against majoritarian rule finds little sympathy. Heinz-Christian Strache, the leader of the Austrian Freedom Party, which built itself on the ruins of the Nazi Party, wrote on his Facebook page on

November 9, 2016: "Little by little, the political left and the out-of-touch and corrupt establishment is being punished by voters and driven from power. This is a good thing, because the law comes from the people." *Gut so, denn das Recht geht vom Volk aus.* (Strache, a dental technician by training, has since become the vice-chancellor of Austria.) The abuse of positive law has opened European societies to the dangers of a populism wherein law is unmoored from transcendent standards.

The ideal of freedom, having been polluted with leftism by the human rights establishment, is now being co-opted by authoritarians. The expansive human rights concept of the international human rights community, especially its preoccupation with centralized wealth redistribution and with enforcing "tolerance" by prosecuting "hate speech," has contributed to the return of reactionary nationalism. It has, ironically and tragically, encouraged the ideal of homogenous, conformist societies in which the individual is an organic part of the state, where there is no line between civil society and the state, and where the rights of the individual against the state are thus irrelevant and unnecessary, as Carl Schmitt, the legal philosopher of Nazism, envisioned.[37]

Collectivist and Restrictive Islamic "Human Rights"

Islamic theocracies assert that they respect human rights by adhering to Sharia law. They do so on the basis of economic and social rights, which form a bridge between the international human rights system and orthodox Islam. Islamic governments find a place for themselves in human rights by way of economic and social rights, and this also allows liberal democracies to accommodate repression in Islamic states, in the hope of defusing political tensions and reducing terrorist threats. International organizations encourage this fallacy in an effort to gain the support of Islamic governments. Economic and social rights help mask the deep incompatibility between Islamic law and authentic human rights.

I am a witness to the variety in global Islam. Many years of defending and working with Muslim communities and human rights activists in the Balkans, Central Asia, and in Chechnya and elsewhere in the Northern Caucasus showed that Islam can coexist with secular governments and with universal standards of human rights. The vice president of the IHF, the late Srdjan Dizdarevic, was a Bosnian Muslim. There is profound diversity among the world's 1.8 billion Muslims. But as the leading anthropologist Clifford

Geertz observed in 1968, the dynamic, reformist element in Islam is oriented toward orthodoxy and militancy.[38] Today, Islam is more dynamic than at any time since the twelfth century. Its various constituents and leaders wish to "shift the frame of reference in the public realm to one in which Islam, in its various interpretations, is a major shaping force."[39] While political, fundamentalist Islam is rising around the world, the lines between fundamentalist and moderate interpretations are not clearly drawn, and are contested by Islamists.

Apologists for Islamism increasingly claim that Sharia law is a doctrine of human rights, and this assertion goes largely unchallenged. Conditioned by multiculturalism to put all cultures on the same moral plane, we seem embarrassed by the fact that human rights is a Western invention, and reticent about the actual nature of human rights. When I met with government-supported human rights activists from Saudi Arabia and heard them claim that the idea of human rights was a pillar of Islam, I failed to respond with the truth. In effect, I was intimidated by the vast gulf that separated our different understandings of human rights, and I feared that casting myself in the role of a teacher with superior knowledge would derail the dialogue we were trying to have. In retrospect, the rigid Saudi position appears as a form of bullying or blackmail. Their viewpoint had to be at least tacitly accepted as a condition for their presence at the discussion.

Claims that any religious doctrine is a human rights doctrine are false and dangerous. There is no genuine human rights provision in Islam, even as regards economic and social rights. Neither can the idea of human rights be found in Judaism, Christianity, or any other religious creed.[40] Religions have given mankind an appreciation for the sanctity of life and the dignity of the human person. They have been the source of values by which humans have tried to overcome the cruelties of the natural world and remedy the failings of human nature. Judaism and Christianity fed into the framework of natural law and natural rights, with their doctrines of a common human nature under a transcendent universal law. International human rights incorporates the moral imperative of protecting the sanctity of individual freedom and dignity, adding legal mechanisms to protect individuals from tyrannical governments.[41]

Fundamentalist Islam upholds no concept of a natural law distinct from positive law and existing in a transcendent moral order. Natural law cannot act as a check against positive law because they are one and the same. Nor is there any line between mosque and state in orthodox Islam. This is a crucial difference from modern Judaism and Christianity, whose historical development led to a distinction in principle between religious and temporal power, even when those powers were of the same religion, and even though they might compete for supremacy. Prophets challenged kings on moral grounds. Clerics aimed to hold rulers to account, and occasionally succeeded. Eventually this division of powers meant that secular authorities would protect the freedom of religion for their subjects or citizens.

By contrast, orthodox Islam is a unitary social and political order as well as a religion. Islamic texts promote respect for human dignity, but they do not promote human rights. Islam emphasizes duties, including the duties of rulers to their subjects, and mutual duties between society and individuals. It is a "social religion," and its doctrines suggest positive social legislation, without offering any legal recourse for the individual against the state. There is no means to lodge legal claims against the ruling powers, which is a technical requirement for a right. Regardless of the de facto freedoms that individuals may experience under an Islamic regime, there are no human rights when there is no legal possibility for individuals to challenge state authorities and to receive remedies for violations.

Under strict interpretations of Islam, individual rights have little meaning, since human nature is realized through the community. In Islam, "Individual freedom ends where the freedom of the community begins, not the other way around."[42] The Islamic approach to human rights, like the Eurasian one, insists that "individual freedoms must be subject to limitations for the protection of the interests of the community."[43] Also like Eurasianism, Islam's religio-political theory claims that freedom lies in submission to authority and to Islamic law. It means freedom from the burden of choice and freedom from conflict with the community and the state, and with God's will.

The national sovereignty of an Islamic theocracy cannot easily be limited by an international human rights treaty. Of all the many conflicts between orthodox Islam and international human rights standards, none is more acute than the issue of apostasy laws that make it a crime for an individual to forsake Islam. In over twenty-four member states of the UN, it is a crime to change one's religion, and in ten of these Islamic states, including members of the UN Human Rights Council, this crime is punishable by death.[44] The reason is that apostasy from Islam is viewed as treason against the state—a state defined by orthodox Islam. Few if any Muslim authors have questioned the idea of sanctions against apostasy.[45] Given the dominance of Islamic states in international forums and the importance those states attach to apostasy laws, they are not even seriously disputed by other countries in those forums, or by UN human rights commissioners.

In 2016, along with two human rights activists, Kamal and Christina Fahmi, I sought meetings with delegations to the UN Human Rights Council from states that criminalize apostasy, in an attempt to open a dialogue on the issue. Speaking to UN officials and to a number of people close to Islamic governments, Kamal, a Christian who grew up in Sudan, used language rarely heard in human rights advocacy: "We are not against anyone," he said. "We are just trying to help Muslims who do not have the right to change their faith. We feel it is not right." None of the delegations representing countries where apostasy is against the law would even agree to meet with us. The UN high commissioner never answered a letter we wrote asking that steps be taken to open discussions about the problem.

The Cairo Declaration on Human Rights in Islam

Over the past several decades, Islamic declarations about human rights have tried to show consistency between Islamic law and international human rights law. They include the Universal Islamic Declaration of Human Rights (1981), which was a nongovernmental initiative; the Arab Charter on Human Rights, by the League of Arab States (1994); and the Cairo Declaration on Human Rights in Islam (1990). The latter, written for an international audience by the Organization of the Islamic Conference (OIC), has been the most widely recognized. To the extent the Cairo Declaration has convinced the international community that Islamic law accords with human rights principles, it is because of the articles that resemble economic and social rights. Were the international human rights system not infected by these bogus human rights, there would be no case, and no thought mechanisms that could harmonize political systems based on Sharia law with human rights.

The Cairo Declaration was adopted by the member states of the OIC as a contribution to the World Conference on Human Rights.[46] Like the Bangkok Declaration, an assertion of "Asian values" that pushed the Vienna conference to institutionalize an emphasis on economic and social rights and the "indivisibility" of human rights, the Cairo Declaration was a challenge to "Western dominance of the human rights agenda."[47] The human rights scholar Eva Brems observed that it is written in the language and style of international human rights law, yet "quite a number of features express an Islamic particularity. The four-paragraph preamble consists almost entirely of religious rhetoric," for example, that "God has made the Islamic Ummah 'the best nation that has given mankind a universal and well-balanced civilization.'"[48] The Cairo Declaration was written, in part, "to protect man from exploitation and persecution, and to affirm his freedom and right to a dignified life in accordance with the Islamic Shari'ah," which is described as "the only source of reference for the explanation or clarification of any of the articles of this Declaration" (Preamble, Article 25).

Despite this overtly sectarian framing, broad elements of the Cairo Declaration were absorbed into the Vienna Declaration on Human Rights, and taken up by the international human rights community generally. These elements include the emphasis on economic and social rights, and a spirit of communalism that renders individual freedom less important than duties to the collective. The Cairo Declaration (Article 13) says, "Work is a right guaranteed by the State and the Society for each person with capability to work." It says that all will have rights to a clean environment, medical and social care, and public amenities provided by the state and society (Article 17): "The States shall ensure the right of the individual to a decent living that may enable him to meet his requirements and those of his dependents, including food, clothing, housing, education, medical care and all other basic needs."

When it comes to civil and political rights, however, there are no references to freedom of religion, freedom of assembly, freedom of association, the right to a fair trial, minority rights, or trade union rights. There is essentially no freedom of expression outside the norms of Sharia. Article 22 states that "Everyone shall have the right to express his opinion freely in such manner as would not be contrary to the principles of the Shari'ah.... Everyone shall have the right to advocate what is right, and propagate what is good, and warn against what is wrong and evil according to the norms of Islamic Shari'ah." It warns that information "may not be exploited or misused in such a way as may violate sanctities and the dignity of Prophets, undermine moral and ethical values or disintegrate, corrupt or harm society, or weaken its faith." The freedom that is recognized is the freedom to live and act within a specific religious and political context, and in harmony with its norms. The Cairo Declaration also regurgitates international anti-hate-speech principles: "It is not permitted to arouse nationalistic or doctrinal hatred or to do anything that may be an incitement to any form of racial discrimination."

The Islamic Human Rights Vision
Goes Mainstream

Faced with both political and terrorist aggression on the world scene, with the growing influence of Islamic populations in liberal democracies, and with the dynamism and increasing power of Islamic fundamentalism, the international community has sought to bend human rights in the direction of the Cairo Declaration, perhaps to integrate and pacify Islamic populations. In important ways, this response resembles the process of formulating the Universal Declaration of Human Rights, a process meant to bring the world together in the name of a common moral purpose. It is also reminiscent of the strategy of bending the UDHR in the direction of communism, when political goals of integration and inclusion and of promoting social-welfare schemes undermined the principle of universality based on natural rights. And once again, it is a process driven by the politics of the left, which finds sympathy with the communalism of Islam and with its challenge to the West's ideal of individual rights and freedoms.

Following the 1993 World Conference, the United Nations increasingly focused on "combating racism, racial discrimination, xenophobia, and related intolerance." It organized major conferences on these topics, which easily became conceptual platforms for limiting freedom, and even for propagating hatred and racial discrimination. The 2001 World Conference Against Racism in Durban, South Africa, provided an arena for equating Zionism with racism, and for relativizing the Holocaust. More particularly, the NGO Forum organized to run in parallel with the conference, and attended by around eight thousand activists, was the scene of blatant anti-Semitism, where a South African group supporting Palestinians distributed copies of the Protocols of the Elders of Zion.[49] The United States and Israel withdrew from the conference, with Congressman Tom Lantos, a human rights leader, saying that it had been "wrecked by Arab and Islamic extremists."[50] Among the human rights activists who protested against the hijacking of the NGO Forum were colleagues from the IHF. Dimitrina Petrova, a founder of the Bulgarian Helsinki Committee and later the European Roma Rights Center, said the NGO documents "contain inappropriate language fuelling precisely the kind of hatred and racism the Durban gathering was meant to challenge."[51]

The Organization of the Islamic Conference (since 2011, the Organization for Islamic Cooperation) repeatedly proposed UN resolutions to protect Islam from "defamation" and to protect Muslims from "Islamophobia." Sixteen such resolutions were introduced in the UN Human Rights Council and were passed with the support of Islamic states. I agree that these resolutions in some cases addressed actual problems; the ridicule of religions is not a healthy practice, and it can lead to crimes and violations of human rights. But this problem should be addressed through moral education, in the context of family, religious institutions and schools. The same goes for Islamophobia, if it means a discriminatory, disparaging and prejudicial attitude toward individuals based on their Islamic faith. But fear of Islam is a feeling, and so too is hate. Feelings cannot be banned by law, and human rights do not protect religions from criticism or even defamation. Human rights do, or should, protect critical speech. The U.S. representative in the Human Rights Council, Eileen Donahoe, rejected a resolution on the defamation of religion, saying clearly that it was because the United States could not "agree that prohibiting speech is the way to promote tolerance, and because we continue to see the 'defamation of religions' concept used to justify censorship, criminalization, and in some cases violent assaults and deaths of political, racial, and religious minorities around the world."[52]

As support for the antidefamation resolutions had been diminishing, both Islamic states and liberal democracies had an interest in ending them. A consensus solution was found in 2011, in the form of Human Rights Council Resolution 16/18, which shifted the focus from combating the defamation of religion to combating "intolerance, negative stereotyping and stigmatization of, and discrimination, incitement to violence and violence against, persons based on religion or belief."[53] The resolution "Condemns any advocacy of religious hatred that constitutes incitement to discrimination, hostility or violence, whether it involves the use of print, audio-visual or electronic media or any other means." The council expressed "concern that incidents of religious intolerance, discrimination and related violence" and of "negative stereotyping" were increasing around the world, and it urged states "to take effective measures...consistent with their obligations under international human rights law, to address and combat such incidents."

Resolution 16/18 was meant to divert the energies of Islamic states away from criminalizing the defamation (or criticism) of Islam, and toward prohibiting "hate speech" against Muslims (and others). But it sneaks through the dangerous hole in human rights law that totalitarian states placed there, in Article 20(2) of the International Covenant on Civil and Political Rights, which says, "Any advocacy of national, racial or religious hatred that constitutes incitement to discrimination, hostility or violence shall be prohibited by law." As noted above, this provision was formerly opposed by liberal democracies. But today, "hate speech" is outlawed in all European countries.

The resolution further compromises one of the basic freedoms and natural rights by urging governments to restrict "incitement to discrimination." That can be interpreted in various ways, and indeed the resolution has been interpreted in different ways since its passage. While it ostensibly focuses on speech that is harmful to persons, in practice it can sweep in speech critical of a religion. According to Deborah Weiss,

> it has become apparent over time that the OIC's definition of "advocacy of religious hatred" includes criticism of Islam. It is not limited to the advocacy of hatred against individuals. In other words, the OIC imbues the "advocacy of religious hatred" phrase with the same meaning that it gave to "combating defamation of religions." It protects the ideology of Islam and prohibits any criticism of it.[54]

Jacob Mchangama wrote that the "putative consensus around Resolution 16/18 is a charade," noting that in a Human Rights Council speech, "the OIC explicitly equated 'defamation of religion,' a broad and nebulous category including religious satire and criticism, with advocacy of religious hatred."[55]

The Western human rights community, which has hardly ever expressed even mild concern about the blatant conflict between hate-speech legislation and freedom of speech, has applauded Resolution 16/18. An NGO concerned solely with freedom of expression, named Article 19 after the provision in the Universal Declaration proclaiming "the right to freedom of opinion and expression," saw the resolution as a "bridge" between opposing perspectives and value systems.[56] The description is apt in ways that perhaps were not intended. There is nothing positive about a bridge between freedom and oppression.

The resolution established the "Istanbul Process," a series of meetings to discuss its implementation. At the opening of one conference in 2015, Iyad bin Amin Madani, the secretary general of the OIC, said that "religious hatred" needs to be confronted "at all levels," and that it is necessary to determine "where freedom of expression ends, and hate speech begins." In a list of instances of incitement to hatred and discrimination, Madani included "printing of senseless caricatures of Prophet Mohammed," which "have all resulted in promoting a culture of discrimination and violence that has also led to loss of innocent lives and wider sense of alienation, isolation, rejection, polarization and exclusion among affected communities." Madani claimed that "OIC has always upheld the principle of openly discussing all ideas, values or beliefs in an environment of tolerance and respect."[57]

In the U.S. House of Representatives, Resolution 569, "Condemning violence, bigotry, and hateful rhetoric towards Muslims in the United States," was submitted in December 2015 to follow up on HRC Resolution 16/18. The European Union embraced the Istanbul Process, and its offer to host a meeting was seen by the secretary general of the OIC as a "qualitative shift in action against the phenomenon of Islamophobia, which spread in many European countries, targeting the Muslim communities there."[58] Among the human rights priorities of the EU are the elimination of racism, xenophobia and related intolerance.[59] And there is a broadening common ground between the EU and the OIC, centered on fighting "hate speech." Federica Mogherini, the EU high representative for foreign affairs and security policy, was quoted on June 24, 2015 as saying, "The idea of a clash between Islam and 'the West'…has misled our policies and our narratives. Islam holds a place in our Western societies. Islam belongs in Europe.…I am not afraid to say that political Islam should be part of the picture."[60]

Resolution 16/18 brought liberal democracies closer to acting on the concerns of Islamic states, and arguably closer to criminalizing criticism of Islam, which should be protected speech under international law that upholds natural rights. But it appears not to have had a parallel effect on Islamic states by focusing their attention on speech that incites hatred of persons; instead, those states have continued their efforts to criminalize the criticism of Islam globally. The resolution has not led to any significant positive changes in the way Islamic states treat religious and political minorities. In 2013, the League of Arab States agreed upon an "Arab Guideline Law for the Prevention of Defamation of Religions," essentially a blasphemy law, which prohibits, inter alia, "Contempt or disrespect [for] or [offense to] any of the religions or by defaming them or insulting them or ridiculing them or infringing on them."[61] The virulent anti-Semitic public speech that is commonplace in many Islamic countries reveals a chasm between this inclusive language and the selective application of the principles.

The Istanbul Process has allowed the leaders of Islamic states to legitimize repression of speech and of religious freedom within the framework of international human rights law, and to justify these actions in the mushy language of tolerance and multiculturalism. Resolution 16/18 is not pulling totalitarian Islamic states toward freedom, instead, it presents an obstacle to those who seek freedom in those states, and is even pulling free states away from freedom. Such "bridging" initiatives are no favor to Muslims who practice or seek an Islam that is compatible with human rights. According to Denis MacEoin, Resolution 16/18 "will very likely assist many Muslims in bringing even more prosecutions against non-Muslim critics or even against moderate Muslims who oppose much that is done in the name of Islam." He sees indications of this effect already in some democratic states, "not least that former bastion of free speech, the United States."[62]

The inclination to limit freedom rights is on the ascendant, and it operates within the framework of international human rights. Liberal democracies increasingly approach fundamental freedoms, in particular the freedom of speech, in a manner not inconsistent with the Cairo Declaration and with Islamic law. Consider the currently popular notion of "trigger warnings" to shield people from ideas that make them "uncomfortable"; or the designation of campuses as "safe spaces" where members of particular ideological communities should never run the risk of being exposed to contrary ideas and challenging information; or the efforts to silence and ostracize those who object to the imposition of a suffocating harmony.[63] In this climate, facts are of little consequence, and the underlying principle clearly echoes the prohibition of "slander" set down in *The Reliance of the Traveller* (Umdat al-Salik), an Islamic manual of jurisprudence written in the fourteenth century and considered to contain absolute legal rulings. It defines slander as "to mention anything concerning a person that he would dislike" (r2.2). Today, we hear that it's indefensible to say anything about Islam or its Prophet that "hurts the feelings of a billion Muslims."

The information space in a fundamentalist Islamic society, and also in a Eurasian one, is tightly controlled by authorities who wield power in the name of upholding values common to the community, and protecting certain people from hurt feelings. Around the world, basic individual human rights are being restricted by essentially fascist and theocratic governments, and also, in a more attenuated but insidious manner, in liberal democracies, and in ways that are asserted to be consistent with the principle of human rights.

The Failure of Liberal Democracies to Protect Natural Rights

Natural rights are increasingly violated in Western societies, under the combined influence of China's coercive economic power, Eurasia's antiliberal agitation, the demands of Islamic regimes and activists, and forces within Western societies that aim to subordinate individual rights to political objectives. The international human rights system, moving toward becoming a global regulatory hegemon, is ill-equipped to respond, and often neglectful of natural rights while spotlighting more trivial concerns. Can we truly commit our moral energies to the question of the availability of fresh vegetables in Northern Canada as a human right? The very idea of natural rights, the moral core of international human rights, has been leeched out of the system by the presence of economic and social rights and collective rights that are based on political assumptions.

The ICESCR and other international treaties make specific political choices mandatory, transferring democratic processes to the realm of international law. The protection of basic freedoms is relegated to a small corner of the sprawling human rights system, which regulates more and more areas of activity. The concept of human rights has been swept into a broad river of campaigns for social justice, global economic development, environmental protection, multiculturalism, tolerance, access to water and sanitation, and more. Natural rights and freedoms are viewed as but one element in a vast web of conditionality, as means to other ends, or even as obstacles to the enjoyment of other human rights. The bright beacon of freedom is being dragged into the dirt by forces whose objectives are threatened by individual freedom and choice, and who hide their *ressentiment* in mobs demanding the imposition of the collective will.

Democratic societies must be free to place duties on individuals in order to achieve shared goals, like ensured levels of health care for all, but if such goals are imposed in the name of human rights, they contradict the very idea of human rights. I am with Yuri Orlov: human rights are not about *what*, but about *how*. Human rights protect the freedom to pursue political goals, but when they are conflated with political goals they can be used to violate the rights of those who oppose them. That is happening today in Western societies, as in the Eurasian and Islamist spheres.

Unrecognized Encroachments
on Natural Rights

The United States government seriously violated the internationally guaranteed human rights of American citizens by using the bureaucratic machinery of the state, specifically the Internal Revenue Service (IRS), to harass and discourage the work of citizens' groups holding critical views about the Obama administration.[64] The government has also snooped on the correspondence and activities of journalists, an invasion of privacy and an affront to the principle of freedom of the press. Government agencies stonewalled attempts to investigate the issue, as is typical in authoritarian states. But no U.S. or international human rights organizations raised concerns about what the IRS or the Department of Justice did; those actions were not seen as human rights issues.

From a global perspective there is certainly nothing exceptional about the Obama administration's abuse of human rights and civil society in those two cases. Many governments around the world violate the freedom of association and the principle of equality before the law in order to persecute their political opponents and to enhance their own power. Monitoring the communications of media is also a standard human rights violation, generally justified in the name of "security." The IRS and the Department of Justice have used playbooks that were perfected by Russia and many other authoritarian states to stifle, intimidate and criminalize opponents.

These issues were apparently never mentioned in the UN Human Rights Council, nor in America's Universal Periodic Review, nor in testimony about violations of the Helsinki standards in the Human Dimension of the Organization for Security and Cooperation in Europe. By contrast, the Bush administration's human rights infringements dominated international human rights discourse. Amnesty International famously called the rendition program a "gulag." American groups and the IHF warned that the United States had squandered its capacity to lead by example because of equivocation on torture and other practices that called into question the country's commitment to human rights. But when the victims were Tea Party and other conservative activists, the human rights community was silent—except for some words of praise for the misdeeds. Julian Bond, a revered civil rights leader and former chairman of the National Association for the Advancement of Colored People (NAACP), praised the IRS for targeting Tea Party groups, while claiming that the NAACP was itself unfairly targeted by the Bush administration. Bond said in an interview that the Tea Party organizations deserved to be scrutinized because they were "racist."

In this context it is worth noting that American civil society groups sometimes try to bring the hand of the state down upon others, also a phenomenon that evokes countries where the rule of law is ignored and where governments and judiciaries arbitrarily apply the law to serve private interests. For instance, Professor Eugene Kontorovich noted in 2016 that the private lobby firm J Street and other progressive groups were campaigning "to get the Treasury Department to pull the tax-exempt status of U.S. charities that provide support to Israeli communities in the West Bank and Golan Heights, i.e., settlements." Summing up the constitutional problem, he wrote, "To put it simply, J Street et al are asking that some non-profits be denied tax exemptions *because they disagree with the President on diplomatic matters.*"[65]

Human rights activists have, correctly, defended the rights of terror suspects who have professed the most violent, anti-Semitic and misogynist views. But they have failed to defend those with whom they apparently disagree more: American citizens on the political right. Many American citizens have lost respect for their own natural rights and seem not to realize when those rights are being trampled.

A profound disregard for the principle of natural rights was on evidence in a European debate surrounding the question of gender quotas in the workplace. In the United States, "affirmative discrimination" has been thoroughly criticized on constitutional grounds, but I believe I am the only human rights activist in Europe to have challenged gender quotas publicly as a violation of human rights.[66] The principle of equality before the law is central to human rights. Giving preference to one group over another, even in the name of achieving equality between groups, is contrary to the rule of law. But that principle was ignored in a long political debate that resulted in an agreement to force Germany's largest business firms to appoint women to 30 percent of positions on corporate boards. The German government passed the law imposing the quota in March 2015.

Racial, religious and other quotas, including those imposed on Jews in the 1930s, have always been defended as "good for society." Future generations too might have less benign reasons for violating equality before the law than attaining gender diversity on corporate boards. Defenders of the German law employed utilitarian arguments that reduced sacrosanct human rights to goals that can be ignored if they conflict with other priorities. They blamed sexual chauvinism for opposition to the quotas, and women's representatives of the German Green Party deemed political friction over the measure to be "unacceptable."

But critics of the legislation also relied on utilitarian arguments, side-stepping the questions of equality and freedom. Opponents said that gender quotas patronize and infantilize women; that they prove women need the strong arm of the state to guarantee their career advancement; and that such quotas undermine respect for women's achievements by holding them to a lower standard. Business groups say the quota will reduce efficiency and that voluntary efforts to improve female representation on corporate boards will eventually bring the desired results. When the European Commission proposed to mandate that private companies' nonexecutive boards be at least 40 percent female by 2020, European states led by the United Kingdom signaled their opposition. But they argued on procedural grounds, saying that such measures should fall within the competencies of member states according to the "subsidiarity principle," rather than be imposed by the EU.

The failure to reject quota proposals as contrary to human rights is fully understandable given the deterioration of human rights discourse over several decades. Quotas as a remedy for discrimination have been legitimized by international human rights treaties like the Convention on the Elimination of All Forms of Discrimination against Women (CEDAW), which has been ratified by virtually every country on earth except the United States and several Islamic theocracies, as well as the Convention on the Elimination of All Forms of Racial Discrimination (CERD). The UN Human Rights Committee has also endorsed quotas, and Article 23 of the European Charter of Fundamental Rights explicitly permits them, saying, "The principle of equality shall not prevent the maintenance or adoption of measures providing for specific advantages in favor of the under-represented sex." The quota policies in Germany and the EU manifest a general diminishing of human rights protections in favor of social policy objectives. Germans will have more women on corporate boards, but they will live in a society where the heavy hand of the state increasingly dictates outcomes.

The Human Rights Campaign against Hate Speech

Freedom of speech is increasingly restricted in Western societies, but these restrictions are not regarded as violations of human rights by intergovernmental organizations, nor by the vast majority of those who make up the human rights community. On the contrary, they are generally supported by that community. Governments and civil society tend to agree on limitations of speech, and the positions of many liberal democratic governments converge with those of authoritarian governments on this issue. International human rights institutions exhibit the same tendency and will likely do so increasingly in the future.

In 2008, the Human Rights Council's mandate on "Promotion and Protection of the Right to Freedom of Opinion and Expression"—one of several special procedures to protect basic rights and freedoms, established in 1993— was forced by authoritarian states to change its remit. At the 7th Session of the Human Rights Council, Egypt, representing the African Group, and Pakistan, on behalf of the Organization of the Islamic Conference (OIC), introduced a measure to add the following language to the duties of the special rapporteur:

> [T]o report on instances in which the abuse of the right of freedom of expression constitutes an act of racial or religious discrimination, taking into account articles 19 (3) and 20 of the International Covenant on Civil and Political Rights, and general comment No. 15 of the Committee on the Elimination of All Forms of Racial Discrimination, which stipulates that the prohibition of the dissemination of all ideas based upon racial superiority or hatred is compatible with the freedom of opinion and expression.[67]

In other words, the job of the UN's top freedom of expression guardian would henceforth be to report on speech violations, as well as violations of the freedom of speech.

Meanwhile, the prosecution of "hate speech" in liberal democracies has brought them closer to the political censorship deployed in totalitarian states like China, and to the form of censorship in the Russian and Islamic spheres in the interest of cultural and religious conformity. In significant measure, censorship has become a human rights tool.

After the Danish newspaper *Jyllands-Posten* published cartoons of Muhammad in 2005 and violent reactions ensued in Muslim communities and societies, taking the lives of about two hundred people, statements by government representatives from diverse states generally agreed on a need to regulate freedom of expression in order to ensure religious tolerance. I witnessed an example at a meeting of the Permanent Council of the Organization for

Security and Cooperation in Europe, soon after the controversy erupted. One after another delegation leader from states of the former Soviet Union, led by a gloating Russian ambassador, said the incident demonstrated that state regulation of the content of mass media was "responsible" and necessary for stability and for domestic and international peace.

There was hardly any disputing of these assertions among representatives of Western democracies, although the OSCE's media freedom representative, Miklós Haraszti, later said that "the right to question all beliefs is itself a cherished tradition in democratic countries."[68] The widespread violence and political turmoil following publication of the cartoons was—and still is—blamed on the decision to publish them, not the decisions to react to them with murderous rage. In the aftermath of the episode, international leaders, including the president of the United States, spoke of the "responsibilities" that go along with freedom of speech. Of course, under the Obama administration, top government officials initially blamed the terrorist attack in Benghazi on incitement by an anti-Muslim video.

The anti-hate-speech clause in international human rights law bans "Any advocacy of national, racial or religious hatred that constitutes incitement to discrimination, hostility or violence." It is perhaps the worst element of international human rights law. The term "incitement to violence" or to "hostility" is a legal vagary that can easily be exploited. How do we define "incitement?" Incitement of whom? How do we define "hostility?" More generally, what is "hate speech?" This kind of legislation is an open invitation to politically motivated censorship.

The 1993 Vienna Declaration gave new life to efforts to restrict the freedom of speech in calling for the "comprehensive elimination of all forms of racism, racial discrimination, xenophobia and related intolerance." Combating "hate speech" has increasingly become a concern of governmental and civil society organizations. Fighting xenophobia and intolerance is now a growth industry within human rights institutions. This has occurred in part because a large political consensus can be found in multilateral institutions among authoritarian states and the human rights advocates in liberal democracies in favor of promoting "tolerance" by limiting expressions that can be labeled "hate speech." The Council of Europe and the OSCE have been paralyzed by political conflict, but programs promoting tolerance provide common ground—another bridge between opposing perspectives. Russian opposition has forced the OSCE to abandon even use of the term "human rights," but "tolerance" projects abound, and at root they signal the international political convergence against liberty. The Council of Europe fights hate speech from within its human rights bureaucracy, as does the OSCE. The European Union's Agency for Fundamental Rights devotes most of its energies to the politically safe problems of hate speech and discrimination.

Hate speech is thought to damage the dignity of the vulnerable person by defaming characteristics that such an individual shares with a group.[69] The grounds for identifying and prosecuting hate speech are expanding. The Council of Europe has introduced the category of "sexist" hate speech:

> Sexist hate speech relates to expressions which spread, incite, promote or justify hatred based on sex. Some groups of women are particularly targeted by sexist hate speech (notably young women, women in the media or women politicians), but every woman and girl is a potential target for online and offline sexist hate speech. The increasing availability and use of Internet and social platforms have contributed to growing occurrences of sexist hate speech. The Council of Europe has started to address this issue by looking at the potential use of existing standards and at policies on combating gender stereotypes.[70]

The Council of Europe says that "allowing sexist hate speech to thrive with impunity does not constitute freedom of expression as it reduces plurality and diversity and is rather another manifestation of gender inequality."

The main target of anti-hate-speech campaigns is so-called "Islamophobia." No one should doubt that discrimination against Muslims exists and has been a real problem, especially following the events of 2001. The IHF issued a special report on the subject. But the charge of Islamophobia is most often used to try to stifle critical discussion of Islam, which should be legally protected speech, rather than to protect Muslims from actual discrimination. For years, European courts have been sentencing and fining citizens for speech critical of Islam, essentially applying Islamic blasphemy law in Western societies, and treating Muslims as a privileged group. The following critique by Jeffrey Tayler is, unfortunately, on the mark:

> Those who deploy the...term "Islamophobia" to silence critics of the faith hold, in essence, that Muslims deserve to be approached as a race apart—not as equals, not as individual adults capable of rational choice, but as lifelong members of an immutable, sacrosanct community, whose (often

highly illiberal) views must not be questioned, whose traditions (including the veiling of women) must not be challenged, and whose scripturally inspired violence must be explained away as the inevitable outcome of Western "interventionism" in the Middle East or racism and "marginalization" in Western countries.[71]

The campaign against "Islamophobia" trivializes the prejudice and discrimination that Muslims often do encounter as members of minority communities in Europe, while it creates widespread fear of speaking openly about radical or fundamentalist Islam. It has also provoked a vicious backlash that arguably makes those problems worse. This reaction helps accomplish what Islamists want: it unifies Muslims in their own eyes, and in the eyes of the world, so that efforts to combat or contain violent Islamic jihadism are seen as attacks on all Muslims everywhere. It collectivizes problems that should properly be seen as matters of individual moral and legal responsibility.

Official efforts to impose tolerance through censorship have added fuel to nationalist-populist movements. The vast majority of prosecutions for "hate speech" have, in effect, served to enforce Islamic law, and this naturally deepens anxieties about immigration and intensifies prejudice against Muslims. According to Douglas Murray, the prosecution of the Dutch politician Geert Wilders for advocating less immigration to the Netherlands by Moroccans is "a nakedly political move. The Dutch courts are behaving like a religious court. They are trying to regulate public expression and opinion when it comes to the followers of one religion."[72] But the case against Wilders has not prevented his political party from becoming the largest in the Netherlands, and has likely contributed to its success.

Speech expressing anxieties about Islamic beliefs and practices has also been prosecuted as a threat to "public peace." For example, in Germany, Michael Stürzenberger was convicted by the District Court of Munich for "insulting" and "belittling" Muslims and Islam. Stürzenberger, the leader of Freedom Bavaria, was fined 2,500 euros for posts on the *Politically Incorrect* free-speech blog, in which he made highly critical remarks about Islam, characterizing it as a cancer that would destroy Germany. The Munich public prosecutor claimed his remarks would disturb the public peace.

Opponents of a plan to build a mosque in Munich were also subject to state intimidation. They were called "right-wing extremists" by the Bavarian interior minister, Joachim Hermann, who said the anti-mosque campaign was intended to arouse "unconstitutional prejudices." Opponents of the mosque have been placed under surveillance by the German domestic intelligence service (Bundesamt für Verfassungsschutz), a decision that was upheld by the Administrative Court of Bavaria. The Forum for Religious Freedom–Europe, an NGO (disclosure: I'm its president), raised concerns about freedom of speech in this case, but they went unacknowledged by the German media, by officialdom, and by civil society.[73]

In the United Kingdom, numerous individuals have been fined and jailed for speech crimes under the Public Order Act and the Communications Act. Both laws contain vague language that puts citizens at risk from expansive legal interpretations and political exploitation. They are representative of bad legislation that is intended to address real dangers to minority populations, but actually creates more hostility by heavy-handed censorship of other citizens' concerns.[74] After a terrorist murder in Woolwich, for example, police arrested ten people for "malicious" or "anti-religious" language in their online effusions, apparently to make examples of them. The arrests took place in the dead of night. One local authority advised that "the consequences could be serious" should citizens fail to heed warnings against such expression of opinion. The vast majority of prosecutions have involved posts on social media. Alleged crimes involving Facebook and Twitter rose by almost 800 percent in the four years prior to 2013, with about 650 people charged during that period.[75] In 2016, a man named Matthew Doyle was charged with "racial hatred" for Twitter posts in which he called a response by an imaginary Muslim interlocutor "mealy mouthed."[76] This clearly represents a highly elastic definition of racial hatred. Yet those prosecuted under this overzealous and chilling campaign against "speech crimes" have not been defended by the country's vibrant human rights community, or at the international political level.

Although hate-speech laws in Europe and other Western countries have primarily been used against critics of Islam, their chilling effect is broader. Human rights commissions have become Orwellian enforcers of political correctness. The head of Australia's Human Rights Commission sought an indictment of the country's leading political cartoonist under Section 18C of the country's Racial Discrimination Act, which bans any speech likely to offend, humiliate or intimidate (an echo of Islamic law on slander). The cartoon in question allegedly insulted Aboriginal people, and members of the commission demanded an explanation from the artist. One journalist concluded, "The Australian Human Rights Commission has as much credibility as any of the tribunals appointed to enforce the official mindset of a totalitarian regime."[77]

In Europe, a legal space for violating freedom of speech has been established by laws prohibiting Holocaust denial. While the impulse behind those laws may be understandable in historical perspective, the principle is flawed. Even the case for opposing them may be seriously misunderstood, as I found when I spoke at a conference in the UN Palace of Nations in Geneva, and denounced such laws as a violation of the freedom of expression. Afterward, several people praised my "courage" as a Jew willing to "tell the truth about what really happened." I felt myself in the chilling presence of Holocaust denial. "That's not what I was saying," I explained to one interlocutor, whereupon she turned around and walked away. There is no doubt that Holocaust denial is a habit of anti-Semites, but no one should be denied the right to hold or express any belief, and courts are not the place to establish truth. But rather than fading away as they should, those laws have spawned more restrictions on speech.

Violating Germany's laws against hate speech and Holocaust denial carries long prison terms. What is more, under new legislation passed in 2017, social media platforms will be held criminally responsible for hate speech posted by users. The law forces self-censorship, saying that social media platforms must remove hate speech within 24 hours or face fines of up to 50 million euros. A leading journalist, Jochen Bittner, warned that the real target of the law seemed to be political activists on the right.[78] It thus offers a vivid example of how anti-hate-speech laws can be exploited for partisan ends.

The government is apparently anxious to prove its vigilance against politically incorrect expression, after being taken to task by the UN Committee on the Elimination of Racial Discrimination. In 2013, the committee charged that Germany had violated the human rights convention it oversees by not "effectively investigating" statements made by a public figure, Thilo Sarrazin, about the economic habits of members of minority groups. German authorities had refused to prosecute Sarrazin, claiming the statements did not promote racial hatred. The UN committee ruled that the statements were illegal because they amounted to disseminating views of racial superiority and hatred, and recommended that Germany review its policies because it had "failed to provide protection against…discrimination."[79] But according to an analysis by two legal scholars, the committee had shown a "dismissive

treatment of the freedom of expression" as well as an "extensive" interpretation of racial discrimination."[80]

The European Court of Human Rights has not protected citizens against
infringements on their right to freedom of speech. When Swedish citizens who
had distributed leaflets critical of homosexuality appealed their conviction in
Swedish courts for using "homophobic" language, the European Court upheld
it. But as Jacob Mchangama observes, "tolerance and equality before the law
are not principles that give the state the right to change the moral outlook
of others or force their conscience on moral issues such as homosexuality."
According to Mchangama, prosecutions under hate-speech laws are becoming
detached from any actual harm to protected groups: "The European approach
to freedom of expression has created legal and cultural space for politicians
and social movements where the banning of undesirable or disagreeable
symbols and speech becomes a goal in itself."[81]

It isn't surprising that hate-speech indictments are so arbitrary when "hate
speech" has not been clearly defined in law. A factsheet produced by the European Court essentially acknowledges how vague the concept is, saying that
the "identification of expressions that could be qualified as 'hate speech' is
sometimes difficult because this kind of speech does not necessarily manifest
itself through the expression of hatred or of emotions. It can also be concealed
in statements which at a first glance may seem to be rational or normal."[82]
The European Union Agency for Fundamental Rights offers a remarkably
capacious definition, saying that hate speech includes "disrespectful public
discourse."[83] A member of the Danish parliament was found guilty of insulting and denigrating Muslims for quoting a statement that was recognized
as factually true, as the truth is no defense against criminal prosecution for
"hate speech."[84]

Concerns about "incitement to discrimination and hatred" grew from the
historical experience of Nazi anti-Semitic propaganda and discourse. The problem that appeared to need a remedy was the potential for a racist demagogue
to arouse a mob against a minority by group defamation. But hate-speech laws
are not used to punish the members of such mobs for their injurious actions,
but rather to punish those whose words may have incited them. This assumes
that the listeners are automatons, without moral agency, incapable of taking
responsibility for their own reactions to speech by others. Hate-speech laws
collectivize and infantilize individuals, reflecting a paternalistic view of society.
They are, like the restrictions in Putin's Russia, a form of moral censorship, to

shield citizens from wrong or unpleasant or unhealthy ideas, on the assumption that people won't be able to govern their own responses. Following the Muhammad cartoon controversy and similar incidents, many non-Muslims have taken the patronizing position that Muslims should not be expected to control their rage over affronts to their religious feelings.

There is no natural right not to be insulted, but one can argue for a duty under natural law to refrain from reacting violently to insults—and also to refrain from acting criminally in response to defamatory statements about others. The proper barriers to incitement lie in civil society, not in courts. But civil society in Western democracies often promotes restrictions on freedom of speech. When schools and universities are declared "safe spaces" to protect students from hearing hurtful or provocative ideas, those students get the message that they have no moral agency or rational capacity to control their reactions, and no responsibility to do so. Instead, others must be silenced, in violation of their natural rights.

In the United States, hate-speech legislation is incompatible with the First Amendment, but this fact is not understood even by mass media journalists. A commentator on a leading television news channel, for example, claimed that "hate speech is excluded from protection" under the First Amendment.[85] And a public opinion poll found over half of Democrats favoring the criminalization of hate speech, while a third of Republicans agreed.[86]

Neither the international human rights system nor civil society is protecting citizens from raw political censorship, and the subject of human-caused "climate change" is one illustration. The Index on Censorship found that debate on climate change was being "stifled," as mass media try to marginalize data that conflict with a theory of global warming, aiming to force a consensus on the issue. National institutions like the British Royal Society have implied that ulterior motives lie behind skepticism about climate change, and the UN secretary general has put his authority behind the position that skeptics are wrong.[87] Promoting and enforcing particular beliefs about climate change under the legal framework of human rights has become de rigueur at the UN. Speaking at a legal conference in 2012, Mary Robinson, formerly the high commissioner for human rights, insisted that climate change is "a huge human rights issue. It is an intergenerational problem which is undermining the fight against poverty and is a gender issue because it primarily affects women in poverty."[88] The UN is trying to shut down debate on climate change, just as it shut down debate on the nature of human rights.

It is politically expedient for climate change activists and for human rights officials to brand climate change a human rights issue, a notion that has gone virtually unchallenged. Skepticism on the subject is now treated as an attack on human rights and worthy of censure. Thus the organization called Ethics and Climate declared, "Given the immensity of the harm from the climate change disinformation campaign, a case can be made that new laws criminalizing disinformation on matters as dangerous as climate change are warranted where the disinformation is transmitted to protect economic interests."[89]

Powerful politicians like the attorneys general of California and New York seek indictments against ExxonMobil for allegedly lying to shareholders on the issue. Should courts have the authority to establish what is scientific truth? Staff from the Obama administration joined climate activists in advocating for a blackball against a university professor who expressed doubts about the veracity of some scientific claims supporting the idea of manmade climate change.[90] I cannot see any difference between these incidents and the censorship practiced by authoritarian states, where intellectuals and journalists have been tried for writings that contradicted officially sanctioned positions on historical events, or that offended officials in ruling parties. Such trials have attracted the attention of international human rights activists, who monitor trials and defend victims, but those activists are silent—or even complicit—when states crack down on challenges to politically correct ideas.

Failure to Protect the First Freedom

Freedom of religion is a priority for human rights protection because it shields our capacity to form our basic moral and intellectual orientations, independent of government control. Freedom of religion is more than the freedom to attend (or not attend) a church or synagogue or mosque; it is the freedom to situate oneself in the moral universe; to find the basis upon which to judge what is true or false, good or bad, right or wrong. Freedom of religion or belief is the freedom to discover and understand moral distinctions. It allows us to reflect on the principles of human rights, and to rank the moral importance of different rights. But the dogma of the international human rights community holds that moral distinctions between human rights do not exist. All have been ruled equal, not through philosophical reflection, but by a process of political alignment, a drive to equate economic and social rights with civil and political rights.

Freedom of religion was the first human right to be understood as natural to the individual, as a universal right that every society and every government is obligated to respect, a right that was central to the understanding of human rights and democracy at the beginning of modern liberalism. Yet it has also been a victim of the campaign to dethrone natural rights and displace them with the politics of the left. It has been relegated to a small corner of the international human rights system. If no human rights are to be considered more important than any others, then freedom of religion will be balanced against the expanding field of what are now called human rights. If a society aims to engineer substantive equality among its members, making the pursuit of equality a quasi-religious crusade, then it will challenge religious beliefs and choices.[91] The state will have replaced religions as our source of moral truth. Totalitarian states cannot abide freedom of religion, as religious belief intrinsically challenges the absolute power of the state.

The failure of international institutions to protect the freedom of religion is in part the result of a more general lack of regard for moral distinctions— between cultures or ideas or principles, as though the freedom of religion were no more important, no more vital, than state-guaranteed employment counseling. This notion is deeply degrading. International human rights has become an ideology that, under the guise of protecting human dignity, paints mankind as a species with little more individual autonomy than insects.

In the deeply conformist world of international human rights, it is dangerous to one's reputation and career to question the false ideas that are repeated by international authorities. Among these false ideas is that freedom of religion must be weighed against any number of other rights or social goals. When the French government instituted a ban on religious clothing, targeting Muslim full-face veils in 2010, many including my colleagues and myself expected that the European Court of Human Rights would overturn the legislation in order to protect the freedom of religion as a priority human right. We were wrong. In upholding the French ban on wearing the burqa or niqab in 2014, the European Court balanced the right to manifest one's religion against other things that are not even human rights at all, but which the court deemed more important. According to the court's registry, the judges "accepted that the barrier raised against others by a veil concealing the face in public could undermine the notion of 'living together.'" The full-face veil would "call into question the possibility of open interpersonal relationships," which are "an indispensable element of community life within the society in question." The court thus accepted France's claim that veils concealing the face "breached the right of others to live in a space of socialization which made living together easier."[92]

The court's flimsy, psychobabble rationale for denying a central human right set a precedent for limiting anything that makes anyone else uncomfortable and may thus be considered "antisocial." This bodes ill for the preservation of basic liberties. The court's language and reasoning were duplicated in 2016 by Germany's interior minister, Thomas de Maizière, who said, "Showing your face is essential for our communication, co-existence and social cohesion and that's why we're asking everyone to show their faces." Chancellor Angela Merkel followed several months later, at a meeting of the Christian Democratic Union, stating that "The full-face veil must be banned, wherever it is legally possible."[93]

There is no question that fundamentalist Islam and Islamism deeply challenge the effort to protect the freedom of religion. Many tenets of the faith are impossible to defend because they arguably call for infringing upon the rights and dignity of others, and encourage violence. My colleague Willy Fautre, a leading expert on the freedom of religion, has forcefully rejected Islamism as "an ideology that wants to radically change the existing nature of a state into a theocracy to be dominated by one religious worldview.... Islamic totalitarianism is a totalitarian ideology inspired by the Quran but it is not a religion."[94] No one would deny that burqas symbolize values that are inimical to gender equality, but studies (including one by Human Rights Watch) have shown that most women who wear burqas do so voluntarily. For those who wish to wear a burqa or niqab, a ban will keep them out of public places, isolating and disadvantaging them. To deny them the right to manifest their religion would create more inequality, not less.

In 2009, Swiss authorities held a successful federal popular initiative "against the construction of minarets." At that time there were four minarets in the country, attached to mosques in major cities. The IHF and Human Rights Watch stated that the ban was a violation of human rights.[95] The response of the UN Human Rights Council was not a demand to protect the freedom of religion, or to condemn the subjection of a question of human rights to a democratic referendum, but an OIC-backed resolution condemning the "defamation of religion," from which Western democracies abstained.[96] In

2011, the European Court of Human Rights declared a challenge to the ban inadmissible, as the applicants had not proved that they had been victims of a violation of the European Convention on Human Rights.[97]

Fundamentalist Islam itself does not respect the principle of religious freedom, as the laws against apostasy demonstrate. For many millions of people, Islam has not been embraced freely. But while the principle of religious freedom must not be exploited to defend coercion and violence in the name of religion, it must remain to defend the manifestations of religious belief that cause no harm to others. Even if Islam politicizes religion, Western authorities must not politicize the question of religious freedom.

In the United States, a country that exists mainly because of the longing for religious freedom, and one that put religious freedom at the head of its list of constitutionally protected rights, the 2016 platform of the Democratic Party included this clause: "We support a progressive vision of religious freedom that respects pluralism and rejects the misuse of religion to discriminate."[98] Perhaps the language sounds anodyne—like a simple call for respecting religious pluralism. But in view of the prominent controversies involving religious freedom at the time, one can see the problem in framing the most basic human right within a political "vision." It is true that government institutions must not use religion to discriminate against some citizens, but private institutions and individuals in civil society should be permitted to make choices in accordance with religious beliefs. Freedom of religion means not being forced to participate in rituals that violate one's religious commitments. When this freedom is seen as just one among many rights, not one of fundamental moral significance for individuals, then it appears no more important than the "right" to the services of a particular wedding photographer or baker for a gay weddings. I believe in the right to marriage for gay citizens, but it should not be allowed to interfere with the freedom of religion, and it need not do so if tolerance is really a two-way street. As Roger Pilon makes the point, "It is one thing to prevent government officials from discriminating against same-sex couples—that is what equal protection is all about—quite another to force private individuals and organizations into associations they find offensive."[99]

It is even more troubling that someone who came close to winning the presidency of the United States expressed the view that people's religious *beliefs* must be changed. At the Women in the World Summit in 2015, while discussing abortion and reproductive health care, Hillary Clinton said that "deep-seated cultural codes, religious beliefs, and structural biases have to be changed."[100] The statement alarmed religious communities, but not human rights communities. Public and official indifference to infringement on religious freedom is a trend in liberal democracies and in the international human rights community.

The freedom of religion, now as in the eighteenth century, tests our ability to defend those whom we may find alien. Few were concerned when European states persecuted the Church of Scientology; I recall arguing with a colleague in the IHF who insisted, "But those people are crazy!" The German government demonized members of the group and even recommended denying places in schools to their children. When one takes a job in a German hospital, one must sign a legal declaration avowing not to be a member. This was not seen as a human rights issue in the German public discourse, only an issue of fighting a "totalitarian cult."

Minority religious "sects" have regularly been subjected to vicious media characterizations, especially in countries like Austria and France, but with no outcry from official anti-hate-speech monitors. They have been denied equal treatment under the law. Hungary has deregistered religions other than several "official" faiths, throwing their legal status into limbo. My colleagues and I have devoted considerable effort to defending members of the Unification Church in Japan, Moldova, Kazakhstan and other countries. Authorities refused to investigate abductions and torture aimed at forcing members to change their faith. We visited numerous delegations to the UN Human Rights Council to try to convince states to pressure Japanese authorities to afford members of the Unification Church equal treatment under the law, but the issue moved almost no one. No other human rights group would take up the problems of the unpopular movement. The United States government has been the only one to provide any support. Eventually, perhaps because we were successful in urging the UN Human Rights Committee to raise the issue with Japanese authorities, and in exposing "deprogrammers" who exploited fears for their personal gain, the kidnappings ceased.

It is true that choices must be made in the vast challenge of defending human rights, and the problems of minority religions in Western societies rarely involve violent abuse. But indifference to the freedom of religion in Western societies is emblematic of a more general failure to appreciate the importance of protecting the "indisputable core of human rights," that is, natural rights. The failure to appreciate the freedom of religion has revealed a fissure in our understanding of human rights, and a disconnect from the moral impulses that gave birth to common human rights standards. Religion is, after all, what the sociologist Peter Berger called our "sacred canopy." Freedom of religion includes the freedom also of unbelievers to formulate their own answers to the ultimate questions, and to cultivate moral principles based on sources of their choosing. It is the freedom to make moral and intellectual choices in the realm of civil society, choices about irreducible principles. It is the freedom to know and act upon natural law and natural rights.

The international community has moved away from a concept of human rights with freedom at its center. Conditioning the realization of freedom on complex state policies, it encourages legislation that limits freedom of speech and freedom of religion. The postmodern international human rights regime, although it grew out of the liberal tradition, in some ways resembles the fascistic Eurasian and Orthodox Islamic ideas of freedom, in which the rights of individuals must yield to collective political goals. What Eurasianists call "spiritual security" is little different from the Western phenomenon of "political correctness," with its hollow notion of diversity. Regaining respect for the freedom of religion and for natural rights may be the first and most important step, and perhaps the hardest step, toward rebuilding human rights in theory and practice.

On the Future of International Human Rights

The debasement of human rights is one of the main reasons for the decline of the "liberal democratic world order." It has exposed deep-seated illusions about the power of international law, and has brought longstanding doubts about its efficacy into sharper focus. It has revealed the difficulty of promoting individual freedom through inclusive international institutions. The international community has lost touch with the natural rights foundation for international human rights standards, while its members have imposed a system of positive international law whose politicized character discredits the idea of human rights. Today, despite the proliferation of international human rights law and intergovernmental human rights mechanisms, more and more people are denied their most basic human rights. Autocracies and dictatorships are gaining ground on the world scene: according to Freedom House, "2016 marked the 11th consecutive year of decline in global freedom." In fewer than half of the world's states do men and women live in freedom.[1]

Unfree states have solidified power over their citizens, abetted by the United Nations human rights system, where the logic of human rights is used to justify repression. And those captive citizens have been deceived into looking toward the "international community" for solutions to their problems, and into believing that "dialogue" and prolonged "transitions to democracy" will bring true political freedom. They have been pacified by the illusion of a functioning international system of justice, and often blame their plight on neglect by other nations. Their hopes have been misdirected to an international system that promotes peace and stability—indeed, the status quo—over freedom. Drawing the focus of human rights activity toward economic and social rights has hampered mobilization against paternalistic and repressive regimes that restrict moral choice and freedom. It gives cover to political agitation for more intrusive government, and for movements promising solutions to social problems that in fact violate true human rights. It legitimizes calls for restricting freedom in order to promote various interpretations of "social justice." It inspires reactionary populist movements that violate basic principles of human rights and the rule of law when they come to power.

Civil society campaigns in the free world are likewise beguiled into seeing international institutions as the optimal platforms for their advocacy. Establishing intergovernmental institutions and "high level" positions offers the illusion of doing something about intractable human rights problems, but it essentially kicks those problems upstairs, into a region of largely symbolic activity shared by a narrow range of actors far removed from the struggles of women and men living under repression. International human rights institutions have no effective power over repressive regimes. But the civil society human rights community has developed an obsession with the authority and prestige of the international political world and its institutions. Members of that community often pour their energies into mechanisms and processes with negligible concrete impact.[2]

At the same time, the idea of the human right to freedom, what Kant called the original right, has lost its magic. Among younger generations in liberal democracies, large percentages attach little value to individual freedom and evince no visceral rejection of totalitarian ideas. According to research conducted by the Victims of Communism Memorial Foundation, 58 percent of "millennials" claimed to prefer socialist, communist or fascist forms of government to capitalism and democracy. The same survey found a serious lack of understanding of how authoritarian political systems actually function and scant knowledge about the extent of the crimes against humanity that have been committed in their name.[3] Young Americans are also deeply ambivalent about their country's most fundamental constitutional human rights protections. According to a survey by the Brookings Institution in 2017, about half do not believe that "hate speech" is protected by law, and think it legitimate to violently shut down speech with which they disagree. Among those identifying as members of the Democratic Party, fully 62 percent hold the latter view. A majority favor rules on university campuses "prohibiting certain speech or expression of viewpoints that are offensive or biased against certain groups of people."[4] Influential public opinion leaders have fallen for what Jean-François Revel termed the "totalitarian temptation," and openly wish for strong and unaccountable state power that could implement changes they favor.[5]

These are but a few examples of how far contemporary society has drifted from a principled respect for natural rights. In this book, I have tried to show how contradictions in our concept of human rights reflect a betrayal of some central principles of our moral and political tradition. This in turn pulls back the curtain on a broad deviation from a path that offered magnificent possibilities following the Enlightenment. A detachment from the ideal of natural rights, whether by an ideological assault or by neglect, is a recipe for the use of raw power to achieve the objectives of the state, unimpeded by the obstacle of "archaic" philosophies and standards. It calls to mind the advice that Niccolò Machiavelli offered in Chapter XV of *The Prince*, recommending that rulers meet political challenges with methods unconstrained by "imaginary" moral principles. Machiavelli wrote that he wanted to deal with the world as it was, not as it should be; he aimed to provide a "useful" guide to political action, one based on "the effectual truth of the thing." Thus the moral rules set forth in scripture and classical philosophy had to be bypassed in order to get things done in politics. Similarly, progressives declared the "old doctrines" to be "inadequate"; the "transpolitical" standard derived from the nature of man was deemed defective. The ancient philosophy set goals that were impossible to fulfill, being utopian and dependent on "imaginary standards."[6]

In the postmodern world, the standards of natural rights have been subordinated to political goals, and this debasement of human rights has impaired their capacity to secure and protect the basic freedoms vital to human fulfillment. The human rights community seeks to dismiss the "ancient philosophy" of Enlightenment universalism. It aims to universalize particular political preferences, while undermining the idea of universal natural rights because it sprang from a specific political tradition. This turns things on their head. What is ordinary and conventional is promoted as transcendent, with a hollow reverence. No moral or substantive difference is recognized between natural law and positive law, between fundamental, universal laws and conventional laws. International human rights law has lost the sense of representing a transcendent standard for nations.

The Disenchantment of Human Rights

Human rights has also become rationalized and routinized, to use concepts from the sociology of Max Weber. International human rights has become a bureaucracy, burdened by an obsession with process and procedure. Under the influence of economic and social rights, it has largely been reduced to small, technical questions. Weber saw modern industrial society moving toward "mechanized petrification," being dominated by "specialists without spirit, sensualists without heart."[7] Human rights defenders have turned into technocrats. Passion for freedom has been drained from their language. Yet contemporary human rights leaders promoting expanded intergovernmental human rights bureaucracies exhibit a deep complacency; in Weber's words, "this nullity imagines that it has attained a level of civilization never before achieved."[8]

In the Fifth Thesis of the "Idea of a Universal History with a Cosmopolitan Intent," Kant had seen the "achievement of a universal civil society which administers law among men" as the goal of human progress. Originally inspired by Kant's vision of rational progress toward freedom and individual rights, Weber later warned that the modern world was becoming an "iron cage" because of the progressive rationalization of social life, leading to a spiritually empty state of disenchantment; it would be a "polar night of icy darkness."[9] Weber rejected the "rational kingdom of ends" advocated by Kant. The hubristic crusade to remove risk, to ensure equality of result, to engineer the "conditions for freedom" with global economic and social rights regulation is without doubt the very perversion of Enlightenment rationalism about which Max Weber despaired.

The disenchantment of human rights has led to a disenchantment *with* human rights. The problem is becoming clear, especially in the Anglo-Saxon realm of political culture, but solutions are not. Conservatives in particular have been thoroughly alienated from human rights, but have no alternative plan for protecting freedom. Over a decade ago, the British Conservative leader Michael Howard blamed his country's Human Rights Act of 1998 for "the avalanche of political correctness, costly litigation, feeble justice, and culture of compensation running riot in Britain today." The act was intended to incorporate the substance of the European Convention on Human Rights into UK law, but the long dispute over how to implement the convention revealed a widespread conservative estrangement from the understanding of human rights that prevails in international institutions. Michael Gove, as justice secretary, complained that "human rights culture…supplants common sense and common law, and erodes individual dignity by encouraging citizens to see themselves as supplicants and victims to be pensioned by the state." Lord Judge, Britain's former chief justice, warned that the European Court of Human Rights disregards democratic processes because it supplants the "sovereignty of Parliament" with rulings by unelected judges.[10]

The absurdity of the new human rights is a dirty little secret, yet a problem too big to address. A leading Liberal member of the European Parliament told me that human rights made sense only if defined and interpreted narrowly, but that idea isn't to be heard in public political discourse. Another member agreed, but warned that the issue was "controversial." In 2017, a proposal was made for a European Parliament workshop to discuss how expansion of the concept of human rights affected efforts to protect human rights, but the idea met stiff opposition.

In the United States, conservatives have blocked the ratification of most major international human rights legislation, not because they are against human rights, but because they reject what they view as the ideological content of treaties, and the potential infringement on national sovereignty and on the individual freedoms of U.S. citizens. American discontent with the human rights agenda at the United Nations has led to calls for withdrawing from human rights institutions and for defunding the UN itself.

International law in general, and international human rights law in particular, may have reached a point of unraveling, as widespread reaction to the prospect of global governance rides on a tide of populism and calls for a renewal of national sovereignty. These movements are not demanding respect for individual rights, but are resisting global or regional social engineering. The fragile remains of natural rights and respect for individual freedom are in danger of being swept away under one or another form of authoritarian collectivism. We have encouraged this retreat from international human rights standards by allowing politicized and overreaching global regulations to become untenable. International human rights law and institutions have come to be associated with social engineering, global centralization, and even global governance. The idea of human rights today carries connotations of moral condescension by a left-wing elite that promotes ideological multiculturalism while scorning national cultural identities. Moreover, most discourse about human rights today consists in complaints about "neoliberalism" and charges that the slide into leftist global politics has not gone far enough. According to Costas Douzinas, "Human rights claims and struggles bring to the surface the exclusion, domination and exploitation and the inescapable strife that permeates social and political life," while the international human rights system keeps a lid on the class struggle by "framing it in terms of legal and individual remedies."[11]

Hubris has dragged international human rights law and institutions in political directions, and consequently, political division is weakening the commitment to human rights in Western societies. What János Kis called the "indisputable core of human rights" is not a matter of ideology. When restricted to narrow, clear, justiciable principles, human rights provide common ground for people of all political stripes who believe in the protection of individual freedoms on principle, and when these freedoms are guarded, societies can solve their problems through democratic means. But human rights become the focus of political disputes when expansive interpretations drag in questions of social policy better left to legislatures, and when proponents of global governance and social transformation schemes try to use human rights law to achieve them.

A backlash against human rights hubris is thus eroding commitment to the very idea of an international human rights system among heirs to the classical liberal tradition that gave birth to the concept. International human rights are predicated on relinquishing an element of sovereignty in adopting universal standards. But political parties and leaders deeply skeptical of international law are gaining power, and when more states are governed by nationalist parties concerned first to defend sovereignty, international institutions will decline. What, then, can be the future for human rights? Will we "throw the baby out with the bathwater"? Will the excesses of economic and social rights bring down respect for freedom rights as well?

An international regime that promotes and protects natural rights would indeed allow politically neutral observers to expose the failings of oppressive governments, but it would not dictate their political choices, nor would it provide a rationale for abusing their citizens. An international regime that supports economic and social rights, on the other hand, threatens the sovereignty of citizens in a democracy more than it does the power of states. Despite their revolutionary pedigree, economic and social rights have proved to be engines of the status quo, while natural rights provide a path toward liberation and rational principles for reform.

The current trend toward reasserting nationalism and national sovereignty will bring the question of human rights back home, to the realm of constitutional law, and this can be either good or bad for natural rights. It has the potential to ground natural rights more securely in national institutions and in the consciousness and allegiances of citizens. But nationalism can also subsume the individual into a state conceived as an organic reality, a state built on denying that "the individual is governed by a rule of conduct superior to the arbitrary decrees of the earthly authority."[12] Nationalist approaches to human rights will likely take the form seen under Vladimir Putin, or the Chinese Communists, or many other authoritarian states: Each nation has its own notion of human rights, with no concept of universal natural rights discernable by reason. Ethnic and nationalist chauvinism is thus a threat to human rights both within states and at the international level.

A Future for Human Rights: "We must think!"

Respect for natural rights is threatened on multiple fronts: by the corrosive force of utopianism and hubris in Western democracies; by the resurgence of nationalist statism and totalitarian Islamism; by leftist intellectual critiques that hold liberal internationalism to be a mask for neoliberal exploitation and oppression of national communities. International human rights institutions are deeply infected by antiliberal forces. If there is to be an international program to protect natural rights in the future, it will likely emerge as a loose coalition of free states that work together to assist freedom movements around the world, while evaluating the legitimacy of governments according to common standards.

Hersch Lauterpacht, in looking over the history of the idea of natural law, saw revivals of respect for the concept in periods of rising nationalism, when fears about the dangers of state power became acute. A renewed respect for natural rights will need to be rooted in the civil societies of national states, and nurtured in educational and philanthropic institutions. Civil society organizations devoted to promoting natural rights need to be fostered. Human rights groups devoted to civil and political rights must be given means of support outside of the mainstream foundations and intergovernmental institutions. Human rights must be understood in philosophical terms, not through "methodological positivism." Respect for individual human rights needs to be firmly rooted in the beliefs and actions of individuals who, like the Soviet human rights dissidents, establish the existence of freedom by their own acts.

There is still a need for inclusive global institutions to provide a platform for discussing challenges to security, for promoting health and environmental protection, and for addressing many other problems that require international cooperation for their solution. But we who uphold the principle of natural rights must come to terms with the fact that the human rights institutions of the United Nations have been victims of a hostile takeover, where levels of hypocrisy have become toxic. The citizens of the world cannot rely on a Human Rights Council composed of members that deny women equal rights; that are controlled by religious extremists and impose the death penalty on those who change their religion; that are autocratic and even totalitarian. Such an institution will not and cannot protect individual rights and freedoms. Perhaps even worse, it is a threat to the very idea of human rights.

States committed to natural rights could stay in those institutions, but if they do, they must articulate and fight for their ideas. Even if we believe those institutions have no future, we can use them to make the case for human rights that is not being made now. It will be expressed not in a toothless international legal regime, but rather in a moral consensus among free peoples to protect their own rights and to express solidarity in concrete ways with the citizens of oppressive states that deny them political freedom. A human rights policy of this form would not rely on multilateral consensus, but would pursue bilateral means to pressure abusive governments and help captive peoples. Citizens of a democratic state that understands and treasures natural rights will likely not be indifferent to the situation of those in other lands who do not enjoy those rights. In the idea of natural rights we find the true foundation of the universality of human rights and the moral obligations it imposes.

The hijacking of human rights as a concept was made possible by a political assault on the idea of freedom, an assault led by condescending leftists seeking greater state power and disrespecting the moral agency of the individual. If we are serious about protecting the idea and the practice of human rights, we must go back to the roots of human rights, declaring that we are not speaking of regulating the fast food industry, the technology available in homes for the elderly, rent control, gender quotas, or reducing carbon emissions. We are speaking about the difference between freedom and coercion, and we are arguing for freedom. If American colonists were ready to die for their natural rights, if Soviet dissidents had the courage to freeze in Gulag camps to uphold their principles, if Chinese students were ready to face slaughter on Tiananmen Square in resistance to totalitarianism, then we must be ready to think deeply about what they sacrificed for, and be prepared to defend it.

The second American president, John Adams, as a young lawyer and revolutionary and an avid student of classical philosophy, declared to his fellow colonists that in order to establish freedom in America, "We must *think!*"[13] Now, as then, citizens everywhere must think about the meaning of human rights if we truly wish to protect and preserve them. Human rights institutions will not be reformed from the top down; the corrupt international superstructure of human rights must be allowed to wither away. A new human rights community must be formed, a community devoted to human rights universalism but skeptical of global governance. It must draw its members from among those concerned to defend individual freedom, from among those who have given up on human rights and need to be convinced that freedom requires human rights. The tectonic shifts underway as this book is being completed seem like grave threats to international human rights, and indeed we are in a period of "deconstruction." But as is often the case, decline and failure open up new possibilities. As international human rights is sailing into a moral vacuum, there is room to revive a human rights understanding based on natural rights. In the debasement of human rights lies a challenge and an opportunity.

Notes

INTRODUCTION

1 Jonah Goldberg, *Liberal Fascism* (New York: Broadway Books, 2007), p. 85.

2 Sonja Biserko, *Yugoslavia's Implosion: The Fatal Attraction of Serbian Nationalism* (Oslo: Norwegian Helsinki Committee, 2012), p. 33.

3 Ibid., pp. 85–86.

CHAPTER 1: THE ACHILLES' HEEL
OF INTERNATIONAL HUMAN RIGHTS

1 The phrase is from an unpublished paper by Jan Edward Garrett, "The Doubtful Descent of Human Rights from Stoicism."

2 Heinrich Rommen, *The Natural Law: A Study in Legal and Social History and Philosophy*, trans. Thomas R. Hanley (1947; Indianapolis: Liberty Fund, 1998), Kindle loc. 593.

3 Hersch Lauterpacht, *An International Bill of the Rights of Man* (1945; Oxford, UK: Oxford University Press, 2013), pp. 18–20.

4 Marcus Tullius Cicero, *The Republic and The Laws*, trans. Niall Rudd (New York: Oxford University Press, 1998), p. 69.

5 Rommen, *The Natural Law*, Kindle loc. 525.

6 Thomas Jefferson said that liberties would not be secure were they not believed to be the gift of God, which was their "only firm basis."

7 Robert P. George, "Natural Law," *Harvard Journal of Law and Public Policy* 31 no. 1 (2007), p. 174.

8 Leo Strauss, *Natural Right and History* (1950; Chicago: University of Chicago Press, 1971), p. 9.

9 Ayn Rand, *The Virtue of Selfishness: A New Concept of Egoism* (New York: Signet, 1964), p. 93.

10 Lord Denning's statement has been reported by his successors as Master of the Rolls, Lord Bingham and Lord Dyson. See, for example, Lord Dyson, "Speech at Magna Carta, Religion and The Rule of Law," Temple, London, June 7, 2014, p. 2, https://www.judiciary.gov.uk/wp-content/uploads/2014/06/mor-speech-magna-carta-religion1.pdf

11 See Jack Donnelly, *Universal Human Rights in Theory and Practice*, 2nd ed. (Ithaca, N.Y.: Cornell University Press, 2003), pp. 72–86.

12 Gregory Johnson, "The First Founding Father: Aristotle on Freedom and Popular Government," in *Liberty and Democracy*, ed. Tibor R. Machan (Stanford, Calif.: Hoover Institution Press, 2002), p. 37.

13 Immanuel Kant, *Groundwork of the Metaphysics of Morals* (6:237), trans. Mary Gregor (Cambridge, UK: Cambridge University Press, 1996), p. 30.

14 Ibid.

15 Clifford Orwin and Thomas Pangle, "The Philosophical Foundation of Human Rights," in *Human Rights in Our Time: Essays in Memory of Victor Baras*, ed. Marc F. Plattner (Boulder, Col.: Westview Press, 1984), p. 8.

16 Ibid., p. 11.

17 Asbjørn Eide, "Economic and Social Rights," in *Human Rights: Concepts and Standards*, ed. Janusz Symonides, UNESCO Publishing (Aldershot, UK: Ashgate, 2000), p. 113.

18 Mark Mazower, "The Strange Triumph of Human Rights, 1933–1950," *Historical Journal* 47 no. 2 (June 2004), pp. 379–98.

19 Ibid., p. 381.

20 A point also made by Mazower in ibid.

21 UNESCO Symposium on Human Rights, 1948, UNESCO/PHS/3(Rev.), Introduction, p. VI, quoted in Moses Moskowitz, *Human Rights and World Order* (New York: Oceana Publications, 1958), p. 84.

22 As recorded in Paul Gordon Lauren, *The Evolution of International Human Rights* (Philadelphia: University of Pennsylvania Press, 1998), p. 221.

23 Thomas Krapf, "The Last Witness to the Drafting Process of the Universal Declaration of Human Rights: Interview with Stéphane Frédéric Hessel," *Human Rights Quarterly* 35 no. 3 (August 2013), pp. 253–68.

24 Ibid.

25 Hessel's *Indignez-vous!* (*Time for Outrage*), first published in 2010 and translated into numerous languages, sold 3.5 million copies.

26 Samuel Moyn, "The Universal Declaration of Human Rights of 1948 in the History of Cosmopolitanism," *Critical Inquiry*, Summer 2014, p. 372.

27 Eide, "Economic and Social Rights," p. 118.

28 See Zühtü Arslan, "Taking Rights Less Seriously: Postmodernism and Human Rights," *Res Publica* 5 no. 2 (December 1999), p. 199.

29 Isaiah Berlin, *Four Essays on Liberty* (Oxford, UK: Oxford University Press, 1969), p. 144.

30 Karl Marx, *On the Jewish Question*, in *Karl Marx: Selected Writings*, ed. David McLellan, 2nd ed. (Oxford, UK: Oxford University Press, 2000), p. 61.

31 Arslan, "Taking Rights Less Seriously," p. 199, n. 26.

32 See, for example, James Ostrowski, *Progressivism: A Primer on the Idea Destroying America* (Buffalo, N.Y.: Cazenovia Books, 2014), Kindle loc. 585ff.

33 David Bernstein, *Rehabilitating Lochner: Defending Individual Rights against Progressive Reform* (Chicago: University of Chicago Press, 2011), p. 44.

34 Ibid., p. 40.

35 President Franklin Roosevelt, State of the Union Address, January 11, 1944.

36 David McCullough writes that Truman was applauded for three minutes by an audience including many of Great Britain's elite academics following the statement, which he made after receiving the honorary degree *Doctoris in Iure Civili* (Doctor of Civil Law) in June 1956. McCullough, *Truman* (New York: Simon & Schuster, 1992), pp. 956–57.

37 For example, Daniel J. Whelan, *Indivisible Human Rights: A History* (Philadelphia: University of Pennsylvania Press, 2010), p. 21.

38 John P. Humphrey, *Human Rights and the United Nations: A Great Adventure* (New York: Transnational Publishers, 1984), pp. 31–32.

39 Christopher N. J. Roberts, *The Contentious History of the International Bill of Rights* (Cambridge, UK: Cambridge University Press, 2014), p. 41.

40 UNESCO, "The Grounds of an International Declaration of Human Rights," Paris, July 31, 1947, http://unesdoc.unesco.org/images/0012/001243/124350eb.pdf

41 Lauterpacht, *An International Bill of the Rights of Man*, p. 90.

42 Ibid., pp. 155–56.

43 Ibid., p. 157.

44 See Jan Narveson, "Collective Rights?" *Canadian Journal of Law and Jurisprudence* 4 no. 2 (July 1991), p. 334.

45 See Aryeh Neier, "Social and Economic Rights: A Critique," Center for Human Rights and Humanitarian Law, *Human Rights Brief* 13 no. 2 (2006), pp. 1–2.

46 See, for example, the policies of Advancing Human Rights, a group started by Robert Bernstein, the disillusioned founder of Human Rights Watch.

47 Charles Fried, *Right and Wrong* (Cambridge, Mass.: Harvard University Press, 1978), p. 110.

48 Frank Holman, "'An International Bill of Rights': Proposals Have Dangerous Implications for U.S.," *American Bar Association Journal* 34 no. 11 (November 1948), p. 1080.

49 Whelan, *Indivisible Human Rights*, p. 6.

50 Moses Moskowitz, *Human Rights and World Order* (New York: Oceana Publications, 1958), p. 25.

51 See, for example, Dianne Otto, "Rethinking the 'Universality' of Human Rights Law," *Columbia Human Rights Review* 29 (1997), pp. 1–46.

52 Mazower, "The Strange Triumph of Human Rights, 1933–1950," p. 397.

53 John Halprin, William F. Schulz and Sarah Dreier, "Universal Human Rights in Progressive Thought and Politics," Center for American Progress, October 2010, https://www.scribd.com/document/38956856/Universal-Human-Rights-in-Progressive-Thought-and-Politics

54 The British philosopher Maurice Cranston made this point in his argument against economic and social rights, in *What Are Human Rights?* (New York: Basic Books, 1964).

CHAPTER 2: THE CONCEPT OF HUMAN RIGHTS DURING THE COLD WAR

1 Jesse Norman and Peter Oborne, *Churchill's Legacy: The Conservative Case for the Human Rights Act* (London: Liberty, 2009), p. 9.

2 Council of Europe, *Collected Edition of the "Travaux Préparatoires" of the European Convention on Human Rights* (The Hague: Martinus Nijhoff, 1976).

3 See, for example, Costas Douzinas, "Human rights or a British bill of rights?" *Guardian*, June 30, 2010.

4 Quoted in Daniel J. Whelan, *Indivisible Human Rights: A History* (Philadelphia: University of Pennsylvania Press, 2010), p. 72.

5 Ibid., p. 129.

6 The terms from Thomas Kuhn, *The Structure of Scientific Revolutions* (1962), are relevant to the development of human rights.

7 See Whelan, *Indivisible Human Rights*, p. 135ff.

8 Asbjørn Eide, "Economic and Social Rights," in *Human Rights: Concepts and Standards*, ed. Janusz Symonides, UNESCO Publishing (Aldershot, UK: Ashgate, 2000), p. 110.

9 Ibid., p. 132.

10 Ibid.

11 Ibid.

12 Ibid., p. 130.

13 Whelan, *Indivisible Human Rights*, p. 144.

14 Ibid., p. 146.

15 Moses Moskowitz, "Implementing Human Rights: Present Status and Future Prospects," in *Human Rights: Thirty Years after the Universal Declaration*, ed. B. G. Ramcharan (The Hague: Martinus Nijhoff, 1979), p. 122.

16 James Ring Adams, "From Helsinki to Madrid," in *Human Rights in Our Time: Essays in Memory of Victor Baras*, ed. Marc F. Plattner (Boulder, Col.: Westview Press, 1984), p. 119.

17 Daniel J. Whelan, "The United States and economic and social rights: past, present ... and future?" Human Rights and Human Welfare Working Paper No. 26, posted February 28, 2005, p. 11, https://www.du.edu/korbel/hrhw/workingpapers/2005/26-whelan-2005.pdf

18 Jacob Mchangama, "The Sordid Origin of Hate Speech Laws," *Policy Review*, December 1, 2011.

19 Ibid.

20 Ibid.

21 See Aaron Rhodes, "Mannomann: Die Frauenquote ist ein Menschenrechtsverstoss," *Zeit Online*, November 12, 2014.

22 Some of the following material has been published in a different form, in Aaron Rhodes, "Human rights concepts in the OSCE region: changes since the Helsinki Final Act," *Central Asian Survey* 36 no. 3 (April 2017), pp. 313–30.

23 Ernest Gellner, "The Pluralist Anti-Levellers of Prague," *Contemporary Thought and Politics*, vol. 2 of *Selected Philosophical Themes* (1974; London: Routledge, 2003), p. 163.

24 Ludmilla Alexeyeva, *Soviet Dissent: Contemporary Movements for National, Religious, and Human Rights* (Middletown, Conn.: Wesleyan University Press, 1985), p. 267.

25 F. C. Barghoorn, *Politics in the USSR* (Boston: Little, Brown, 1966), p. 47.

26 Árpád Kadarkay, *Human Rights in American and Russian Political Thought* (Lanham, Md.: University Press of America, 1982), p. 168ff.

27 Aviezer Tucker, *The Philosophy and Politics of Czech Dissidence from Patočka to Havel* (Pittsburgh: University of Pittsburgh Press, 2000), p. 120.

28 Alexeyeva, *Soviet Dissent*, p. 292.

29 Valery Chalidze, *To Defend These Rights*, trans. G. Daniels (London: Collins & Harvill Press, 1975), p. 60.

30 Alexeyeva, *Soviet Dissent*, p. 268.

31 Andrei Amalrik, *Will the Soviet Union Survive Until 1984?* (New York: Harper & Row, 1970).

32 Valery Chalidze, *The Soviet Human Rights Movement: A Memoir* (New York: Jacob Blaustein Institute for the Advancement of Human Rights, American Jewish Committee, 1984), p. 3.

33 Ibid., p. 4.

34 It was, according to the Helsinki Commission of the United States Congress, the most persecuted of all the Helsinki watch organizations.

35 Chalidze, *The Soviet Human Rights Movement*, p. 28.

36 Valery Chalidze and Richard Schifter, *Glasnost and the Primacy of Social and Economic Rights* (Washington, D.C.: Freedom House, 1988), p. 5.

37 Andrei Sakharov, *Memoirs*, trans. Richard Lourie (New York: Random House, 1990), p. 418.

38 Tucker, *The Philosophy and Politics of Czech Dissidence*, p. 116.

39 The distinction was made by Jean-Paul Sartre in *Search for a Method* [Questions de méthode], trans. Hazel E. Barnes (New York: Alfred A. Knopf, 1963).

40 Tucker, *The Philosophy and Politics of Czech Dissidence*, p. 173.

41 Chalidze, *To Defend These Rights*, p. 4ff.

42 Tucker, *The Philosophy and Politics of Czech Dissidence*, p. 120.

43 See Jack Donnelly, *Universal Human Rights in Theory and Practice*, 2nd ed. (Ithaca, N.Y.: Cornell University Press, 2003), p. 10ff.

44 *Human Rights in the Democracy Movement Twenty Years Ago—Human Rights Today*, Conference in Budapest, November 21–22, 2005, ed. David Roberts Evans and Ferenc Köszeg (Budapest: Hungarian Helsinki Committee, 2006), p. 60.

CHAPTER 3: BIRTH OF THE POST–COLD WAR
HUMAN RIGHTS DOGMA

1 Leo Strauss, *Natural Right and History* (1950; Chicago: University of Chicago Press, 1971), p. 2.

2 Richard Rorty, "Human Rights, Rationality and Sentimentality," in *Wronging Rights? Philosophical Challenges for Human Rights*, ed. Aakash Singh Rathore and Alex Cistelecan (London: Routledge, 2011), p. 108. I made some of the same points expressed here in "Human Rights in the 'New Europe': Some Problems,"

a chapter in *The Politics of Human Rights*, ed. The Belgrade Circle (London: Verso, 1992).

3 The same basic point was made by Michael Ignatieff when he argued against any metaphysical human rights claims as "divisive," in *Human Rights as Politics and Idolatry* (Princeton, N.J.: Princeton University Press, 2002), p. 54.

4 G. Fackre, letter to the *University of Chicago Magazine*, June 1994.

5 James Ceaser, "What Next for the Left?" *Weekly Standard*, February 8, 2016.

6 Address by Secretary-General Boutros Boutros-Ghali at the opening of the World Conference on Human Rights, Vienna, June 14, 1993, in *The United Nations and Human Rights, 1945–1995*, The United Nations Blue Book Series, vol. 7 (New York: United Nations Department of Public Information, 1995), doc. 84, pp. 441–48, at p. 442.

7 Ibid., pp. 442, 443.

8 Ibid., p. 443.

9 Fareed Zakaria, "The Rise of Illiberal Democracy," *Foreign Affairs*, November 1, 1997.

10 James Finn, "Human Rights in Vienna," *First Things*, November 1993.

11 Vienna Declaration and Programme of Action, Adopted by the World Conference on Human Rights in Vienna, A/CONF.157/24 (June 25, 1993).

12 The Center for Women's Global Leadership, Rutgers University, New Jersey.

13 Charlotte Bunch, "The Global Campaign for Women's Human Rights: Where Next Year After Vienna?" *St. John's Law Review* 69 (1995), p. 171ff.

14 Hilary Charlesworth, "Human Rights as Men's Rights," in *Women's Rights, Human Rights: International Feminist Perspectives*, ed. Julie Peters and Andrea Wolper (New York: Routledge, 1995), pp. 103–13. See also Hilary Charlesworth and Christine Chinkin, *The Boundaries of International Law: A Feminist Analysis* (Huntington, N.Y.: Juris Publishing, 2000).

15 "UN human rights office accused of 'bizarre' behaviour after condemning the 'free market,'" *Telegraph*, September 6, 2016.

16 United Nations, "In hard-hitting speech, UN human rights chief warns against populists and demagogues," UN News Centre, September 6, 2016.

17 UN Human Rights Council, Opening Statement by Zeid Ra'ad Al Hussein, September 13, 2016.

18 Vienna Declaration and Programme of Action, Part I, Article 5.

19 See, for example, Heiner Bielefeldt, "Misperceptions of Freedom of Religion or Belief," *Human Rights Quarterly* 35 no. 1 (February 2013), pp. 33–68.

20 Asbjørn Eide, "Interdependence and Indivisibility of Human Rights," in *Human Rights in Education, Science and Culture: Legal Developments and Challenges*, ed. Yvonne Donders and Vladimir Volodin (Aldershot, UK: Ashgate, 2007), p. 11.

21 James Nickel, statement at the "Rethinking Human Rights" seminar organized by the Freedom Rights Project, King's College London, May 8–9, 2013.

22 UN Committee on Economic, Social and Cultural Rights, Contribution at the World Conference on Human Rights, Vienna, A/CONF.157/PC/62/Add.5 (March 26, 1993).

23 According to Aryeh Neier, an American human rights leader, this is the origin of the term "social rights." See his *International Human Rights Movement: A History* (Princeton, N.J.: Princeton University Press, 2012), p. 83ff.

24 Hon Gareth Evans QC, Minister for Foreign Affairs of Australia, "Human Rights and the New World Order," Speech to the World Conference on Human Rights, Vienna, June 15, 1993, available at http://www.gevans.org/speeches2.html

25 Kevin Boyle, "Stock-taking on Human Rights: The World Conference on Human Rights, Vienna 1993," *Political Studies* 43, Issue Supp. 1 (August 1995), p. 80ff.

26 Moses Moskowitz, "Implementing Human Rights: Present Status and Future Prospects," in *Human Rights: Thirty Years after the Universal Declaration*, ed. B. G. Ramcharan (The Hague: Martinus Nijhoff, 1979), p. 125, quoted in Daniel J. Whelan, *Indivisible Human Rights: A History* (Philadelphia: University of Pennsylvania Press, 2010), p. 177.

27 Yoani Sanchez, "Cubans Are Trapped in a Myth," *Huffington Post*, https://www. huffingtonpost.com/yoani-sanchez/cubans-are-trapped-in-a_b_2959496.html

28 Erika Guevara-Rosas, "Fidel Castro's human rights legacy: A tale of two worlds," quoted by Amnesty International, November 26, 2016.

29 *Washington Post*, June 9, 1993, cited in Andrew Clapham, "Creating the High Commissioner for Human Rights: The Outside Story," *European Journal of International Law* 5 (1994), p. 560.

30 UN General Assembly, "High Commissioner for the promotion and protection of all human rights," A/RES/48/141 (December 20, 1993).

31 Clapham, "Creating the High Commissioner for Human Rights," p. 556.

32 Brian Tamanaha, *The Rule of Law* (Cambridge, UK: Cambridge University Press, 2004), p. 34.

33 Jan Edward Garrett, "The Doubtful Descent of Human Rights from Stoicism," unpublished paper, p. 8.

34 Roger Scruton, "Nonsense on Stilts," prepared for a Conference on Human Rights, Lincoln's Inn, London, 2011, http://www.morec.com/scruton/nonsense. html

35 Ibid.

36 Tamanaha, *The Rule of Law*, p. 43.

37 For example, in 2017, when members of the European Parliament asked for a critical discussion about how an expansive concept of human rights had affected the protection of human rights, the proposal was opposed by a majority of the Parliament's Human Rights Subcommittee.

CHAPTER 4: TOWARD HUMAN RIGHTS
WITHOUT FREEDOM

1 UN Office of the High Commissioner for Human Rights, "Analytical study on the relationship between climate change and the human right of everyone to the enjoyment of the highest attainable standard of physical and mental health," A/HRC/32/23 (May 6, 2016).

2 See for example, Anna Walnycki, "Recognizing urban rights: global debates and local struggles," International Institute for Environment and Development, June 14, 2016.

3 James Griffin, *On Human Rights* (Oxford, UK: Oxford University Press, 2008), p. 2.

4 Jacob Mchangama and Guglielmo Verdirame, "The Danger of Human Rights Proliferation," *Foreign Affairs*, July 24, 2013.

5 See my own article, "Does Universal Human Rights Mean Anything Anymore?" *American Thinker*, August 19, 2012.

6 UN Committee on Economic, Social and Cultural Rights, General Comment No. 12, "The right to adequate food (Art. 11)," E/C.12/1999/5 (May 12, 1999), par. 15.

7 Ibid., par. 26.

8 Michael Astor, "UN Expert: Junk Food is a Human Rights Concern," Associated Press, October 25, 2016.

9 UN General Assembly, "The human right to water and sanitation," A/RES/64/292 (July 28, 2010).

10 "Trickle Down: Is Access to Clean Water a Human Right?" *Scientific American*, April 6, 2011.

11 UN Committee on Economic, Social and Cultural Rights, General Comment No. 14, "The right to the highest attainable standard of health (article 12 of the International Covenant on Economic, Social and Cultural Rights," E/C.12/2000/4 (August 11, 2000), par. 9.

12 UN Human Rights Council, "Access to medicines in the context of the right of everyone to the enjoyment of the highest attainable standard of physical and mental health," A/HRC/RES/32/15 (July 1, 2016).

13 Shreerupa Mitra-Jha, "UN Human Rights Council adopts landmark resolution on access to medicines," *Firstpost*, July 2, 2016.

14 United Nations Population Fund (UNFPA), State of world population 2012, "By choice, not chance: family planning, human rights and development," Summary, http://www.unfpa.org/sites/default/files/resource-pdf/EN-SWOP2012-Summary. pdf

15 Eithne Dodd, "Is There a Human Right to Contraception?" *RightsInfo*, January 3, 2018.

16 See Molly Moorhead, "In Context: Sandra Fluke on contraceptives and women's health," *Politifact*, March 6, 2012.

17 Chris Grove and Daniela Ikawa, "Historic step towards access to justice for ESCR violations at UN," Open Democracy, December 1, 2015.

18 ParentalRights.US,"Why We Oppose It—Problems with the CRPD," *Watchman*, January 8, 2014, http://www.watchman.parentalrights.us/articles/why-we-oppose-it-problems-with-the-crpd_4.html

19 UN Committee on the Rights of Persons with Disabilities, "Concluding observations on the initial report of the European Union," CRPD/C/EU/CO/1 (July 14, 2016), par. 9.

20 Ibid., par. 21.

21 European Parliament, Report on the implementation of the UN Convention on the Rights of Persons with Disabilities, with special regard to the Concluding Observations of the UN CRPD Committee, 2015/2258(INI) (June 9, 2016).

22 Richard W. Rahn, "Resist the UN's Disability Convention," *Washington Times*, August 7, 2012.

23 Joel Hirst, "A Sad OAS General Assembly Meeting," *Huffington Post*, September 8, 2012.

24 Manuela Picq, "Is the Inter-American Commission of [*sic*] Human Rights too progressive?" *AlJazeera*, June 9, 2012.

25 European Commission, EU Charter of Fundamental Rights, http://ec.europa.eu/justice/fundamental-rights/charter/index_en.htm

26 Damian Chalmers, Gareth Davies and Giorgio Monti, *European Union Law: Cases and Materials* (Cambridge, UK: Cambridge University Press, 2010), p. 239.

27 Navanethem Pillay, "Strengthening the United Nations human rights treaty body system," Report by the UN High Commissioner for Human Rights, June 2012.

28 See Jacob Mchangama and Aaron Rhodes, "The Call for a Global Tax," *National Review*, May 22, 2012.

29 See UN Watch, "U.N. to Endorse Hero of Holocaust Deniers, Alfred De Zayas," December 20, 2015.

30 Philip Alston, "Reconceiving the UN Human Rights Regime: Challenges Confronting the New UN Human Rights Council," June 2006, p. 11, https://ssrn.com/abstract=907471

31 Ibid., pp. 20–22.

32 UN General Assembly, "Human Rights Council," A/Res/60/251 (April 3, 2006), par. 4. Cf. Manfred Nowak et al., "UN Human Rights Council in Crisis: Proposals to Enhance the Effectiveness of the Council," in *European Yearbook on Human Rights 2011*, ed. Wolfgang Benedek et al. (Cambridge, UK: Intersentia, 2011), p. 48.

33 Nowak et al., "UN Human Rights Council in Crisis," p. 56. Italics in the original.

34 Radhika Balakrishnan and James Heintz, "Economic Reform Is a Human Right," *Nation*, March 13, 2014.

35 Balakrishnan is the director of the Center for Women's Global Leadership at Rutgers University. She is also coeditor (with Diane Elson) of *Economic Policy and Human Rights: Holding Governments to Account* (London: Zed Books, 2011).

36 European Commission, "EU researchers and policymakers debate European human rights challenges," Community Research and Development Information Service (CORDIS), June 29, 2016.

37 UN Office of the High Commissioner for Human Rights, "Austerity measures may violate human rights," November 5, 2012.

38 United Nations, "UN independent experts call for EU banking sector reform in line with human rights obligations," UN News Centre, October 5, 2012.

39 UN Office of the High Commissioner for Human Rights, "Economic inequality and financial crises undermine human rights, UN expert says in new report," March 15, 2016.

40 UN Committee on Economic, Social and Cultural Rights, "Concluding Observation on the sixth periodic report of the United Kingdom of Great Britain and Northern Ireland," E/c.12/GBR/CO/6 (July 14, 2016).

41 "UN Report Says UK Economic Policies Are a Violation of Human Rights," *Mother Jones*, July 1, 2016.

42 Jamie Burton, "Austerity and Human Rights in an 'Anti-Factual' Brexit," *Social Europe*, July 12, 2016.

43 "Govan Law Centre gives evidence to UN on Scots rights for adequate housing," *Scottish Housing News*, July 8, 2016.

44 Caroline Mortimer, "Government austerity policy a breach of international human rights, says UN report," *Independent*, June 29, 2016.

45 "Honduras' Fight Against Neo-Liberalism," Report by 54 Honduran NGOs to the UN Committee on Economic, Social and Cultural Rights.

46 UN Human Rights Council, Report of the Special Rapporteur on the right to food, Olivier De Schutter, A/HRC/22/50/Add.1 (December 24, 2012).

47 See Jacob Mchangama and Aaron Rhodes, "UN distorting human rights yet again," *Commentator*, May 11, 2012.

48 Olivier De Schutter, "Climate change is a human rights issues—and that's how we can solve it," *Guardian*, April 24, 2012.

49 Joseph Klein, "The U.N.'s Land Redistribution Scheme," *FrontPage*, October 25, 2010.

50 "Trump turning the US into 'world champion of extreme inequality', UN envoy warns," *Guardian*, December 15, 2017.

51 Mchangama and Rhodes, "The Call for a Global Tax."

52 Constitution Act, 1982, Part I, Canadian Charter of Rights and Freedoms, Article 7: "Everyone has the right to life, liberty and security of the person and the right not to be deprived thereof except in accordance with the principles of fundamental justice."

53 Quoted in Althia Raj, "Canada Defends Record on Economic, Social Rights at UN," *Huffington Post*, February 25, 2016.

54 Canada Without Poverty, "UN tells Trudeau government—human rights are not optional," February 24, 2016.

55 Liam Thornton, "The European Convention on Human Rights: A Socio-Economic Rights Charter?" in *Ireland and the European Convention on Human Rights: 60 Years and Beyond*, ed. S. Egan, L. Thornton and J. Walsh (London: Bloomsbury, 2014), pp. 249–50, available at http://researchrepository.ucd.ie/handle/10197/6132

56 Marijke De Pauw, "McDonald v. the United Kingdom: A step forward in addressing the needs of persons with disabilities through Article 8 ECHR," Strasbourg Observers, June 4, 2014.

57 Jacob Mchangama and Aaron Rhodes, "The Problem with European 'Human Rights,'" *Wall Street Journal*, April 24, 2012.

58 European Court of Human Rights, Grand Chamber, Case of *M.S.S. v. Belgium and Greece* (application no. 30696/09).

59 See "Human rights are not 'abstract ideas,' must be main tool in meeting development targets – Ban," UN News Centre, July 12, 2016. See also Aaron Rhodes, "The UN's Politicized Human Rights Vision," *American Thinker*, August 3, 2016.

60 Strasbourg Observers, "European Court tackles unacceptable traffic noise pollution," December 1, 2010.

61 "Views of the United States of America on Human Rights and Access to Water," Submitted to the Office of the United Nations High Commissioner for Human Rights, June 2007, Article 1.

62 Meera Karunananthan, "Is the UN turning its back on the human right to water?" *Guardian*, June 19, 2014.

63 UN Human Rights Council, "Promotion of the right to peace," A/HRC/RES/20/15 (July 17, 2012).

64 UN Office of the High Commissioner for Human Rights, "One step closer to a real right to international solidarity in a world of ever deepening inequalities," June 17, 2014.

65 Joanne Pedrone, J.D., and Andrew Kloster, J.D., draft paper, "Human Rights Treaty Body Reform: New Proposals," p. 27ff, available at https://ssrn.com/abstract=1885758

66 UN Committee on the Elimination of Discrimination against Women, CEDAW General Recommendation No. 24: Article 12 of the Convention (Women and Health), 1999, A/54/38/Rev.1, chap. I, par. 11.

67 Nicole Haberland et al., *It's All One Curriculum: Guidelines and Activities for a Unified Approach to Sexuality, Gender, HIV and Human Rights Education* (New York: Population Council, 2009).

68 Moses Moskowitz, "Implementing Human Rights: Present Status and Future Prospects," in *Human Rights: Thirty Years after the Universal Declaration*, ed. B. G. Ramcharan (The Hague: Martinus Nijhoff, 1979), p. 122.

69 Clifford Rob, ed., *The International Struggle for New Human Rights* (Philadelphia: University of Pennsylvania Press, 2009).

70 Ibid., p. 8.

71 Ibid., p. 11.

72 Ibid., pp. 112–13.

73 Ibid., pp. 117–18.

74 Ibid., p. 11.

75 Ibid., p. 13.

76 Ibid., p. 116.

77 Ibid., p. 119.

78 See Aaron Rhodes, "Does Universal Human Rights Mean Anything Anymore?" *American Thinker*, August 19, 2012.

79 Ibid.

80 UN Office of the High Commissioner for Human Rights, "UN Human Rights Chief offers her support for a new Convention on the rights of older persons," April 8, 2014.

81 This according to a confidential memo from the EU's Working Party on Human Rights (COHOM).

82 See Aaron Rhodes, "The False Promise of a Business and Human Rights Treaty," *Huffington Post*, July 10, 2014.

83 Ibid.

84 John G. Ruggie, "A UN Business and Human Rights Treaty Update," Harvard Kennedy School, May 1, 2014.

85 Human Rights Watch, "Human Rights in Supply Chains: A Call for a Binding Global Standard on Due Diligence," May 30, 2016.

86 WeMove.EU, "Stop corporate abuse: we need rights for people and rules for business," https://you.wemove.eu/campaigns/stop-corporate-abuse

87 See Noha Shawki, "New Rights Advocacy and the Human Rights of Peasants: La Via Campesina and the Evolution of New Human Rights Norms," *Journal of Human Rights Practice* 6 no. 2 (July 2014), pp. 306–26.

88 UN Human Rights Council, A/HRC/21/L.23 (September 27, 2012).

89 Mark B. Smith, "Social Rights in the Soviet Dictatorship: The Constitutional Right to Welfare from Stalin to Brezhnev," *Humanity*, June 11, 2014.

90 Quoted in Doriane Lambelet, "The Contradiction between Soviet and American Human Rights Doctrine," *Boston University International Law Journal* 7 (1989), p. 61.

91 Elliott Abrams, "The Return of the Soviet Standard," *National Review*, August 26, 2009.

92 See Aaron Rhodes and Jacob Mchangama, "UN Reviews Show Dysfunction of Human Rights Discourse and Practice," *Huffington Post*, May 13, 2013; updated July 13, 2013.

93 See Aaron Rhodes, "Wide Acclaim for China's State-Centered, Collective Human Rights," *Huffington Post*, October 24, 2013; updated January 23, 2014.

94 See Aaron Rhodes, "The Inadvertent Vulnerability of China's Leaders," *Washington Times*, August 29, 2013.

95 Ashifa Kassam and Tome Phillips, "Chinese minister vents anger when Canadian reporter asks about human rights," *Guardian*, June 2, 2016.

96 Justin Tang, "Ontario Minister Michael Chan defends China's human-rights record," *Globe and Mail*, June 8, 2016.

97 UN Human Rights Council, Report of the Commission of Inquiry on Human Rights in the Democratic People's Republic of Korea, A/HRC/25/63 (February 7, 2014).

98 UN Human Rights Council, Report of the Working Group on the Universal Periodic Review: Democratic People's Republic of Korea, A/HRC/27/10 (July 2, 2014).

99 See Aaron Rhodes, "Turkmenistan Faces Second UN Human Rights Review," *Chronicles of Turkmenistan*, October 1, 2013.

100 UN Human Rights Council, Report of the Working Group on the Universal Periodic Review: Islamic Republic of Iran, A/HRC/28/12 (December 22, 2014).

101 UN Human Rights Council, Report of the Working Group on the Universal Periodic Review: Belarus, A/HRC/30/3 (July 13, 2015).

102 Human Rights Watch, "Cuba's International Human Rights Obligations," 1999, https://www.hrw.org/reports/1999/cuba/Cuba996-02.htm

103 Garry Leech, "The Bias of Human Rights Watch," *Critical Legal Thinking*, March 21, 2013.

104 See Aaron Rhodes, "Hört auf zu schweigen," *Zeit Online*, October 31, 2013.

CHAPTER 5: THE LOSS OF AMERICA'S
HUMAN RIGHTS EXCEPTIONALISM

1 Alexis de Tocqueville, *Democracy in America* (New York: Vintage, 1945), vol. 2, p. 36.

2 Dan Wright, "Hillary Clinton Takes Mantle of George W. Bush, Promises Regime Change," *Shadowproof*, September 1, 2016.

3 Ayn Rand, "Man's Rights," in *The Virtue of Selfishness* (London: Penguin, 1964), p. 53. Emphasis in the original.

4 Philip A. Hamburger, "Natural Rights, Natural Law, and American Constitutions," *Yale Law Journal* 102 no. 4 (January 1993), pp. 907–32.

5 Donald S. Lutz and Charles S. Hyneman, eds., *American Political Writing During the Founding Era: 1760–1805*, 2 vols. (Indianapolis: Liberty Fund, 1983); see also Ellis Washington, "Reply to Judge Richard A. Posner on the Inseparability of Law and Morality," *Rutgers Journal of Law and Religion* 3 (2001), pp. 1–130.

6 James Otis, *Rights of the British Colonies Asserted and Proved* (Boston & London: J. Almon, 1764), p. 52. Available at the Online Library of Liberty.

7 Resolves of the Pennsylvania Assembly on the Stamp Act, September 21, 1765, http://avalon.law.yale.edu/18th_century/penn_assembly_1765.asp

8 Resolutions of the House of Representatives of Massachusetts Assembly, October 29, 1765, from *The Founders' Constitution*, vol. 1, chap. 17, doc. 11 (University of Chicago Press, 1987), http://press-pubs.uchicago.edu/founders/documents/v1ch17s11.html

9 Harvey J. Kaye, *Thomas Paine and the Promise of America* (New York: Hill & Wang, 2005), p. 43.

10 Thomas Paine, *Rights of Man* (London: Penguin Classics, 2001), p. 68.

11 Richard Bland, "An Inquiry into the Rights of the British Colonies," 1766, http://teachingamericanhistory.org/library/document/an-inquiry-into-the-rights-of-the-british-colonies/

12 Hamburger, "Natural Rights, Natural Law, and American Constitutions," p. 923ff.

13 Cf. Gordon S. Wood, *The Radicalism of the American Revolution* (New York: Vintage, 1993), p. 213ff.

14 James R. Stoner, "Declaration of Independence," Natural Law, Natural Rights and American Constitutionalism (The Witherspoon Institute, 2017).

15 Hadley Arkes, *Constitutional Illusions and Anchoring Truths: The Touchstone of the Natural Law* (Cambridge, UK: Cambridge University Press, 2010), p. 46.

16 According to David Armitage, natural law would underlie a law of nations in the absence of an imperial global authority, with nature itself as a standard and world opinion its court. See David Armitage, *The Declaration of Independence: A Global History* (Cambridge, Mass.: Harvard University Press, 2007).

17 James Wilson, "Of the Natural Rights of Individuals," 1790, http://teachingamericanhistory.org/library/document/of-the-natural-rights-of-individuals/

18 Hamburger, "Natural Rights, Natural Law, and American Constitutions," p. 919.

19 Ibid., p. 921.

20 James Madison, "Memorial and Remonstrance," 1785, in *The Writings of James Madison: 1783–1787* (New York: G. P. Putnam's Sons, 1787), p. 185.

21 Ján Figel',"Religious Freedom 'Is a litmus test of overall freedom' says EU special envoy," *World*, October 27, 2016.

22 Edward Shils, "The Intellectuals and the Powers: Some Perspectives for Comparative Analysis," in *The Intellectuals and the Powers and Other Essays*, Selected Papers vol. 1 (Chicago: University of Chicago Press, 1972), p. 3.

23 Wood, *The Radicalism of the American Revolution*, p. 193.

24 Michael S. Greve, *The Constitution: Understanding America's Founding Document* (Washington, D.C.: AEI Press, 2013), p. 58.

25 Wood, *The Radicalism of the American Revolution*, p. 213ff. See also Dwight Burlingame, ed., *Philanthropy in America: A Comprehensive Historical Encyclopedia* (Santa Barbara, Calif.: ABC-CLIO, 2004), vol. 1, p. 393ff.

26 J. M. Opal, "General Jackson's Passports: Natural Rights and Sovereign Citizens in the Political Thought of Andrew Jackson, 1780s–1820s," *Studies in American Political Development* 27 no. 2 (October 2013), pp. 69–85.

27 George Combe, *The Constitution of Man in Relation to the Natural Laws* (1828; New York: Cassell Publishing Co., 1893), Preface, p. v.

28 Lysander Spooner, *The Unconstitutionality of Slavery* (1845; Boston: Bela Marsh, 1860).

29 John C. Calhoun, "A Disquisition on Government," 1851, in *Selected Writings and Speeches* (Washington, D.C.: Regnery Gateway, 2003), p. 33ff.

30 Abraham Lincoln, Letter to Henry L. Pierce and Others, April 6, 1859, http://www.abrahamlincolnonline.org/lincoln/speeches/pierce.htm

31 Herman Belz, "Abraham Lincoln and the Natural Law Tradition," Natural Law, Natural Rights, and American Constitutionalism (The Witherspoon Institute, 2011).

32 Cf. Hadley Arkes, "The Drift from Natural Rights," chap. 2 of *Natural Rights and the Right to Choose* (Cambridge, UK: Cambridge University Press, 2002).

33 See Stephen M. Feldman, *Neoconservative Politics and the Supreme Court: Law, Power, and Democracy* (New York: NYU Press, 2012), p. 14ff.

34 Josiah Royce, *Selected Writings* (Mahwaw, N.J.: Paulist Press, 1988).

35 William James, "What Pragmatism Means," in *Essays on Pragmatism* (New York: Hafner Press, 1969), p. 142.

36 Thomas P. Whelan, "Pragmatism and Natural Rights," *Marquette Law Review* 12 no. 2 (February 1928), pp. 156–57.

37 Ibid., pp. 158–59, quoting Roscoe Pound.

38 Ibid., p. 159.

39 Cf. Arkes, "The Drift from Natural Rights."

40 Charles Edward Merriam, *A History of American Political Theories* (1903; New York: Macmillan, 1920), p. 305.

41 Ibid., p. 310.

42 John Dewey, *The Ethics of Democracy*, 1888, in *The Early Works of John Dewey*, ed. Jo Ann Boydston, vol. 1: 1882–1888, Early Essays and *Leibniz's New Essays* (Carbondale: Southern Illinois University Press, 1969), p. 239.

43 John Dewey, *The Public and Its Problems* (New York: H. Holt & Co., 1927).

44 John Lachs and Robert B. Talisse, eds., *American Philosophy: An Encyclopedia* (Abingdon-on-Thames: Routledge, 2008), p. 528.

45 Tibor Machan, "Natural Rights," *Daily Bell*, July 30, 2014.

46 John Dewey and James Tufts, "Responsibility and Freedom" and "Rights and Obligations," excerpts from "Social Organization and the Individual," chap. 22 of *Ethics* (New York: Henry Holt, 1908).

47 Jean M. Yarbrough, "Theodore Roosevelt: Progressive Crusader," Heritage Foundation, September 24, 2012.

48 Theodore Roosevelt, Speech in Osawatomie, Kansas, on September 1, 1910.

49 See Ronald J. Pestritto, "Founding Liberalism, Progressive Liberalism, and the Rights of Property," in *Liberalism and Capitalism*, ed. Ellen Frankel Paul, Fred D. Miller and Jeffrey Paul (Cambridge, UK: Cambridge University Press, 2012), p. 70.

50 Robert P. George, "Natural Law," *Harvard Journal of Law and Public Policy* 31 no. 1 (2007), p. 171.

51 Frank Goodnow, *The American Conception of Liberty and Government* (Providence, R.I.: Standard Printing Co., 1916), p. 57.

52 See Ronald Pestritto, "The Birth of the Administrative State: Where It Came From and What It Means for Limited Government," Heritage Foundation, November 20, 2007.

53 Jonah Goldberg, *Liberal Fascism: The Secret History of the American Left, from Mussolini to the Politics of Change* (New York: Doubleday, 2008), p. 119.

54 Woodrow Wilson, *The State: Elements of Historical and Practical Politics* (1898; Lexington, Mass.: D. C. Heath, 1918), p. 651.

55 Goldberg, *Liberal Fascism*, p. 86.

56 Woodrow Wilson, "An Address to the Jefferson Club of Los Angeles," May 12, 1911, in *The Papers of Woodrow Wilson*, ed. Arthur S. Link, vol. 23 (Princeton, N.J.: Princeton University Press, 1977), p. 34. See Ronald J. Pestritto, "Progressivism and America's Tradition of Natural Law and Natural Rights," Natural Law, Natural Rights, and American Constitutionalism: Critics of the Natural Law Tradition (The Witherspoon Institute, 2017).

57 President Franklin Roosevelt, State of the Union Address, January 11, 1944. See also Sidney Milkis and Jerome Mileur, *The New Deal and the Triumph of Liberalism* (Amherst: University of Massachusetts Press, 2002), p. 33.

58 Cass R. Sunstein, *Conspiracy Theories and Other Dangerous Ideas* (New York: Simon & Schuster, 2014), p. xii.

59 For a discussion, see Patrick J. Austin, "Expansive Rights: FDR's Proposed 'Economic' Bill of Rights Memorialized in the International Covenant on Economic, Social, and Cultural Rights, but with Little Impact in the United States," *Chicago-Kent Journal of International and Comparative Law* 15 no. 1 (January 2015), p. 9.

60 President Calvin Coolidge, Address at the Celebration of the 150th Anniversary of the Declaration of Independence, Philadelphia, July 5, 1926.

61 Philip Alston, "Putting Economic, Social and Cultural Rights Back on the Agenda of the United States," CHRGJ Working Paper No. 22 (2009), pp. 2–3.

62 Daniel J. Whelan, "The United States and economic and social rights: past, present ... and future?" Human Rights and Human Welfare Working Paper No. 26, posted February 28, 2005, p. 11, https://www.du.edu/korbel/hrhw/workingpapers/2005/26-whelan-2005.pdf

63 Mary Ann Glendon, *The World Made New: Eleanor Roosevelt and the Universal Declaration of Human Rights* (New York: Random House, 2001), p. 186.

64 Austin, "Expansive Rights."

65 Glendon, *The World Made New*, p. 190.

66 Ibid., p. 186.

67 Quoted in Henry Shue, *Basic Rights: Subsistence, Affluence, and U.S. Foreign Policy* (Princeton, N.J.: Princeton University Press, 1996), p. 221, n. 5.

68 Alston, "Putting Economic, Social and Cultural Rights Back on the Agenda of the United States," p. 3.

69 Whelan, "The United States and economic and social rights," p. 7.

70 Quoted in ibid., p. 8.

71 Alston, "Putting Economic, Social and Cultural Rights Back on the Agenda of the United States," pp. 3–4.

72 Undated memo from Griffin Smith to James Fallows, quoted in Hauke Hartmann, *Die Menschenrechtspolitik unter Präsident Carter: Moralische Ansprüche, strategische Interessen und der Fall El Salvador* (Frankfurt: Campus Verlag, 2004), p. 75.

73 Quoted in Whelan, "The United States and economic and social rights," pp. 10–11, citing Hauke Hartmann, "US Human Rights Policy under Carter and Reagan, 1977–1981," *Human Rights Quarterly* 23 no. 2 (2001), p. 423.

74 Quoted in Philip Alston, "U.S. Ratification of the Covenant on Economic, Social and Cultural Rights: The Need for an Entirely New Strategy," *American Journal of International Law* 84 no. 2 (1990), p. 378.

75 Ibid.

76 Carter Center, "U.S. Finally Ratifies Human Rights Covenant," June 28, 1992.

77 See for example, Clair Apodaca, *Understanding U.S. Human Rights Policy: A Paradoxical Legacy* (New York: Routledge, 2006).

78 Cf. William Safire, "Human Rights Victory," *New York Times*, November 5, 1981.

79 Quoted in ibid.

80 E. Michael Myers, "State Department says Hague committed to human rights," UPI, November 5, 1981.

81 U.S. Department of State, *Country Reports on Human Rights Practices for 1982*, submitted to the Committee on Foreign Relations, U.S. Senate, and Committee on Foreign Affairs, U.S. House of Representatives, February 1983 (Washington, D.C.: U.S. Government Printing Office).

82 Paula Dobriansky, Deputy Assistant Secretary for Human Rights and Humanitarian Affairs, "U.S. Human Rights Policy: An Overview," Address to the American Council of Young Political Leaders in Washington, D.C., June 3, 1988, reprinted in U.S. Department of State, Bureau of Public Affairs, Current Policy No. 1091 (1988), pp. 1–3.

83 Noam Chomsky, *Failed States: The Abuse of Power and the Assault on Democracy* (London: Penguin, 2007), p. 232.

84 See Julia Häusermann, "Realisation and Implementation of Economic, Social and Cultural Rights," in *Economic, Social and Cultural Rights: Progress and Achievement*, ed. Ralph Beddard, Ralph Hill and M. Dilys (London: Palgrave Macmillan, 1992), p. 51.

85 Conference on Security and Co-operation in Europe, "Concluding Document of the Vienna Meeting of Representatives of the Participating States," *International Legal Materials* 28 no. 2 (March 1989), pp. 533–34, par. 13–14.

86 See Sarah B. Snyder, *Human Rights Activism and the End of the Cold War: A Transitional History of the Helsinki Network* (Cambridge, UK: Cambridge University Press, 2011), p. 141ff.

87 Amnesty International, "Economic, Social and Cultural Rights: Questions and Answers," p. 6, adapted from *Human Rights Education: The Fourth R*, 9:1 (Spring 1998), https://www.amnestyusa.org/pdfs/escr_qa.pdf

88 United Nations, Press Conference on the Results of the 54th Session of the Commission on Human Rights, April 24, 1998, quoted in William F. Schulz, *The Future of Human Rights: U.S. Policy for a New Era* (Philadelphia: University of Pennsylvania Press, 2008), p. 293, n. 16.

89 Strauss's supposed political influence was detailed by Anne Norton in *Leo Strauss and the Politics of American Empire* (New Haven: Yale University Press, 2004). Jenny Strauss Clay, Leo Strauss's daughter, wrote a stinging refutation of the notion of a "Straussian cabal," in an op–ed, "The Real Leo Strauss," *New York Times*, June 7, 2003.

90 International Helsinki Federation for Human Rights, "Counter-terrorism measures and the prohibition on torture and ill-treatment," November 2006, http://www.refworld.org/docid/46963ae90.html

91 Philip Alston, "Putting Economic, Social and Cultural Rights Back on the Agenda of the United States," in *The Future of Human Rights*, ed. Schulz, p. 131.

92 Quoted in ibid., p. 124.

93 Statement of the United States of America delivered by Richard Wall, "Item 10: Economic, Social and Cultural Rights," at the 59th Session of the United Nations Commission on Human Rights, April 7, 2003, quoted in ibid., p. 126.

94 Charles Kesler, "The Nature of Rights in American Politics: A Comparison of Three Revolutions," Heritage Foundation, September 30, 2008.

95 Laurence Tribe, "Clarence Thomas and 'Natural Law,'" *New York Times*, July 15, 1991.

96 Hadley Arkes, *Natural Rights and the Right to Choose* (Cambridge, UK: Cambridge University Press, 2002), p. 18.

97 Hon. Diarmuid F. O'Scannlain, "The Natural Law in the American Tradition," *Fordham Law Review* 79 no. 4 (2011), p. 1514.

98 Ibid., p. 1515.

99 Robert E. Shapiro, "Natural Rights—Requiescant in Pace," *Litigation* 39 no. 3 (Summer 2013), pp. 55–58.

100 Hillary Clinton, "Remarks on the Human Rights Agenda for the 21st Century," Georgetown University, December 14, 2009, U.S. Department of State, https://2009-2017.state.gov/secretary/20092013clinton/rm/2009a/12/133544.htm

101 Jay Nordlinger, "Hillary Clinton and Human Rights," *National Review*, August

26, 2009, http://www.nationalreview.com/corner/186118/hillary-clinton-and-human-rights-jay-nordlinger

102 "Clinton: Chinese human rights can't interfere with other crises," CNN, February 22, 2009.

103 "Only a Matter of Speech? Secretary of State Hilary [*sic*] Clinton's China Blunder," *The XL File*, February 26, 2009, http://bricks-for-jade.blogspot.com/

104 Francesca Chambers, "Angry Castro lectures America on its failures on the human right to healthcare, education and pensions (but his denial that Cuba has any political prisoners was limper than Obama's hand)," *Daily Mail*, March 21, 2016.

105 See Aaron Rhodes, "Obama's Human Rights Betrayal," *Huffington Post*, March 22, 2016.

106 "The Obama Legacy: Lowering standards and betraying human rights in Cuba," *Notes from the Cuban Exile Quarter*, May 29, 2016.

107 Mary Anastasia O'Grady, "Obama Betrayed Cuba's Dissidents," *Wall Street Journal*, August 14, 2016.

108 Nora Gámez Torres, "Cuban officials and Communist Party members can now get U.S. remittances and more," *Miami Herald*, October 21, 2016.

109 Dorothy Rabinowitz, "The Alien in the White House," *Wall Street Journal*, June 9, 2010.

110 See Harold Koh, "Why Transnational Law Matters," *Penn State International Law Review* 24 no. 4 (2006), p. 746.

111 Brett Shaefer, "Obama's Miss at the UN," Heritage Foundation, September 26, 2012.

112 Observation from correspondence with Cathy Fitzpatrick, a human rights activist.

113 See Jacob Mchangama and Aaron Rhodes, "The Call for a Global Tax," *National Review*, May 22, 2012.

114 UN Human Rights Council, National Report submitted in accordance with paragraph 15 (a) of the annex to Human Rights Council resolution 5/1, United States of America, A/HRC/WG.6/9/USA/1 (August 23, 2010), p. 4.

115 Ibid., p. 17.

116 Ibid.

117 Ibid., p. 13.

118 Ibid., p. 18.

119 Roger Pilon, "Wrong about Human Rights," *Philadelphia Inquirer*, September 1, 2010.

120 UN Human Rights Council, Report of the Working Group on the Universal Periodic Review, United States of America, A/HRC/16/11 (January 4, 2011), par. 87.

121 Ibid., par. 88.

122 UN Human Rights Council, Summary prepared by the Office of the High Commissioner for Human Rights in accordance with paragraph 15 (c) of the annex to Human Rights Council resolution 5/1, United States of America, A/HRC/WG.6/9/USA/3/Rev.1 (October 14, 2010).

123 Ibid.

124 Joshua Kurlantzick, "Obama must be more aggressive on human rights," *Washington Post*, December 13, 2009.

125 Elliott Abrams, "The Soviet Standard Returns: Hillary Clinton mouths an old Communist bromide," *National Review*, August 26, 2009.

126 Rabbi Abraham Cooper and Harold Brackman, "Obama, what about human rights? A world of work awaits," *New York Daily News*, September 24, 2009.

127 Caroline Glick, "Our World: Ideologue-in-Chief," *Jerusalem Post*, June 29, 2009.

128 Quoted in Eli Lake, "Human rights groups see Obama wavering," *Washington Times*, October 7, 2009.

129 Kenneth Roth, "Obama's Hesitant Embrace of Human Rights," *International Herald Tribune*, March 3, 2010.

130 Colum Lynch, "U.S. Faces Doubts About Leadership on Human Rights," *Washington Post*, September 22, 2009.

131 Jackson Diehl, "Obama's national security strategy is light on the human rights agenda," *Washington Post*, May 31, 2010.

132 Bret Stephens, "Does Obama Believe in Human Rights?" *Wall Street Journal*, October 19, 2009.

133 Jimmy Carter, "A Cruel and Unusual Record," *New York Times*, June 24, 2012.

134 Eli Lake, "Why Obama Let Iran's Green Movement Fail," *Bloomberg*, August 24, 2016.

135 Anne R. Pierce, *A Perilous Path: The Misguided Foreign Policy of Barack Obama, Hillary Clinton and John Kerry* (New York: Post Hill Press, 2016); see also my review, "Obama's Weak Human Rights Record," *Huffington Post*, August 15, 2016.

136 Pierce, *A Perilous Path*, p. 287.

137 Alan Dowd, "Word Choice: 'Freedom' Absent from First Presidential Debate, Part of Troubling Trend," *Providence*, September 30, 2016.

138 See Multilateralism Survey Results in Josh Busby, Will Inboden and Jon Monten, "American Foreign Policy Is Already Post-Partisan: Why Politics Does Stop at the Water's Edge," *Foreign Affairs*, May 30, 2012, http://files.foreignaffairs.com/legacy/attachments/classics/TablesMay22.pdf

139 Pierce, *A Perilous Path*, pp. 55, 58.

CHAPTER 6: A CONVERGENCE AGAINST LIBERTY

1 The term is taken from Robert Jay Lifton, *Thought Reform and the Psychology of Totalism: A Study of "Brainwashing" in China* (New York: Norton, 1961). A "thought-terminating cliché" is used in brainwashing to quell cognitive dissonance and justify erroneous logic.

2 Liu Huawen, "World recognizes China's progress in human rights protection," *People's Daily*, November 3, 2016.

3 See, for example, "China Stresses Right to Development at UN Human Rights Commission," *China Through a Lens*, March 23, 2002.

4 See, Wu Zurong, "Respect for China's Right to Development Is Essential," *China/US Focus*, February 20, 2014.

5 John Samuel, "Rise of unfreedom," *My Republica*, November 17, 2016.

6   Reuters, "New U.N. chief, in China, calls for human rights respect," November 28, 2016.

7   Some of this material has been published in a different form in my article "Human rights concepts in the OSCE region: changes since the Helsinki Final Act," *Central Asian Survey* 36 no. 3 (April 2017), pp. 313–30.

8   See, Political Capital Research and Consulting Institute, "The Russian Connection: The Spread of pro-Russian policies on the European far right," March 14, 2014.

9   Russian Orthodox Church, "Basic Teaching on Human Dignity, Freedom and Rights," 2008, https://mospat.ru/en/documents/dignity-freedom-rights/

10 See, for example, Aaron Rhodes, "Combating Eurasia's challenge to basic human rights," *Washington Times*, June 25, 2014.

11 Robert Coalson, "Russian Conservatives Challenge Notion of 'Universal' Values," RFE/RL, December 10, 2008.

12 Andrei Illarionov, Remarks at the NATO Parliamentary Assembly, May 31, 2014. The speech in Russian can be found here: http://300tube.com/watch?v=Uk3OjC8fEE0; and a transcript here: https://echo.msk.ru/blog/aillar/1338912-echo/

13 Liah Greenfeld, *Nationalism: Five Roads to Modernity* (Cambridge, Mass.: Harvard University Press, 1992), p. 243.

14 Paul Goble, "Putin Says Cultural Unity, Not Passport Nationality, Is What Matters," *Window on Eurasia*, New Series, April 24, 2014, http://windowoneurasia2.blogspot.com/2014/04/window-on-eurasia-putin-says-cultural.html

15 Timothy Snyder, "How a Russian Fascist Is Meddling in America's Election," *New York Times*, September 20, 2016.

16 Sohrab Ahmari, "How the Kremlin Sees Trump's Re-Reset with Moscow," *Wall Street Journal*, November 17, 2016; updated November 20, 2016.

17 Julie Elkner, "Spiritual Security in Putin's Russia," *History and Policy*, January 1, 2005.

18 See, Forum for Religious Freedom–Europe and Human Rights Without Frontiers, "Condemn Russia's Jehovah's Witnesses Ban," Statement for the Supplementary OSCE Human Dimension Meeting, June 22–23, 2017.

19 Human Rights Watch, "Russia: Halt Orders to Block Online Media," March 23, 2014.

20 Jill Dougherty, "How the media became one of Putin's most powerful weapons," *Atlantic*, April 12, 2015.

21 Paul Goble, "After Crimea, 'One Spark' Could Engulf Russia in Pogroms, Moscow Observers Say," *Window on Eurasia*, New Series, May 17, 2014, http://windowoneurasia2.blogspot.de/2014/05/window-on-eurasia-after-crimea-one.html

22 Anna Dolgov, "United Russia Bill Seeks to Protect Kids From 'Distortions' of Patriotism," *Moscow Times*, May 11, 2014, https://themoscowtimes.com/articles/united-russia-bill-seeks-to-protect-kids-from-distortions-of-patriotism-35310

23 Alexander Dugin, *The Fourth Political Theory* (London: Arktos, 2012), p. 191.

24 Human Rights First, "Spread of Russian-style Anti-Propaganda Laws," February 27, 2014.

25 Human Rights First, "Russia Includes Transgender Status on List of Driver's License Medical Restrictions," February 27, 2015.

26 Dugin, *The Fourth Political Theory*, p. 169.

27 Giuliano Adriano Malvicini, "Dugin on the Subject of Politics," Counter-Currents Publishing, September 12, 2014.

28 Dugin, *The Fourth Political Theory*, p. 154.

29 Coalson, "Russian Conservatives Challenge Notion of 'Universal' Values."

30 Miklós Haraszti, *The Velvet Prison: Artists Under State Socialism*, trans. Katalin and Stephen Landesmann (New York: Basic Books, 1987), p. 8.

31 Human Rights Education Centre, Belarus, "Non-Human Rights Education in Belarus," Document submitted to the OSCE Human Dimension Implementation Meeting, October 2, 2009, OSCE, HDIM.NGO/0423/09.

32 See Rhodes, "Combating Eurasia's Challenge to Basic Human Rights."

33 Adam Michnik, "The Uncanny Era of Post-Communism," 1991, in *An Uncanny Era: Conversations between Václav Havel and Adam Michnik*, ed. Elzbieta Matynia (New Haven: Yale University Press, 2014), p. 52.

34 See, for example, Sergey Lavrov, "Russia's Foreign Policy: Historical Background," from *Russia in Global Affairs*, March 3, 2016, posted by The Ministry of Foreign Affairs of the Russian Federation, http://www.mid.ru/en/foreign_policy/news/-/asset_publisher/cKNonkJE02Bw/content/id/2124391

35 Political Capital Research and Consulting Institute, "The Russian Connection."

36 Political Capital Research and Consulting Institute, and Social Development Institute, "'I am Eurasian'—The Kremlin connections of the Hungarian far-right," March 2015.

37 Carl Schmitt, *Constitutional Theory* (1928), trans. Jeffrey Seitzer (Durham, N.C.: Duke University Press, 2008), pp. 233–38.

38 Clifford Geertz, *Islam Observed: Religious Development in Morocco and Indonesia* (Chicago: University of Chicago Press, 1968).

39 Nijib Ghadbian, *Democratization and the Islamist Challenge in the Arab World* (Boulder, Col.: Westview, 1997), p. 59.

40 Point made also by Jack Donnelly in *International Human Rights* (Ithaca, N.Y.: Cornell University Press, 2003).

41 See Aaron Rhodes, "Exploiting Chinese Culture to Justify Repression," *China Perspective*, November 26, 2014.

42 Eva Brems, *Human Rights: Universality and Diversity* (The Hague: Martinus Nijhoff, 2001), p. 205.

43 Ibid., p. 206.

44 Angelina E. Theodorou, "Which countries still outlaw apostasy and blasphemy?" Pew Research Center, July 29, 2016; see also Set My People Free, "Countries where apostasy and blasphemy laws in Islam are applied," http://freedom2worship.org/images/docs/map-laws-oct2016r.jpg

45 Brems, *Human Rights: Universality and Diversity*, p. 211.

46 UN General Assembly, "Status of Preparation of Publications, Studies and Documents for the World Conference: Contribution of the Organisation of the Islamic Conference," A/CONF.157/PC/62/Add.18 (June 9, 1993).

47 Brems, *Human Rights: Universality and Diversity*, p. 261.

48 Ibid., p. 260.

49 Steven L. Jacobs and Mark Weitzman, *Dismantling the Big Lie: The Protocols of the Elders of Zion* (Jersey City: Ktav Publishing House, 2003), p. 8.

50 Barnaby Phillips, "UN Conference in Tatters," BBC News, September 3, 2001, http://news.bbc.co.uk/2/hi/africa/1523905.stm

51 European Roma Rights Center, "ERRC Dissociates Itself from WCAR NGO Forum," September 5, 2001.

52 Ambassador Eileen Chamberlain Donahoe, "Combatting Defamation of Religions: U.S. Explanation of Vote," Statement to the UN Human Rights Council, March 25, 2010, U.S. Mission to the UN, https://geneva.usmission.gov/2010/03/25/combatting-defamation-of-religions-u-s-explanation-of-vote/

53 UN Human Rights Council, "Combating intolerance, negative stereotyping and stigmatization of, and discrimination, incitement to violence and violence against, persons based on religion or belief," A/HRC/RES/16/18 (April 12, 2011).

54 Deborah Weiss, Esq., *The Organization of Islamic Cooperation's Jihad on Free Speech*, Civilization Jihad Reader Series (North Charleston: CreateSpace Independent Publishing Platform, 2015).

55 Jacob Mchangama, "A Questionable Victory for Free Speech," *National Review*, March 4, 2013.

56 Article 19 (NGO), "Implementation of Resolution 16-18 is the test of UN HRC's effectiveness," April 5, 2016.

57 Inaugural Statement by His Excellency Iyad Ameen Madani, Secretary General of the OIC, during 5th Meeting of Istanbul Process, in Jeddah, Kingdom of Saudi Arabia, June 3–4, 2015, published by the Universal Rights Group, http://www.universal-rights.org/wp-content/uploads/2015/02/Appendix-IV.-Selected-presentations.pdf

58 World Turkish Coalition, "Islam versus Europe: 'The increasing role of the extreme right in Western politics is beyond our abilities to counter them,'" Turkish Forum English, January 5, 2012, http://www.turkishnews.com/en/content/2012/01/05/islam-versus-europe-the-increasing-role-of-the-extreme-right-in-western-politics-is-beyond-our-abilities-to-counter-them/

59 See for example, Council of the European Union, *Annual Report on Human Rights and Democracy in the World 2015* (Luxembourg: Publications Office of the European Union, 2016), http://www.consilium.europa.eu/media/29703/qc0216616enn.pdf

60 "Federica Mogherini's remarks at 'Call to Europe V: Islam in Europe', FEPS conference," European Union External Action, June 25, 2015.

61 Cf. Jacob Mchangama, "No Blasphemous Miming Here," *National Review*, March 25, 2014.

62 Denis MacEoin, "Free Speech vs Islamic Law?" Gatestone Institute, February 13, 2016.

63 See Alan Levinovitz, "How Trigger Warnings Silence Religious Students," *Atlantic*, August 30, 2015.

64 See Aaron Rhodes, "Left Wing Governments Also Violate Human Rights," *Huffington Post*, July 29, 2013.

65 Eugene Kontorovich "Progressives push to strip groups of nonprofit status for opposing administration foreign policy," *Washington Post*, October 7 2016. Emphasis in the original.

66 Aaron Rhodes, "Mannomann: Die Frauenquote ist ein Menschenrechtsverstoss," *Zeit Online*, December 28, 2014.

67 UN Human Rights Council, "Mandate of the Special Rapporteur on the promotion and protection of the right to freedom of opinion and expression," A/HRC/RES/7/36 (March 28, 2008).

68 Organization for Security and Co-operation in Europe, "OSCE Media Freedom Representative defends papers' right to publish controversial cartoons, asks for mutual respect for traditions," OSCE Newsroom, February 3, 2006.

69 Cf. Jeremy Waldron, *The Harm in Hate Speech* (Cambridge, Mass.: Harvard University Press, 2012).

70 Council of Europe, "Combatting Sexist Hate Speech," 2016, https://www.coe.int/en/web/genderequality/sexist-hate-speech

71 Jeffrey Tayler, "Free Speech and Islam—The Left Betrays the Most Vulnerable," *Quillette*, May 5, 2016.

72 Douglas Murray, "Europe's New Blasphemy Courts," Gatestone Institute, November 4, 2016.

73 FOREF Europa, "Deutschland: Muslime haben das Recht eine Moschee zu bauen sowie die Gegner das Recht haben den Islam zu kritisieren," November 11, 2014.

74 Cf. Aaron Rhodes, "Post-Woolwich arrests violate human rights principles," *Commentator*, May 31, 2013.

75 Tom Whitehead, "Twitter cases 'threat to freedom of speech,'" *Telegraph*, February 3, 2013.

76 "Man arrested after 'mealy mouthed' Brussels tweet," BBC News, March 24, 2016.

77 Piers Akerman, "We've hit a Triggs-er point on mind control," *Daily Telegraph*, November 5, 2016.

78 Jochen Bittner, "Recht gegen 'rechts,'" *Zeit Online*, May 25, 2017.

79 UN Committee on the Elimination of Racial Discrimination, CERD/C/82/D/48/2010 (April 4, 2013).

80 Mads Andenas and Eirik Bjorge, *A Farewell to Fragmentation: Reassertion and Convergence in International Law* (Cambridge, UK: Cambridge University Press, 2015), p. 315.

81 Jacob Mchangama, "The European Court of Human Rights versus freedom of expression," *Commentator*, February 21, 2012.

82 Council of Europe, "Hate Speech," Factsheet, updated November 2008, https://www.coe.int/t/DC/Files/Source/FS_hate_en.doc

83 European Agency for Fundamental Rights, *Homophobia and Discrimination on Grounds of Sexual Orientation and Gender Identity in the EU Member States*, Part II, *The Social Situation* (2009), http://fra.europa.eu/fraWebsite/attachments/FRA_hdgso_report_part2_en.pdf

84 Eugene Volokh, "Danish Member of Parliament (Jesper Langballe) Guilty of 'Insult[ing] or Denigrat[ing]' Muslims," *Volokh Conspiracy*, January 13, 2011,

http://volokh.com/2011/01/13/danish-member-of-parliament-jesper-langballe-guilty-of-insulting-or-denigrating-muslims/

85 Eddie Scarry, "CNN's Chris Cuomo: Hate speech 'excluded from protection' in Constitution," *Washington Examiner*, May 6, 2015.

86 David Harsanyi, "The First Amendment Is Dying," *National Review*, November 13, 2015.

87 Index on Censorship, "Debate on climate change stifled," Human Rights House, January 19, 2007, http://humanrightshouse.org/Articles/7715.html

88 Mary Robinson, Interview at the International Bar Association Annual Conference, 2012, Dublin, https://www.ibanet.org/Conferences/Mary_Robinson.aspx

89 Donald A. Brown, "The Climate Change Disinformation Campaign: What Kind of Crime Against Humanity, Tort, Human Rights Violation, Malfeasance, Transgression, Villainy, or Wrongdoing Is It? Part One: Is the Disinformation Campaign a Crime Against Humanity or a Civil Tort?" *Ethics and Climate*, January 30, 2013.

90 Roger Pielke Jr., "My unhappy life as a climate heretic," *Wall Street Journal*, December 2, 2016.

91 Cf. David Bernstein, "How Anti-Discrimination Became a Religion, and What It Means for Judaism," *Mosaic*, August 8, 2016.

92 European Court of Human Rights, "French ban on the wearing in public of clothing designed to conceal one's face does not breach the Convention," Press Release (ECHR 191), July 1, 2014; see also, Aaron Rhodes, "Schleierfreiheit," *Zeit Online*, August 13, 2014.

93 Harry Farley, "Burqa Ban in Germany 'Wherever Legally Possible,' Says Merkel," *Christianity Today*, December 6, 2016.

94 Willy Fautre, "About the Islamic Totalitarianism," Human Rights Without Frontiers newsletter, December 15, 2017.

95 Human Rights Watch, "Switzerland: Minaret Ban Violates Rights," December 4, 2009; and International Helsinki Federation for Human Rights, "Ban on Minarets Would Violate Switzerland's International Human Rights Commitments and Promote Intolerance Against Muslims," June 5, 2007.

96 UN Human Rights Council, "Combating defamation of religions," A/HRC/RES/10/22 (March 26, 2009).

97 European Court of Human Rights, "Prohibition on building minarets in Switzerland: applications inadmissible," Press Release (ECHR 101), August 7, 2011.

98 The 2016 Democratic Party Platform, https://www.democrats.org/party-platform

99 Roger Pilon, "Whatever Happened to Religious Freedom?" *Wall Street Journal*, July 13, 2015.

100 Quoted by Marc A. Thiessen, "Hillary Clinton is a threat to religious liberty," Op-Ed, *Washington Post*, October 13, 2016.

CONCLUSION: ON THE FUTURE
OF INTERNATIONAL HUMAN RIGHTS

1 Freedom House, "Freedom in the World 2017: Populists and Autocrats: The Dual Threat to Democracy," https://freedomhouse.org/report/freedom-world/freedom-world-2017

2 See Aaron Rhodes, "Does Multilateralism Benefit Human Rights?" *Providence*, October 3, 2016.

3 YouGov, *Annual Report on US Attitudes towards Socialism*, Victims of Communism Memorial Foundation, October 2017.

4 John Villasenor, "Views among college students regarding the First Amendment: Results from a new survey," Brookings, September 18, 2017.

5 See, for example, Thomas L. Friedman, "Our One-Party Democracy," *New York Times*, September 8, 2009. In May 2010, during a *Meet the Press* interview, Friedman wondered, "what if we could be China for a day…to authorize the right solutions…." See: "Friedman: America Should be 'China for a Day,'" *FrumForum*, May 25, 2010.

6 See Leo Strauss and Joseph Cropsey, *History of Political Philosophy*, 2nd ed. (Chicago: Rand McNally & Co., 1972), pp. 251–52, 258.

7 Max Weber, *The Protestant Ethic and the Spirit of Capitalism*, trans. Talcott Parsons (New York: Charles Scribner's Sons, 1958), p. 182.

8 Ibid.

9 Max Weber, *Weber: Political Writings*, ed. Peter Lassman and Ronald Speirs (Cambridge, UK: Cambridge University Press, 1994), p. xvi.

10 See Aaron Rhodes, "The Fruits of Human Rights Hubris," *WorldPost*, May 15, 2015.

11 See Costas Douzinas, *Human Rights and Empire: The Political Philosophy of Cosmopolitanism* (London: Routledge-Cavendish, 2007), p. 80. For a discussion of the work, see Bill Bowering, *The Degradation of the International Legal Order? The Rehabilitation of Law and the Possibility of Politics* (London: Routledge, 2008).

12 Hersch Lauterpacht, *An International Bill of the Rights of Man* (1945; Oxford, UK: Oxford University Press, 2013), p. 19.

13 David McCullough, *John Adams* (New York: Simon & Schuster, 2001).

Index